W9-AHJ-577

Close Encounters of All Kinds

➤ **Close Encounters of the First Kind:**

In these encounters, UFOs are seen at close range, and possibly heard, but the observer doesn't touch them or get touched by them. The UFOs depart without leaving behind any sign of their presence. This sort of experience may be profoundly disturbing psychologically, despite the lack of physical contact.

➤ **Close Encounters of the Second Kind:**

These encounters are much like the Close Encounters of the First Kind, but with the addition of physical indications of a UFO's presence. Common events include scorched ground where the UFO landed, flattened vegetation, and broken tree limbs. Car engines or radios may suddenly stop, or electronic devices may not work while the UFO is present. These effects usually stop after the UFO leaves.

➤ **Close Encounters of the Third Kind:**

Close Encounters of the Third Kind involve watching intelligent alien beings in or around a (usually landed) UFO. The possibilities of a third-kind encounter range from merely seeing the beings to speaking with them (usually telepathically) or having some other interaction.

➤ **Close Encounters of the Fourth Kind:**

Also called "alien abductions," these are cases where aliens take humans aboard a craft against their will to examine them physically and/or mentally and possibly talk with them (again usually telepathically) before returning them whence they came. These experiences are often accompanied by loss of memory for a specific period of time, as well as powerful psychological reactions.

The Ten Signs

The following are ten signs to tell whether you've been abducted by aliens:

➤ Missing periods of time

➤ Frequent nightmares about aliens and UFOs

➤ Sleep disorders

➤ Unusual body sensations upon awaking

➤ Unexplained marks or scars on the body

➤ Feelings of being watched

➤ Repeated sightings of UFOs

➤ Partial memories of alien encounters

➤ Sudden unexplained healing of a long-term illness or affliction

➤ Phobic reaction to discussions of UFOs or extraterrestrials

tear here

alpha books

The 5-5-5 Scale

The 5-5-5 scale can be used to measure the reliability of a UFO sighting. There are three parts to it: the credibility of the observer, the credibility of the observation, and the clarity of the observation. Each of these is rated from 5, the most reliable, to 1, the least reliable. My version of the scale looks like this:

The Observer

5. The observer is someone with status in the community—such as a bishop or judge—who is known for his or her veracity, has no reason to lie, and probably would just as soon not tell the story at all.

4. The observer is a professional pilot or military or police officer, trained to know what he or she is looking at and with no reason to lie.

3. The observer is a random civilian with nothing to gain from reporting the observation.

2. The observer has seen and written about many flying saucers, and has a mission to save the world.

1. The observer is Geraldo Rivera.

The Observation

5. The observation was made by multiple observers who were at different locations and who don't know each other.

4. The observation was made by several observers at the same location who don't know each other.

3. The observation was made by a small group friends at the same location.

2. The observation was made by a single, random observer whose background can be checked.

1. The observation was given by an observer who refused to be identified, or it was phoned in anonymously.

The Clarity

5. The alien craft landed close enough to touch and left an artifact behind, or the observer was able to take clear pictures.

4. The alien craft landed close and left behind indentations of the landing gear, broken tree limbs, or the like, or the observer took fuzzy, out-of-focus pictures.

3. The craft flew by low and slowly, close enough for markings, if any, to be made out.

2. The craft flew by high, but low enough for its shape to be made out, maneuvering in an unearthly way.

1. The observer just got a glimpse of a high-flying craft.

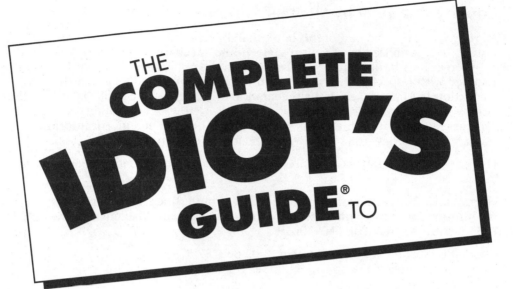

THE COMPLETE IDIOT'S GUIDE® TO

Extraterrestrial Intelligence

by Michael Kurland

alpha books

A Division of Macmillan General Reference
A Simon & Schuster Macmillan Company
1633 Broadway, New York, NY 10019-6785

Macmillan Publishing books may be purchased for business or sales promotional use. For information please write: Special Markets Department, Macmillan Publishing USA, 1633 Broadway, New York, NY 10019.

International Standard Book Number: 0-02-862387-8
Library of Congress Catalog Card Number: 98-85119

01 00 99   8 7 6 5 4 3 2 1

Interpretation of the printing code: the rightmost number of the first series of numbers is the year of the book's printing; the rightmost number of the second series of numbers is the number of the book's printing. For example, a printing code of 99-1 shows that the first printing occurred in 1999.

Printed in the United States of America

Note: This publication contains the opinions and ideas of its author. It is intended to provide helpful and informative material on the subject matter covered. It is sold with the understanding that the author and publisher are not engaged in rendering professional services in the book. If the reader requires personal assistance or advice, a competent professional should be consulted.

Contents at a Glance

Contents

Foreword

Though we like to think of the debate over extraterrestrial life as modern, its roots are in antiquity. Independent of the pseudo-histories of "ancient astronauts," serious scholars like Steven J. Dick and Michael J. Crowe have demonstrated that the debate over "a plurality of worlds" began with Democritus and occupied the analyses of many of the great philosophers and scientists (ranging from Aristotle and Kant to Huygens and Lowell), well before 1900. What was once heresy, in fact, has now become orthodoxy. The scientific Search for Extra-Terrestrial Intelligence (SETI) now has become highly popularized for us through fiction and films. Gallup polls over the last 20 years consistently show that about half of the U.S. population believe Unidentified Flying Objects (UFOs) are real and not imaginary, that our government is covering up information about it, and nearly as many (46%) believe that there are "people somewhat like ourselves living on other planets outside our universe." And a late 1997 Yankelovich poll suggests a 6% increase in UFO belief from the 1996 level.

Though scientists like the late Carl Sagan preferred to separate the topics of SETI and UFOs, they are historically and culturally intertwined. And though one may be skeptical towards UFOs while advocating SETI, we need to remember that there are scientific critics of both areas.

Ever since Kenneth Arnold initiated the Age of Flying Saucers by telling of his bizarre aerial sighting on June 24, 1947, we have been inundated not only with reports but with literally thousands of tomes on UFOs. Those books range from the near sublime to the outright ridiculous, and it has come to the point that no one person could read them all. But Michael Kurland has given it a great try. This book is informed, broadly comprehensive, provocative, witty, and often charming. Perhaps most important, though, it is a delightful guide for the uninitiated yet contains some items that will probably be new even to those already neck-deep in the wondrous worlds of SETI and UFOlogy. In short, there is probably something in here for everyone interested in these topics, whatever our opinions of the reality behind what are now probably a million reports of strangeness in our skies.

Hawkers at sport events still like to yell, "You can't tell the players without a program." With this introductory, but far-ranging book, Kurland gives us such a program, and with it, we can all better enjoy the game.

And it is indeed a game, with players ranging from the hard-headed and super skeptical to the super credulous with minds so open that, as the saying goes, their brains seem to have started spilling out. Through this minefield of opinions and speculations, Kurland cuts a moderate path for us to follow.

A story is sometimes told about a group of skeptics on a train from London on their way to an international conference on UFOs scheduled to take place in Edinburgh. One looked out the window and, commenting on what he saw, said, "I did not know the sheep in Scotland were black."

A second skeptic replied., "What you should have said was that you didn't know that *some* of the sheep in Scotland were black."

A third added, "I think what you really meant to say was that you did not know that *one side* of some of the sheep in Scotland was black."

"No," said the fourth skeptic. "What you should have said was that you did not know that one side of some of the sheep in Scotland was black *some of the time.*"

This little tale exemplifies much that goes on among many critics of belief in UFOs and poses the central question of just how skeptical one should be in appraising the UFO enigma. For in this exotic world of reputed aerial anomalies, seeming facts often turn into mere anecdotes; sightings are usually just reports of sightings; photos may be fabrications; and human testimony may result from both gross error and attention-seeking deception.

Orthodox scientists remind us of "Pascal's Principle," that evidence should be proportionate to the extraordinariness of the claim. For the most conservative, that pretty much necessitates that the existence of UFOs must be established beyond a reasonable doubt, that all other possible explanations must be eliminated. But that extreme burden of proof goes too far and seems to have kept astronomy from accepting the claims that meteorites emerged from the heavens until about 1803—even though eyewitness testimony had been plentiful.

Balancing Pascal's Principal, most scientists also recall "Hamlet's Dictum" which reminds us that there are far more things in heaven and earth than are dreamed of in our philosophies. While we do not want to "know things that ain't so," we don't want to "know things ain't so that actually are." As astronomer and UFOlogist J. Allen Hynek liked to remind us, "Absence of evidence does not constitute evidence of absence." So scientists need to keep the door open for what may prove to be convincing new evidence.

Besides, interest in UFOs and extraterrestrial contact has long gone beyond science and become involved with our religion, folklore, and popular culture. Even if mostly myth, UFOs are obviously a prominent part of contemporary culture.

So, to paraphrase Bette Davis, "Put on your seat belts. It's going to be a bumpy ride." But, with Michael Kurland as your chauffeur and guide to smooth the way, you'll get to see the most interesting sites.

—Marcello Truzzi, Ph.D.

Dr. Marcello Truzzi is currently the Director for the Center for Scientific Anomalies Research, the editor of its journal, *Zetetic Scholar*, and a Professor of Sociology at Eastern Michigan University (in Ypsilanti, Michigan). He received his doctorate in sociology from Cornell University in 1970; and he has taught at Cornell University, the University of South Florida, the University of Michigan, New College (in Sarasota, Florida), and Eastern Michigan University (where he was also Department Head during 1974-1986).

Dr. Truzzi has published a dozen books and many articles in a wide range of journals over several fields including psychology, folklore, anthropology, and the history of science, as well as in sociology. His most recent book (written in collaboration with Arthur Lyons) is *The Blue Sense: Psychic Detectives and Crime* (N.Y.: Mysterious Press/ Warner Books) published in 1991 (paperback in 1992). He is a member of many professional societies including the American Sociological Association, the American Psychological Association, the American Anthropological Association, the American Folklore Society, the Parapsychological Association, and the Society for Scientific Exploration, of which he is a past Councilor.

Introduction

There is life in the universe, that's for sure. Don't let anybody tell you otherwise.

We're it!

But what about elsewhere in the vastness of space—on one of the planets circling the billions and billions of stars in the billions of galaxies that make up our universe?

Well, nobody knows for sure, but most people have an opinion. You've probably heard or read several of them, ranging from "There's probably nothing out there—or they would have contacted us by now," to "There are aliens from another planet among us right now, but there's a massive government conspiracy to cover it up."

If you watch television, it's hard to avoid the occasional "reality" show that attempts to reveal the "truth" about flying saucers. Like most of us, you probably wonder what to believe, and just what it all means to you anyway.

What's Out There?

Numerous questions need to be answered regarding the possibility—or the reality—of extraterrestrial life and, more exciting, extraterrestrial *intelligent* life.

➤ Are there alien creatures beyond the earth?

➤ Do they possess human—or possibly super-human—intelligence?

➤ If aliens are out there, should we try to contact them?

➤ How would we go about doing this?

➤ Have these beings visited us in the past?

➤ Do they have any plans to visit us in the future?

➤ What sort of welcome should we give them if they do?

➤ Could it be that aliens are already here and the facts are being kept from us?

➤ If extraterrestrial intelligences exist and we manage to stumble across them, how important might they be to us and to our future?

I'll do my best to answer these questions and many others, but you should know that some of the answers will begin, "It is believed…" or "Nobody really knows…" or "It seems certain that…" The full answers to many of the questions discussed in this book are not known for sure. Some groups of people claim to know many of the answers, but because each of these groups has a different answer to the same question, sorting them out remains a problem. The truth is out there, however, and we will do our best to determine what it is.

I think my background puts me in a good position to consider the facts in a fair and reasonable manner. I'm the author of several books about criminalistics, the process of using scientific methods to catch criminals and determine the truth of what happened at a crime scene. This has given me some pointers in how to analyze the conflicting evidence in so many UFO sightings. I have also written about a dozen science-fiction novels, an art form that demands the writer to keep an open mind and consider all possibilities.

In this book, I examine the facts and evidence, as well as the opinions, suppositions, claims, and stories, and I'll do my best to make sure that you can tell the difference. You'll then have the information to decide for yourself what is true—and what is important—about the probability of extraterrestrial life and the possibility of our having been visited by alien intelligences.

Questions that are usually considered to be in the field of religion, such as the objective reality of God (or multiple gods), angels, devils, and saints, or the possible locations of either Heaven or Hell, will be considered only as they touch on the discussion of the existence of real, material beings from elsewhere. There will also be scant discussion in this book of the possible existence of fairies, gnomes, trolls, sprites, and other preternatural beings.

What You Will Find in This Book

The basic question that we all find ourselves asking in one form or another is: "What's it all about?" We often divide this question into: "What are we doing here?" and "What is the purpose of life?" and "Are we alone?" Using stories and information gathered by scientists, philosophers, and observers for the past 2,000 years, I will look at the third question, "Are we alone?" to come up with the best possible answer and see what light the answer sheds on the other questions.

The Complete Idiot's Guide to Extraterrestrial Intelligence is divided into five Parts. Each Part examines a different part of the question and relates it to the rest. I will also refer you to other sources where you can get an in-depth look at anything that particularly interests you.

Part 1: Are We Alone in the Universe?

Some people feel excited by the possibility of extraterrestrial life—especially intelligent life—other than our own, whereas some people feel threatened. Some world views embrace this idea, whereas others deny it vehemently. I'll show you who thinks what, where some of these ideas came from, and how they've developed over the centuries.

Part 2: How Early Were the Astronauts?

Did the Pharaohs of ancient Egypt receive unearthly help in building the pyramids? Are there ancient flying saucer landing strips in Peru? We'll consider these possibilities as well as look at UFOs in biblical prophecy. We'll also look at the precursors to the flying saucers in the Middle Ages and up to the 19th century.

Part 3: Weather Balloons of the Gods

The UFO phenomenon began in earnest in 1947 with sightings around the country and throughout much of the world. We'll look at how the phenomenon has grown since then and discuss close encounters of all kinds, crop circles, mutilated animals, and the many people who believe they have been abducted by aliens.

Part 4: It's Out There—Isn't It?—The Scientific Search for Extraterrestrials

Lacking the sort of proof that they can accept of extraterrestrials' presence on earth (a spaceship to take apart, an alien appearing on *The Oprah Winfrey Show*, and so forth), scientists devise ways to determine whether intelligent life exists elsewhere in the universe and whether we can contact them. This part covers that search, exploring the methods, the hopes, and the problems these scientists encounter.

Part 5: Take Me to Your Agent: Extraterrestrials in Popular Culture

Books, movies, and television shows are replete with alien life forms. They may be fictional, but from the 2nd century romances of Lucian of Samosata to the television show *Third Rock from the Sun*, their tales help to create our ideas and opinions about the existence of extraterrestrial life. We'll look at these creations and see how the idea of extraterrestrial life has changed over the centuries.

Thoughtful Asides

Throughout the book are boxed bits of information with guiding symbols to their significance. These are:

Contact

These boxes will explain terms that you might be unfamiliar with or that are used with a different meaning by UFOlogists (people who study unidentified flying objects).

Report from the Field

In these boxes, people involved in the search for extraterrestrials, and those who have met up with them, will report in their own words.

Earthlings Beware

These boxes will help you watch out for possible misinformation and will alert you to problems you might meet in the study of UFOs.

Sighting

These boxes will help to explain what you're reading at that point, and will give helpful hints about what to do, where to go, and whom to see—depending on the circumstances.

Close Encounter

These boxes will be full of more lengthy gobbets of information expanding on the surrounding text.

Acknowledgments

This is where the "thank you's" go. And a big and much-deserved thank you:

To Keith Kahla, for his understanding.

To Gary Krebs, for his unfailing good humor and timely assistance.

To Dick Lupoff, for his infinite wisdom.

To Pat Lupoff, for her suggestions and assistance.

To Tom Ogden, for his support from the beginning.

To Linda Robertson, for her patient and intelligent aid and support.

To Faithe Wempen, for her patience and precision.

To Diana White Eagle, for her fine and steady hand and accurate eye.

And to Xnalgapfa Zrqycc, for giving me a glimpse of how the mind of an alien works.

Part 1
Are We Alone in the Universe?

As you lie on the soft grass on a summer night staring up at the stars, do you find yourself wondering if someone—or something—up there is staring back? If so, you're not alone. Millions of people around the world want to know whether we are alone in the universe, or whether intelligent beings inhabit some of the millions of planets that, according to the latest scientific findings, are circling distant stars. Many people are convinced that we are being visited by beings from elsewhere—from an intergalactic civilization, an alternate dimension, or a different plane of reality—somewhere other than the good solid earth we are standing on. There's still a vast universe out there, and who knows what awaits us around the next bend in interstellar space.

Chapter 1

Life on Other Worlds

In This Chapter

➤ A billion billion stars

➤ Are we alone?

➤ The sun and the moon

➤ The prospect for life elsewhere

➤ Visitors from far away

Some nights when I can't sleep I spend restless hours staring into the dark, pondering the important questions. Among them, along with who does the cigarette-smoking man really work for and what makes George Steinbrenner think he can run a baseball team, are: Is there really life in the universe elsewhere than the planet earth? And is any of this possible life as intelligent—or more intelligent—as we are?

This brings up other questions, such as if there are alien beings out there, will we ever meet them? Or—and here's one that has caused me to turn on the light by my bed and draw the covers up close around me—*are they already here?*

Universal Understanding

On the next clear night, when the moon is absent from the sky or just a sliver near the horizon, go into the countryside far from city lights and look up at the sky. You will be looking at a universe containing more stars than there are people on the planet earth, more stars than there are grains of sand on all the beaches on the planet earth. You'll be able to see only about 6,000 of them with the naked eye, but that 6,000 presents a

Contact

When we speak of the **universe**, we are giving a name to everything that exists: matter, energy, and empty space, as far as you can go in any direction—or as far as a photon of light can go, since we humans really can't go much past the moon yet. For more about what we know of the universe, see Chapter 22.

wonderful and wondrous spectacle. And the others, although so far away as to be invisible to the unaided eye, are out there.

Billions and Billions of Stars

There are stars big enough to swallow the earth without a hiccup if they were where the sun is, and stars small enough to fit comfortably inside the circumference of the earth. If you see a fuzzy white band stretching from horizon to horizon, looking as though a celestial milkmaid had poured her pitcher of milk across the sky, that is our view of the Milky Way Galaxy, home of billions of stars, including our own sun. And the Milky Way is just one of billions of galaxies that make up our *universe*.

Over the past century astronomers have peered farther into the universe and deepened their understanding of what they are looking at, and their sense of wonder has grown with their knowledge. Wherever they look they see stars: old stars, young stars, dying stars, stars in the process of being born. Most of these stars are arranged in galaxies like our own Milky Way: giant clumps of billions of stars shaped like whirling spirals with extended arms or clustered together in a dense clump. Although it was seriously doubted by the experts until recently, it now seems clear that many of these stars have planets circling them much as earth circles the sun.

One Creation or Many?

As we will see in Chapter 22, astronomers using techniques such as spectrography and radio astronomy can now tell you pretty much what the stars are made of, how far away they are, and how old they are. One of the great accomplishments of the past decade is that we now know that there are planets circling many of these distant stars. But what we have yet to find out for sure is whether there is life on any of the worlds circling these stars. We don't even know for sure yet whether there is life on any of the other worlds in our own solar system, although we've done a little poking around on the moon, Venus, and Mars and haven't found any alien life yet.

Scientists are still arguing over whether we will find life, and more particularly intelligent life, elsewhere in the universe. One group would have it that life on earth is a miraculous accident, that the conditions favorable to life are so rare that if any of them were changed slightly, life here would never have gotten started. Therefore, the chance of life developing elsewhere in the universe is so small as to be effectively impossible.

Another group—and these days it seems to be in the majority—holds that the conditions aren't all that rare, and that anyway, with countless billions of stars out there, even the longest odds will eventually come out a winner. After all, the odds of winning the lottery are one in a couple of million, but people do win. As the British astronomer John Macvey put it:

> Our galaxy is some 10,000 million years old and contains something on the order of 100,000 million stars. It is hard to believe that in all this myriad host of suns and throughout all these countless millennia not one race has developed without achieving a degree of practical interstellar capability.

—from *Interstellar Travel: Past, Present, and Future*

As we'll see in Chapter 23, astronomers are now taking the possibility of intelligent life elsewhere in the universe so seriously that they are attempting to see whether beings from elsewhere are sending messages we can pick up with our radio telescopes.

Sighting

Mars is still a possibility, at least for the simpler forms of life, as we will see in Chapter 21, but the moon, with no atmosphere and no available water, and Venus, with a surface temperature hot enough to melt lead, can both probably be ruled out.

Strange, Nonhuman Creatures: Ogres or Aliens?

The possibility of nonhuman intelligence, whether it exists and what it would be like, has been of concern to scientists, philosophers, and the rest of us for as far back as we have any records. For much of that time nobody pondered the existence of life on other planets until we became aware that the planets are separate worlds. But the earliest literature we are aware of, the Babylonian *Saga of Gilgamesh* and the Greek *Odyssey* (attributed to a blind poet named Homer) were both composed centuries before the birth of Christ. Both tales take their hero into strange lands where they meet strange people who are certainly not human. King Gilgamesh visits the underworld and meets the demigods who control it, while Odysseus (the hero of the Odyssey—we usually call him Ulysses) meets, among other nonhumans, the cyclops, a one-eyed monster; Circe, who can turn men into swine; and the sirens, whose song can charm men to their death.

The ogres and goblins, nymphs and sprites, elves, djinni, fairies, gnomes, cyclops, harpies, and other creatures that abound in our myths and fairy tales were not just

Contact

A **light year** is the distance a particle of light (called a *photon*) travels in one year. The speed of light is 186,282 miles per second, so in a year light travels 5,878,500,000,000 miles (five trillion, eight hundred and seventy-eight billion, five hundred million miles).

diversions to amuse children. They were the imaginings of the bards and philosophers of the past as they pondered what beings with intelligences other than human might be like.

Now, as we are developing the ability to reach out and contact these probable beings from a million possible worlds, our view of what they might be like emerges from myth and embraces science. We need to have some idea of how an alien intelligence might be like our own and what are the basic qualities of intelligence that are shared by all intelligent creatures. Whether we are considering listening in to the radio broadcasts of beings *light years* away from earth or worried about communicating with the gray-skinned alien that has just abducted our mother-in-law, we have to have some idea of how an alien might think to understand what it is trying to tell us.

What Our Ancestors Believed

For most of our recorded history we have believed our species (*Homo sapiens*, or "thinking humans," which is the rather conceited scientific name we have given to ourselves) to be at the center of everything, both literally and figuratively. Creation myths from many cultures tell of how the gods (or the one God) picked mankind to be master and steward of all other life on earth. And our view of the universe was that it consisted of the earth with a dome above it across which the sun crossed daily and the stars nightly. The dome was thought to be somewhere between 50 and 200 miles up and made of a miraculous substance called "firmament," in which the stars were stuck like tiny points of light. And at or above that was the domain of Jupiter or Isis or Zeus or The Great Spirit or Ahura-Mazda. Under the earth was the Underworld, home of Pluto or Hades or Rhadamanthus or Vritra, depending on which temple your family prayed at.

But the Earth Is Round

Gradually, from about 500 B.C., learned people in China, Greece, and elsewhere began to accept the observable fact that the earth was a globe and that the moon was another globe circling the it. From this came the thought that the planets, which moved through the static backdrop of stars and followed the same arc across the sky as the moon, might also be globes, and thus, possibly, worlds like the earth.

Close Encounter

The earth is so big that it's hard to tell just by looking that it's a ball and not an infinite plane. The best clues we had before we could fly around it and look for ourselves was that the masts of ships appear to sink lower and lower as the ships sailed away from the observer, and also because shadows cast by objects in sunlight at noon were of different lengths at different locations on the planet—effects caused by the curvature of the earth.

When the Polish Astronomer Nicolaus Copernicus published *The Revolutions of the Celestial Orbs* in 1530, he confirmed the 1,500 year-old theory of the Greek philosopher Pythagoras that the earth went around the sun instead of the other way around. (Some theories are confirmed faster than others.) Copernicus's discovery removed humans from the center of the universe and put the other planets—which Copernicus had shown also circled the sun—on an even footing in importance with the earth. It wasn't long before speculation began as to whether these orbs might also be home to living beings.

But espousing new theories can be dangerous. Galileo Galilei, the 17th-century Italian astronomer, was forced to renounce his teaching of Copernicus's theory, which went against the church's doctrine that the earth was the center of the universe. The Italian philosopher Giordano Bruno was not so lucky. In 1600, he was burned at the stake for teaching that the sun was but one star in an infinite universe of innumerable worlds.

The Man in the Moon

Once the moon was seen to be a world similar to the earth, the idea that there might be life on it was a natural one. Writers began to speculate on what that life might be like.

The theme of possible life on the moon quickly became a popular one. In 1633, a book called *Somnium* (A Dream), by the noted astronomer Johannes Kepler, recounted how the hero reached the moon in a dream and found plants, animals, and people there. In 1638, John Wilkins, an English bishop, discussed the possibility of finding life on the moon in his book *The Discovery of a World in the Moone*. In the same year, a fictional account by Bishop Francis Godwin called *The Man in the Moone* was published. His hero reached the moon in a chariot pulled by a flock of geese and found people living there.

A careful observer could tell the moon was a world and not just a round disc in the sky, because the phases of the moon showed that it shined by light reflected from the sun; only that part of the moon facing the sun was lighted. Unless it passed through the earth's shadow—an effect we call a lunar eclipse—we could see both the light and the dark side and all the possibilities in between as the moon circled the earth. Shine a flashlight at a basketball in a dark room and look at it from all around and you'll see what I mean.

The Solar System Gets Bigger and More Interesting

Astronomers spent the next three centuries steadily expanding the known universe. To the six known planets in our own solar system; Mercury, Venus, Earth, Mars, Jupiter, and Saturn (in order of their orbits' distance from the sun) were added three more: Neptune, Uranus, and Pluto. The Asteroid Belt, an area where thousands of hunks of rock travel in orbit around the sun between the orbits of Mars and Jupiter, was discovered, and some astronomers thought that they marked the remains of a world that had blown up many thousands of years ago. It was even speculated that intelligent inhabitants had blown up their planet in a great atomic war. A less romantic view is that the asteroids are a scattering of interplanetary debris that somehow just never formed into a planet.

Scientists considering the solar system decided that the planets with the best chance for providing a home to life were Mars and Venus. Both are slightly smaller than the earth but not so small that all the atmosphere would have leaked away due to weak gravity. Venus is closer to the sun, so its temperature would presumably be hotter, and Mars is farther away, so it would probably be cooler, but nobody was sure just how much hotter or cooler they would be. When astronomers thought they saw canals on Mars it looked like a good bet for intelligent life, but they were sadly mistaken.

We Probe the Planets

American and Russian space probes sent to survey Venus in the 1960s found that the temperature on the surface of Venus was 480 degrees Centigrade, much hotter than expected and hot enough to melt lead, and, therefore, inhospitable to any form of life we can imagine. As for Mars, the two Viking probes that landed on Mars in 1976 found no canals. The landers performed chemical experiments that showed the possibility of life on the planet to be very doubtful but did not rule it out completely. If there is any sort of life on Mars, however, it is probably not much larger or more complex than earthly bacteria.

As astronomers learned more about the solar system it became increasingly probable that there could be nothing higher than the most elementary life—bacteria or lichen perhaps—on the other planets circling the sun, but nothing like the highly developed plants and animals found on earth. Therefore, it was almost certain that the solar system harbored but one intelligent life form—if you believe that human beings are an intelligent life form. (There are a couple of other possibilities on earth: perhaps elephants and orcas are brighter than we realize and it is just human chauvinism that prevents us from realizing it.)

Extraterrestrial Professions

Now that we are sending space probes to our sister planets with some regularity and seriously considering the possibility of life on planets circling other stars, several new professions have come into being to study what lies beyond the earth, which, in the grand scheme of things, is almost everything. In inventing the new names for some of these jobs, scientists merely stuck the Greek prefix *exo*, meaning "outside," in front of some more familiar titles. Among these new career paths are the following:

Sighting

For more moon madness and a good look at Mars and its absent canals, see Chapter 3. For more on what scientists think it takes to make a planet a possible home for life, see Chapter 20. Chapter 25 has an account of The Great Moon Hoax that was published in the *New York Sun* newspaper in 1835.

➤ An **exogeologist** examines the mineral and rock composition of a planet and tries to determine how it got that way. A surprising amount of this can now be done using sophisticated instruments from unmanned spacecraft in orbit around the subject planet.

➤ An **exobiologist** or **astrobiologist** is concerned with what forms of life might originate on other planets with surface temperatures and atmospheres vastly different from our own. Being able to recognize an alien life form might not be as easy as it seems. As of 1999, the University of Washington in Seattle will offer the first Ph.D program in astrobiology.

➤ An **exometeorologist** discovers how the weather works on a planet with a different atmosphere. This is important, for example, for finding safe places to land our exploration craft.

Don't Bother, They're Here

While scientists began to search for life in the reaches of the universe beyond the solar system, many people came to believe that intelligent aliens have already found us. There are ancient carvings in South America that could be interpreted to be 1,000 year-old depictions of astronauts. There are ancient roads in Peru that go nowhere but when seen from the air form line drawings and geometric designs. There are 2,000 year-old walls that are made of stones fitted so close together that we would have trouble duplicating them with modern technology.

These discoveries, and others, make some experts, like writer Erich Von Däniken, think that extraterrestrial visitors dropped by sometime in the distant past—a notion we will look at in Part 2 (Chapters 5–9).

And if the ancient astronauts were here and left, they may have come back. Or perhaps a second group has arrived to check up on the first. For the past 50 years there have been reports from around the world, at least two or three a week, sometimes many more, of strange objects darting about the sky at tremendous speeds or hovering silently over cars and beaming lights down at the passengers. People have reported seeing UFOs, chasing UFOs, being chased by UFOs, visiting UFOs, being visited by creatures from UFOs, and being abducted by UFOs.

Many thousands of people have had one degree of interaction or another with UFOs, and although most of these happenings are believed to have mundane explanations, there are a certain number that have never been satisfactorily explained. There are people who have been—or think they have been—abducted by alien beings and probed, peered at, and examined against their wills.

Close Encounter

In 840 A.D., Agobard, archbishop of Lyons, rescued three men and a woman who were about to be burned to death as witches by a mob. The four had been seen descending to the ground from a ship in the clouds. What happened to them after the rescue is not known.

Those who were abducted report being poked and prodded by the aliens from the UFOs, being medically examined by the aliens, and having strange objects implanted in their bodies by the aliens. Most of them claim to have then been hypnotically ordered to forget their experiences and, in some cases, furnished with false memories of what happened during the time they were gone.

Whether these tales are objectively true or not, it is clear that many of the people reporting them believe in what they are saying. We'll look at some of these cases in Chapters 13–15, and see what they have in common, how they differ, and what that might mean.

In this book we will examine the possibility that life, and more particularly intelligence, is not unique to earth, and that beings from the stars may already have visited us. A good and believable case can be made either way for both of these propositions; I won't lead you by the hand to any conclusions. But by the end of this book, you'll have a good idea what all the fuss is about and just why it might be important for us to do our best to find out the truth.

I Define Myself

Here are some definitions of UFO-related terms you will find throughout this book. There are other meanings, but this is what I mean when I use these words. More words will be defined through the course of the book as we need them; see Appendix A for a complete glossary.

➤ **Abductee:** One who has been, or believes he or she has been, abducted by aliens.

➤ **Alien:** An intelligent being from another planet.

➤ **Close Encounter:** An interaction with a UFO or an alien. To learn more about the four kinds of close encounters, see Chapter 13.

➤ **Contactee:** One who has been, or claims to have been, in direct conversation or more intimate contact with an alien.

➤ **Extraterrestrial:** Same as alien but more often used to describe aliens thought of as friendly.

➤ **Flying Saucer:** A disc-shaped flying object or, by extension, any UFO. (The name is based on a misunderstanding; see Chapter 10.)

➤ **Foo Fighters:** Mysterious small discs or globes of light that played tag with our fighters and bombers during World War II (see Chapter 10).

➤ **MIB (Men In Black):** Conservatively dressed men who occasionally show up at the site of a UFO incident to interview, or some say intimidate, the observers. Some UFOlogists believe they are government agents, some believe they are aliens, and some believe they are imaginary.

➤ **UFO (Unidentified Flying Object):** The blanket term for any of the various craft that have been sighted or claimed to have been sighted that do not correspond to any known human flying machines. If you've seen some lights in the sky that are probably the landing lights of an airplane, but you can't identify just what sort of plane it is, that doesn't make it a UFO. The craft has to be seen clearly enough for you to believe that it isn't an airplane, or it has to be behaving in a way, such as making sharp right-angle turns, that earthly aircraft are incapable of in order for it to be a UFO.

➤ **UFOlogist:** One who seriously studies UFOs.

> ## The Least You Need to Know
>
> ➤ The universe is made up of billions of galaxies, each of which contains billions of stars.
>
> ➤ Astronomers have recently determined that there are planets circling at least some of these stars.
>
> ➤ We do not know whether there is intelligent life—or indeed any sort of life—elsewhere in the universe, but more and more scientists today consider it probable.
>
> ➤ Many people believe that there are intelligent beings elsewhere in the universe, that some of them have visited our planet, and that they may still be here.

Chapter 2

Myth, Mind, and Magic

> ### In This Chapter
>
> ➤ The meaning of myth
>
> ➤ Do you believe in UFOs?
>
> ➤ The many possible truths about UFOs
>
> ➤ Why so many believe on so little evidence

There is something about a discussion of the possibility of extraterrestrial life—and more particularly extraterrestrial *intelligent* life—that provokes strong opinions among those involved. Human interest in the subject has been strong for hundreds, perhaps thousands, of years. Before our ancestors had a reasonably accurate idea of the composition of the sky, while most people thought it was a dome along which the sun traveled daily from the Eastern Ocean to the Western Sea, and the stars were pin pricks in the dome letting the celestial light shine through, there were important myths about nonhuman intelligences and unearthly beings. The folk legends of many groups tell of people who came from the sky; as gods, as demons, as leaders, or as poor lost souls.

To See Ourselves as Others See Us

We have been pondering, musing, and dreaming about the possible shape and character of intelligences other than our own for as far back as we know. Many of us talk to dogs, cats, trees, and stuffed animals in the fond hope that they might someday talk back. Long ago we realized that we could learn much about the universe, about ourselves, and about the meaning and value of intelligence if we could, however briefly, see through the eyes of another intelligent species.

Sighting

The **Epic of Gilgamesh** was found inscribed on clay tablets in the library of Ashurbanipal, king of Assyria, at his palace at Nineveh. The tablets date back to around 650 B.C. and are believed to be copies of a story that was already ancient at that time.

And we have tried, if only in our imagination, to see ourselves as others see us. The stories about humans interacting with nonhuman intelligences go back past the start of written records. Animals, plants, and rocks that speak, puppets that come to life, creatures that are half animal and half human, as well as beings that are in some way either more or less than human—imps, demons, angels, and gods—have become a part of the collective mythology of mankind. In the *Epic of Gilgamesh*, which dates back more than 2,500 years to ancient Babylon, King Gilgamesh deals with gods, ghosts, and creatures of the underworld.

It is a natural continuation of this interest in nonhuman beings that, as we discovered the vastness of the universe, we wondered what sort of beings might live "out there." At first, as our view of the solar system expanded, it didn't occur to anyone to doubt that there was life on other planets. Every place we had explored had proved to be home to life, and we knew of no reason why that should not continue to be the case on the moon, Mars, Venus, and even the sun.

In their writings early fantasists and philosophers populated the planets with beings much like us, and "moon-men" and Martians entered our mythology.

The Stuff of Myth

When we call something a *myth* we are not saying that the story isn't true. The tale may be strictly true, or it may be based in truth but so transformed and laden with

Contact

A **myth** is a story, often about a god or a hero, that somehow speaks to the human condition, perhaps that teaches us something of what it is to be a member of the society that created the myth.

An **archetype** is a person or object that represents and stands for a whole class of things.

meaning that the actual facts are no longer important. It might be based on specific happenings, or it could be an *archetype*, a sort of composite truth based on many separate events. Psychologist C. G. Jung considered true archetypes to exist in "the collective unconscious" and to be part of the human inheritance. Writers have created characters who represent classical archetypes. Romeo and Juliet are archetypical young lovers; Don Juan is the image of the womanizer; Sherlock Holmes is the archetypical detective; d'Artagnan the archetypical hero.

Take the legend of King Arthur, for example. There was a King Arthur, actually Artorius, back around 450 A.D. He was undoubtedly a good king, and an ancient round table has been found that might have been his. But whether the real Arthur was the son of Uther Pendragon and had a resident magician named Merlin and a covey of noble knights who did good deeds is important only to historians. The King Arthur that we need to raise our spirits and help us think noble thoughts is the Arthur of Tennyson's *The Idylls of the King*, the Arthur of legend.

In some cases myths have grown up around true stories that happened so long ago that the direct history of the event has been lost in the mists of time. Thirty centuries ago a blind Greek poet named Homer was supposed to have written the *Iliad*, a wondrous tale of the siege of Troy over the kidnapping of Helen, the beautiful wife of the king of Sparta. There are gods and heroes and mighty battles and great deeds.

No one knew where Troy was to be found, however, and there was no historical record of a Helen or, for that matter, a Homer. Historians came to think that the story was really the weaving together by many ancient storytellers of many ancient tales into one great myth.

Report from the Field

"Humans need order, which comes both from knowledge and myth. The flying saucer and alien myths are really about how one makes order out of his world. The idea of disk-shaped alien spaceships becomes the symbol for hopes and fears about the world."

—Curtis Peebles, *Watch the Skies!: A Chronicle of the Flying Saucer Myth*

Then, in 1893, an amateur archeologist named Heinrich Schliemann found the fabled city of Troy, and now we know that at least part of the legend is true.

Ancient Wisdom

So, to get back to our original theme, it could be that visitors from the stars really have been among us in the distant past and have taught us many things. If so, the actual accounts of those visits have long since been lost, and vague and distorted stories, told over and over until the details have been obscured, now regarded as myths or fairy tales, may be all that remain.

Let us suppose that hundreds, or even thousands, of years ago intelligent beings from somewhere else came to earth, stayed for a while, and then went away. For some time and in great detail we would retell the story of their stay among us, and how they flew about with wondrous machines and helped with great building projects; how they cured the sick, restored vision to the blind, made the lame walk; how they smote with thunder and lightning anyone foolish enough to oppose them.

Then, in a few generations, the stories would be regarded as legends, as tales of the distant past when heroes walked the earth, or as stories of bogeymen used to frighten children into good behavior.

We have many such tales. There are giants mentioned in the Bible that came to earth and mated with human women (see Chapter 6 of this book). There are the "white gods" of Inca legends that the Inca chiefs mistook the Spaniards for, making the Spanish takeover of South America even easier than it otherwise would have been.

Report from the Field

"Myths are folk narratives that deal with transcendental issues such as the relationship between humans and unearthly beings."

—Charles Ziegler, Coauthor, *UFO Crash at Roswell: The Genesis of a Modern Myth*

There are goblins and imps and sprites and fairies and elves and a host of other creatures whose origins are lost in pre-history.

There are, as we shall see in Part Two (Chapters 5–9), centuries-old stories of odd-looking people visiting various parts of the planet in flying ships of many different sorts. There are stories of sightings and encounters and abductions and sexual liaisons, many paralleling the sort of UFO encounters we hear about today.

Do You Believe?

If someone were to ask you "Do you believe in UFOs?" what would your response be? As a science-fiction writer, I have often been asked the question. Whenever I would do a newspaper interview, or speak to a school group, or appear on a television show, or even just meet someone at a party, it was always one of the first questions I was asked.

Close Encounter

As writer Gertrude Stein lay dying, her lifelong friend Alice B. Toklas leaned over her and murmured, "Gertrude, what's the answer?"

Gertrude, with her last breath, replied, "What's the question?"

As Gertrude Stein knew, the answers you get depend on the questions you ask. And this lady, who loved to play with words in her works, also knew that the same word or phrase can mean many different things depending on who's saying it and to whom it is being said (or written).

What I discovered was that, although the words were the same, I was actually being asked many different questions. The questioner brought to the question his or her idea of the universe and some notion as to what the correct answer should be. Some of the questions that were actually being asked, hidden behind that simply worded query, were:

➤ Do you believe in the possibility of extraterrestrial life?

➤ Do you think it possible that we might be visited by alien beings?

➤ Do you think we're even now being investigated by beings from other worlds?

➤ Are you the sort of nut who thinks little green (or gray or snow-white) men are running around the countryside kidnapping people?

➤ Will you listen sympathetically to my story of being kidnapped by little green men?

➤ Do you feel that parasympathetic vibrations from the astral plain could manifest themselves as what are known to the uninitiated as "flying saucers?"

➤ Do you realize that we're all being duped by self-serving frauds who are lying about their UFO experiences to get their 15 minutes of fame or sell their story to the tabloids?

➤ Are you aware there is a vast government conspiracy to cover up the fact that we've been contacted by superior beings from another galaxy?

➤ You, as an intelligent person, cannot possibly believe that our planet is actually being visited by superior beings from another galaxy. To what do you attribute the current wave of sightings and reports? Is it mass hysteria, contact hypnosis, or what?

Report from the Field

"Flying saucers are real. Too many good men have seen them that don't have hallucinations."

—Captain Eddie Rickenbacker, World War I flying ace and aviation expert

From Primal Soup to Persistent Nuts

To help determine the truth, or at least the most probable scenario, it will help to look at the whole range of possibilities for the existence of extraterrestrial life. I'll put them in order from the most negative (assuming there's no such thing) to the most positive (assuming unearthly beings are among us even now). This is not in any way a chart of the probability of these events or of my belief in any of them, just a list of what might be. There are people who believe—or profess to believe—each of these possibilities.

Look at the following list and decide which numbered item most closely corresponds with your present attitude about the existence of extraterrestrial life. When you've finished this book you might find it interesting to come back to the list and see whether you then pick a different number.

1. We are unique in the universe, a sheer accident that has not been repeated and will not be. Nowhere in the billions upon billions of stars is there any other life except that on earth.

2. There is some life elsewhere, on planets circling stars scattered throughout the universe, but it is a very rare event. And in any case none of it has developed anything approaching intelligence.

3. There has been life on other planets that developed intelligence, and even civilizations. But these civilizations exist for brief moments—say a few thousand years or so—before self-destructing. The odds of any of these other civilizations existing at the same moment as our own are vanishingly small, and even if one did exist it would almost certainly be hundreds of thousands if not millions of light years away. By the time any signals from this civilization could reach us, it—or we—would be long extinct.

4. There are many other civilizations, and we may eventually pick up radio or other signals from one or more of them. But Einstein's cold equations hold, and there is no way to exceed the speed of light (186,282 miles per second). Even though that is very fast, the other stars are so exceedingly far from us that we are isolated on our little planet. Interstellar travel will never be accomplished.

5. There are many other intelligent life forms out there, and they communicate regularly with each other. Although actually traveling between the stars takes a very long time, information is regularly exchanged. When we manage to locate the first signals and send our reply, their antennas will be turned in our direction and we will become part of a true interstellar community.

6. There is a galactic civilization out there, and they have perfected a faster-than-light drive for their space ships. But either they have not found us yet, or they have looked us over and found us not to be the sort of beings they want to associate with. Perhaps we are in a sort of interstellar quarantine, with other races forbidden to contact us until we show some signs of growing up and being able to live in peace with our neighbors.

7. An alien race came to earth many tens of thousands of years ago and seeded it with life in their image. Every once in a while they come back to see how we're doing. The question is, the next time they come will they say, "Wonderful! Things are going according to plan." or "Damn, what a mess! We'd better erase this lot and start over."

8. Regardless of whether there is intelligent life elsewhere in the universe, it has not arrived here yet. The current sightings of UFOs, as numerous and continuous as they are, are merely symptoms of a mass psychosis brought on by the fear of nuclear war. It is the modern equivalent of the witch hunts of medieval Europe, where hundreds of respectable people claimed to have seen witches riding around on their broomsticks blighting the crops and souring milk.

9. Alien beings are keeping a close watch on us. They are forbidden by their rules of contact from letting an inferior race such as us know they are there, but every once in a while we get a glimpse of one of their ships.

10. Extraterrestrial beings of great intelligence have selected some among us to be their representatives, to obey their rules, and to prepare for a wonderful future. These chosen few will be glad to tell you all about it.

11. Extraterrestrials have been watching us for some time, and several of their scout craft have accidentally crashed in various places around the planet, with the crews dying in the crashes. Secret government organizations have sequestered the crashed space ships and the bodies of the aliens to try to discover their secrets.

12. Beings from other worlds are actively investigating earth and its inhabitants. Occasionally, they kidnap humans and subject them to a battery of tests and probe their bodies with strange instruments. Some people have had this happen many times, as though they were part of a controlled experiment. The aliens have the ability to make their subjects forget the experience, which can then only be brought out by hypnosis.

Sightings

An alternate theory is that in the distant past an alien space ship landed on an earth that was devoid of life, perhaps to make repairs or fill their water tanks. The aliens dumped their garbage before they left, and all life on earth, including us, is descended from the microbes in that garbage.

13. There are aliens among us right now. The government has made a secret pact with the extraterrestrial leaders to get their technology. They are even now working with our scientists in secret labs in the western desert. In return we are going to let them settle in Nevada, or perhaps Los Angeles, where nobody will notice them.

Or Perhaps...

There are people who believe in the existence of UFOs, but who do not think they come from other planets. Their theories include:

➤ **Time Travel**: The ships come from the far future to their past, which is our present, in order to change the present to improve our future, which becomes their past. If you can't follow that, that's okay.

➤ **Alternate Universes**: The UFOs come from a different dimension to spy on our dimension, or possibly to steal our natural resources.

➤ **The Hollow Earth**: The saucers come from a hole in the earth, usually believed to be located at the North Pole (see Chapter 16).

➤ **The Secret Civilization**: We are being watched by a civilization of not-quite-humans who live in secret underground cities located around the world. One of them is under Mount Shasta in Washington State. They may be remnants of lost Atlantis.

➤ **The Supernatural Theory**: UFOs are actually manifestations of the spirit world, along with ghosts, poltergeists, banshees, elves, and fairies.

➤ **The Secret Weapon Theory**: UFOs are secret weapons being tested by our government, by the Soviets (now the Russians), by a group of resurgent Nazis, or by your favorite bogeyman.

What Does It All Mean?

In one sense it doesn't matter whether the flying saucers are real or are a figment of our collective imagination. It will certainly matter if one lands on the White House lawn and invites us to join the Galactic Federation; but until that happy day the elusiveness of UFOs defines their category.

It is the readiness of many of us to believe in UFOs with little or no evidence that speaks to who we are as a culture and what we need from our fellows and from the universe.

Close Encounter

A recent Gallup Poll (September, 1996) showed that 76 percent of Americans believe in the probable existence of extraterrestrial life. This is up from 57 percent in 1978. Also, 71 percent of those polled believed that our government knows more about UFOs than it is telling.

I do not speak of those happy few who have—or believe they have—actually seen UFOs close enough to be sure of their alien manufacture, or have spoken to the aliens inside and know their origin and their goals. They have reason to believe in what they have seen, whatever the world might think.

It's the rest of us who have grown up in this society and have been constantly bombarded with untruths and distortions disguised as truth in tabloid weeklies, media advertising, and television commercials. We have learned, one would think, to be selective in what we choose to believe. And yet many—most—of us choose to believe in the literal existence of UFOs.

In the following chapters we'll see if we can figure out why, and just what it is that so many of us believe in. We'll also take a look at the current scientific attempts to contact intelligent beings on planets circling distant stars.

The Least You Need to Know

➤ Nonhuman intelligences have long been an important part of the myths of different cultures.

➤ If aliens have had visited earth centuries ago, the details of that visitation would by now have merged with other myths.

➤ Belief in UFOs can range from a belief that they are possible to a belief that they are here right now.

➤ Most Americans do believe in the existence of flying saucers.

Chapter 3

The Man in the Moon and Other High Places

In This Chapter

➤ The myths of the sun and moon

➤ Ancient Greek philosophers consider life elsewhere

➤ Early tales of travel to the sun and moon

➤ Fictional visits to Mars

Way back sometime before the dawn of recorded history (which was about 5,000 years ago), we humans began wondering about those heavenly bodies closest to us: the sun, the moon, and the five naked-eye planets (Mercury, Venus, Mars, Jupiter, and Saturn in order out from the sun). They are the only celestial objects that can be seen to move about in the seemingly fixed field of stars, and therefore have always been objects of fascination and occasionally fear.

In this chapter, we'll take a look at ancient views of the sun, the planets, and the stars, and show how the interest in them evolved into our modern understanding.

The Gods Look Down

Our ancestors saw their lives as hemmed in by events they could not understand caused by forces over which they had no control. They practiced *polytheistic* and *pantheistic* religions that attributed godlike or supernatural qualities to everything around them. There were gods of the forest and the river, gods of the mountain and the valley, rain gods, harvest gods, and gods of the hunt. If these gods were appealed to, using just the right prayers and incantations, sacrificing just the right animal or virgin, they might be induced to behave in a reasonable manner and allow the tribe to sustain itself for one more season.

Contact

Polytheism is a belief in many gods. **Pantheism** is the belief that God and the universe are one, that God is in everything.

The gods of the sky were seen as especially powerful, as the sky was out of our reach and yet contributed greatly to the success or failure of human endeavor. The sky gods could withhold rain and kill the crops, or cause floods to wash the crops away. They could sometimes cause a full moon to disappear briefly in the middle of the night and, much scarier, cause the sun to be swallowed up in the middle of the day. (Today we know these phenomena to be lunar and solar eclipses.) Thunder was frightening, and lightning even more so. (All through the Middle Ages, priests had a hard time explaining why God so often destroyed churches during lightning storms.)

The Sun in the Morning

The sun, of course, was the most important celestial object. It occupied the daytime sky basically unopposed. (Yes, I know, the stars are there during the daytime, we just can't see them because the sun is too bright—but our ancestors didn't know that.) Oh, occasionally the moon hung around during the day, or the planet Venus could be seen in the early morning or at dusk, but they seemed much dimmer compared to the radiance of the sun.

Sighting

Our English word "sun" comes from the Scandinavian sun god *Sunna*, who also drove across the sky daily, and lived in constant fear of the wolf Fenris, who devoured the sun every time there was an eclipse.

The sun, as the source of light and heat and the object that dominates the daytime sky, was regarded as a god by just about every primitive culture. The Assyrian *Shamash*, the Chaldean *Merodach*, the Zoroastrian *Ormuzd* were all sun gods, as was *Ra* in Egypt and the Aztec *Tezcatlipoca*. The Greek sun god *Helios*, known to the Romans as *Sol*, drove the chariot of the sun across the sky from the eastern ocean to the western sea every day, to bring us daylight and warmth. Helios was often identified with Apollo, who went around telling people how handsome he was.

The Moon at Night

The moon was Diana ("the huntress") or Hecate or Cynthia ("she who hunts the clouds"), and the crescent moon was Astarte. As the Babylonian Ishtar (Phoenician Astoreth), she was the goddess of fertility. The moon was always female, as the sun was always male. The moon was associated with magic and sorcery and hidden things.

Balls in the Sky

It is a peculiar and wonderful ability of human beings to hold two or more contrary views at the same time. About 3,000 years ago, even as the myths of the gods were becoming ritualized, some people were taking a look at the available evidence and coming to different conclusions. They thought of themselves as what we would call natural scientists, but we reach back into history and label them philosophers.

These philosophers taught that rational thought was the process by which we could understand the universe, and possibly even each other. They didn't have much luck convincing the multitudes then, and their spiritual descendants are not having much luck today. Their observation and analysis showed them that the sun was not a god, but a fiery ball high in the sky. And the moon was another ball, probably lit by the reflected light of the sun, and it could be seen to have dark and light areas that could be mountains and valleys, and possibly even seas.

A World Much Like Our Own

Sometime around the year 280 B.C., the Greek philosopher Anaxagoras proposed that the sun was not a god, but a white-hot stone about the size of southern Greece. He was arrested, tried, and sent into exile for making fun of the gods. He also believed that the moon was a world much like the earth. If this was so, there was no reason that he knew of to suppose that the moon couldn't have living beings on it, and probably intelligent beings.

One hundred and twenty years later, the Greek astronomer Hipparchus invented trigonometry and used it to determine the distance from the earth to the moon. His figure was 240,000 miles, which is almost right. (The accepted distance today is 239,000 miles—after all, we've been there.)

Lost Hopes and Forgotten Dreams

One fanciful view of the moon that took hold during the Middle Ages held that it was the destination of all lost objects, including not only that missing sock, but also lost hopes and forgotten dreams and misspent time and broken vows. The Italian poet Ariosto, in his great epic *Orlando Furioso* (Orlando the Mad), written in 1532, has his hero Orlando lose his wits, which are taken to the moon. Orlando's buddy Astolpho goes to the moon in the prophet Elijah's chariot, finds it full of lost prayers, forgotten poems, courtiers' gifts to princes, and Orlando's lost wits, which he brings back in an urn.

In *The Rape of the Lock*, Alexander Pope (1688–1744) takes up this theme, telling us that on the moon:

> There heros' wits are kept in pond'rous vases,
> And beaux' in snuff-boxes and tweezer-cases,
> There broken vows and death-bed alms are found
> And lovers' hearts with ends of ribbon bound.
> The courtier's promises, and sick man's prayers,
> The smiles of harlots, and the tears of heirs
> Cages for gnats, and chains to yoke a flea,
> Dried butterflies, and tomes of *casuistry*.

25

Trips to the Moon and Sun

Even before the formal invention of science fiction—let us say it started with Jules Verne in the late 19th century—writers with fanciful imaginations and something to say about the state of the world had their heroes visiting the moon and, often, the sun. One way of demonstrating the problems with the society you live in is to contrast it with a society somewhere else. And if there is no society that embraces those social or intellectual values that you want to discuss, why then you make one up and put it somewhere your readers have never been so they can't argue with you.

In *Gulliver's Travels* (1726), for example, Jonathan Swift casts his hero among the Lilliputians, tiny people whose tiny problems mirror the ridiculousness of some human concerns. (For example, they are prepared to go to war over which end of a soft-boiled egg to crack.) Gulliver then travels on to Brobdingnag, where giants exemplify the grossness of humans from the point of view of someone able to examine them closely, and to Laputa, where the people are normal sized but preoccupied with science and logic to the point of idiocy. Finally Gulliver arrives at the land of the admirable Houyhnhnms, who look like horses but behave like reasoning beings, and the Yahoos, who look human and behave like animals.

Contact

Casuistry is the study of problems of conscience and morality and how to resolve them. The word implies the ability to use sophisticated logical distinctions to allow you to do what you wanted to do in the first place.

Swift put his mythical lands on far-off islands hidden in the vastness of the ocean, but many writers preferred to go even farther afield, to the moon and beyond.

Close Encounter

Jonathan Swift (1667–1745) was born in Dublin, Ireland, and became a cleric in the Church of England, spending several years as Dean of St. Patrick's Cathedral in Dublin. His biting satires included *A Modest Proposal for Preventing the Children of Poor People from Being a Burden to their Parents or the Country*. Published as a pamphlet in 1729, it recommended that the problem of starving children in Ireland be solved by feeding them to the rich.

The better writers influenced our ideas of what life elsewhere might be like, and also of how we should conduct ourselves here on earth. Among the more noted of these early writers are the following.

Lucian

A True History, which despite its title is the first fictional account of a trip to the moon, was written in 165 A.D. by the Greek writer Lucian of Samosata. In the story Lucian is one of the passengers on a ship that is carried into the atmosphere by a waterspout and then blown to the moon. They encounter warriors riding huge fleas, people with artificial genitals, and other wonders, and discover that the king of the moon is at war with the king of the sun over the planet Jupiter. They return to earth, landing in the ocean, where they are swallowed by a whale. After this the tale gets truly strange.

Lucian followed this with a second work, *Icaromenippus*, in which his hero Menippus flies from Mount Olympus to the moon using one wing from an eagle and one from a vulture. Finding only spirits living on the moon, and noting that the earth was, indeed, round, he went on to the sun. This annoyed the gods, who took away his wings and sent him back to earth.

Sighting

A Greek humorist in the time of the Roman Empire, Lucian of Samosata (ca. 120–200 A.D.) was known for his mordant wit and unconventional thinking, which earned him the nickname "the Blasphemer." His work has been compared with that of Swift and Voltaire. The influence of his fantastic, ribald, funny, irreverent writings stretched from François Rabelais to Jonathan Swift to Mark Twain.

Kepler

The famous astronomer Johannes Kepler (1571–1630) wrote *Somnium* ("dream" in Latin), a romance of life on the moon, in 1634. His moon is divided into two zones—a freezing one facing away from the sun, and a burning one facing the sun. It has air and water and is populated with monsters. As Kepler could not conceive of any scientific way to reach the moon, his hero gets there in a dream.

Godwin

Francis Godwin (1562–1633), an English bishop, wrote *The Man in the Moone*, or, *A Discourse of a Voyage Thither by Domingo Gonsales*, the first book on this theme to be written in English. It was first published in 1638, five years after his death. In it, Gonsales flew to the moon behind several large swan-like birds called "gansas." There he found a peaceful race of tall beings who sent all potential troublemakers to earth. The book has been reprinted many times since its initial publication, and has influenced many subsequent writers.

Cyrano

Cyrano de Bergerac did Lucian one better by actually reaching the sun in his stories. A king's musketeer, poet, and author, de Bergerac was made famous as the title character of Edmond Rostand's 19th-century play. The real Cyrano wrote a pair of space-travel romances that were published together as *The Comical History of the States* and *Empires of the Worlds of the Moon and Sun* (1651). In the first, he invented the rocket ship, reaching the moon by using large gunpowder rockets to blast off from the earth. His four-legged moon men kept sunlight in clear globes. Having only rudimentary ideas of sex, they put him in a cage with Domingo Gonsales (the hero of Bishop Godwin's book), hoping that the two would mate. In his next trip, he went to the sun in a phone booth-sized box on a 22-month trip to "the great plains of day," meeting with the Kingdom of Birds, intelligent flying creatures who put him in prison because he is a disgusting human being. The work is both a satire and a serious metaphysical reflection on humanity's place in the universe.

Russen

In 1703, David Russen wrote *Iter Lunare*, or, *A Voyage to the Moon*. In it he examines the books of Godwin and Cyrano and explains how the science in them is wrong; birds couldn't fly to the moon because there's no air in the space between, a giant clockwork (one of Cyrano's methods) would merely cause the vehicle to spin about without getting anywhere, and similar errors in logic. He seems to have taken their flights of fantasy very seriously. But, interestingly, the one thing he does not dispute is the possibility of finding life on the moon.

Voltaire

Some writers went further afield for their aliens. In Voltaire's story *Micromégas* (1752), Micromégas is a being from the star Sirius, and is rather large as earth beings compute size. The circumference of Sirius, Voltaire explains, is 21,600,000 times that of earth, and the beings that live there are in proportion. Micromégas is 120,000 feet high.

Micromégas is exiled from his home star for the heresy of writing a book in which he suggests that it might be possible for beings to live elsewhere in the universe than Sirius, so he decides to travel about the universe to prove that his theory is true. A master of the laws of gravitation, he is able to flit about the universe from star to star with little effort.

With a pal that he meets on Saturn, he muses about the futility of life. ("Our existence is a point, our duration an instant, and our globe an atom."—and this about the planet Saturn, which could swallow the Earth without noticing, and his character's lifespan of 15,000 years.) Coming to the earth, these giant creatures wander around convinced that the planet is uninhabited, since all earthly life is so much smaller than they. When by accident they discover the existence of microscopic (to them) human beings, they marvel that such tiny creatures can have any intelligence at all. But they don't think much of our intelligence. When told about war, they are astonished that thousands of lives will be taken over a plot of land smaller than Micromégas's heel, and that these thousands are fighting to support rulers they've never seen. When told about religion, and the belief that the universe is made for mankind's pleasure, they break up laughing.

Mars and Its Channels

In 1877, when the planet Mars was as close as it ever gets to the earth, the Italian astronomer Giovanni Schiaparelli was observing Mars through one of the best telescopes available at that time, and he saw something that no astronomer before had noticed: a pattern of long, thin lines connecting the various dark places on the surface. He labeled the lines *canali* on his map, which is Italian for channels. But just what were the lines? And, for that matter, what were the dark places? Mars was seen to have white areas at the planet's north and south poles during its winters, but they faded away during the summer. Could these be ice? This would mean that there wasn't much water on the planet, since it melted away during the summer. On earth the poles hold vast oceans of water locked away permanently as ice.

Sighting

Voltaire was the nom de plume of François Marie Arouet (1694–1778), a practicing playwright, novelist, essayist, historian, poet, satirist, philosopher, and skeptic who was noted for his humanist viewpoint and the scalpel-like precision of his wit.

Close Encounter

Actually one other astronomer had seen lines on Mars. Back in 1869, another Italian, Pietro Angelo Secchi, had recorded *canali*, but his were much shorter and plumper and there were not as many of them. It was Schiaparelli's extensive network of long, thin *canali* that caught the attention of his brother astronomers and the public.

And, if there was water, but only a little, couldn't Schiaparelli's *canali* be not channels but *canals* purposely cut through the Martian deserts by the intelligent design of the Martians to bring water to the dark spots, which must then be irrigated areas producing the food on which the Martians depended?

Mars Becomes Popular

When reports of Schiaparelli's discovery got out, the popular press ran with the story. The channels were promptly turned into canals, and speculation about the possible inhabitants of the red planet became a popular pastime.

Over the next 40 years, the interest in Mars grew tremendously, as a new generation of astronomers, working with the best instruments, expanded and refined Schiaparelli's *canali* until the maps of Mars showed a network of canals criss-crossing the planet.

Extravagant theories were advanced about these canals and the beings who had created them. It was said that the Martians were an old race with great intelligence on a dying planet, doing their best to preserve what little water was left to them. They had created the network of canals, going from pole to pole, to bring the melting ice down to where it was needed for irrigation.

Apergy

The fictional accounts kept pace with the facts, and the stories of travel to Mars were written with a veneer of the purest pseudo-science. In *Across the Zodiac* (1880), Percy Greg has his hero travel to Mars in his space ship the *Astronaut* by means of an anti-gravity force called "apergy." He finds that evolution on Mars has paralleled earth, and the people are much like us. But their science is a thousand years ahead of ours; they have electric cars, dirigibles, typewriters that take dictation, three-dimensional movies, and they practice polygamy. You can't get much more advanced than that.

In 1894 John Jacob Astor took Greg's ideas a step further and, in *A Journey in Other Worlds*, had his apergy-powered space ship *Callisto* travel to Jupiter and Saturn. Jupiter is inhabited by dinosaurs and mastodons and other prehistoric bests. Saturn is the abode of the spirits of the departed, and they impart much other-worldly wisdom to the hero.

A Steel Globe

In Robert Cromie's 1891 novel, *A Plunge into Space*, his heros construct a large steel spaceship shaped like a globe. In a burst of sheer imaginative brilliance, they name it the *Steel Globe*, and set off for Mars. As before, they find the natives of Mars much like the natives of earth, but more advanced, living in "The City of Delight, which had streets lined with flowering shrubs."

Barsoom

Edgar Rice Burroughs, creator of Tarzan, took his readers to Mars with his 1912 novel *A Princess of Mars*. His Mars was called Barsoom, and there was nothing scientific about his stories; they were outright sword-and-buckler adventure novels. But Barsoom was based on the Schiaparelli Mars, replete with canals.

John Carter, Burroughs's hero, arrives on Barsoom by a strange sort of out-of-body astral projection, and finds it occupied by a decadent race of red men, mixed descendants of white, reddish-yellow, and almost black earlier races. There is also a race of tall, green, four-armed barbarians (and I will resist the temptation to add here that four-armed is forewarned), and a black-bearded, yellow people at the north pole.

The races on Burroughs's Mars resemble humans—give or take an extra pair of arms—except that they are not mammals. The women do not give birth to live babies, but lay eggs. The eggs take several years to mature, and once hatched a Barsoomian will live

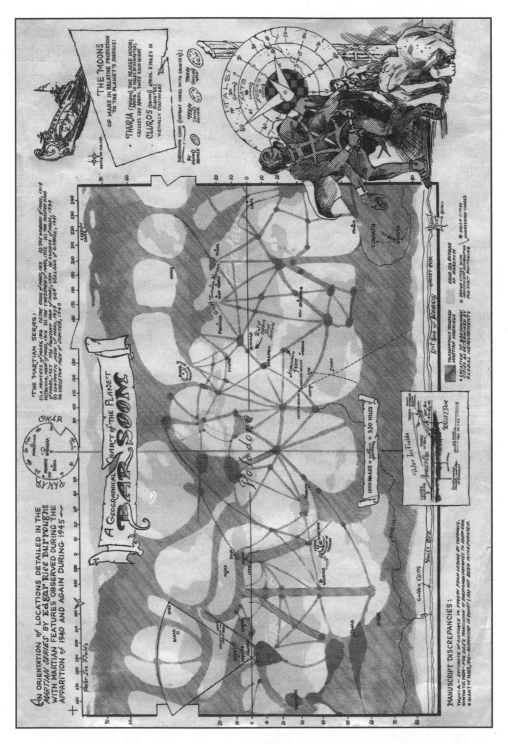

A map of the canals of Mars, with the cities of Edgar Rice Burroughs's Barsoom added.

Sighting

Burroughs's Barsoom resembles the Mars of Edwin Lester Arnold's 1905 *Lieut. Gulliver Jones: His Vacation.* Jones gets to Mars by way of a grubby magic carpet rather than astral projection, but the decadent civilization and the powerful and savage barbarian nomads or Arnold's Mars are echoed in Borough's Barsoom.

for about a thousand years, if he or she doesn't get killed off in one of the constant wars.

The War of the Worlds

In H. G. Wells' *The War of the Worlds* (1898), the Martians come to Earth, with dire consequences for all concerned. We'll look at that, as well as the Great Moon Hoax and other more recent excursions into the literature of extraterrestrial intelligence in Chapters 25 and 26.

The Canals Disappear

The belief in the canals of Mars and its probable intelligent inhabitants persisted for over a hundred years. It wasn't until the voyages of the two unmanned Viking spacecraft in 1975 that close-up photographs established that there were no canals on the surface of Mars. The canali had been artifacts of Schiaparelli's telescope and the viewing conditions, and the imaginations of the later astronomers.

But there are questions about life on Mars, and on even more distant planets and moons in our solar system, that are still not resolved, as we'll see in Chapter 21.

The Least You Need to Know

➤ The sun and the moon were regarded as gods by our ancestors.

➤ About 2,000 years ago, philosophers in Greece and elsewhere reasoned that the sun and moon were worlds much like the earth—except in the case of the sun, much hotter.

➤ Early writers such as Lucian, Cyrano de Bergerac, and Voltaire used stories of trips to the moon as satirical ways of examining the follies of those here on earth.

➤ When the astronomer Schiaparelli thought he discovered canali (channels) on Mars, the popular press promptly turned them into canals, dug and maintained by intelligent Martians, and his fellow astronomers extended the network of canals in their viewings until they covered the planet from pole to pole.

➤ It wasn't until the recent unmanned voyages to Mars that we established for sure that the canals were an artifact of the viewing conditions, and did not exist on the surface of Mars.

Truths Found in Ancient Manuscripts

In the long-ago days of the pharaohs, the Egyptian priests taught that the god Thoth brought writing down from the gods to mankind. The other gods warned Thoth against such a frivolous act, as no good could come of increasing the knowledge of humans, but he did it anyway. The word for "writing" in ancient Egyptian translates as "language of the gods."

In Greek mythology, it was Cadmus, the son of Agenor, king of Phoenicia, who brought the alphabet to Greece. Cadmus was on a quest to find his sister Europa, who had been taken to Crete by Zeus, king of the gods, for reasons of his own. In order to guard and protect Europa, Zeus had a mechanical man made out of bronze, who marched around the shores of Crete and sank any ships foolish enough to try to come ashore. Cadmus was assaulted by a dragon, which he fought and killed. The goddess Minerva instructed him to sow the dragon's teeth in a field, and in their place warriors in full armor sprang up. Cadmus and the warriors went on to found the city of Thebes.

Here, in these earliest myths to be recorded (with the new invention, writing), we see several related tales that could be interpreted as suggesting the presence of alien intelligences greater than our own coming from outerspace, or at least somewhere unearthly; the "gods" bringing a new invention "down" to benefit us dumb earthlings; and the creation of what we today would call a robot several thousand years before such mechanical contrivances were possible.

Significant Stories

What are we to make of such stories? It is always tempting to look over these ancient myths and find in them, not allegories or attempts by a primitive people to explain what they could not understand, but tales of deep significance, concealing important truths.

The problem is that one man's truth is another's idiotic babbling. And so many "truths" can be found in the same narrative that it's clear that what preconceptions you bring to a tale are the strongest influence on what you will get out of it. The story of the gods bringing writing down to earth can be seen in any of the following ways:

➤ Literal truth. There are these gods, Ra and Thoth and so on, and Thoth brought writing down to earth.

➤ An attempt to re-create and explain a past event the truth of which has long been forgotten.

➤ A tale for children and the childlike, to explain in simple terms important truths that are too complex to be easily understood.

➤ Wonderful allegory, showing the art of writing to be important enough to be one of the gifts of the gods.

➤ A way of emphasizing the value of writing and those who use it, and thus enhancing the prestige of the priests and scribes, who were the only ones who could read or write.

➤ A vague cultural memory of a real past event, where an alien being, with seemingly godlike power, created an alphabet for the use of we poor mortals.

➤ A story spread by the Devil to distract people from coming to the path of the True Religion (whatever that may be).

This is the way it is with most of the history and myth and legend that is being looked at with the more sophisticated vision of today and reinterpreted to include the possibility of alien visitation. It is possible that extraterrestrials were involved in one or more of

Report from the Field

"It is in the literature of religion that flying objects from celestial countries are most commonly encountered, along with descriptions of the organization, nature, and philosophy of their occupants. Indeed, several writers have consistently pointed out that the fundamental texts of every religion refer to the contact of the human community with a 'superior race' of beings from the sky."

—Jacques Vallee, *Passport to Magonia* (1969)

these myths, but it is only one possibility among many, and we should look for stronger proof before betting the family jewels on any particular answer.

Sanskrit Stories

These superior beings from outerspace were not always believed to be friendly. The Hindu epic *Mahabharata*, which was written in Sanskrit, was compiled over many centuries and completed in the 3rd century A.D. It tells of "*vimanas,*" flying discs that caused great destruction. The epic records that the city of Varanasi, "burned with all its princes and their followers, its inhabitants, horses, elephants, treasures and granaries, houses, palaces, and markets. The whole of a city… was thus wrapped in flames by the vimanas…and was totally destroyed. The vimanas then, with unmitigated wrath, and blazing fiercely… returned to the hand of Vishnu."

Rama's Celestial Car

In the *Ramayana*, a Hindu scripture telling of Rama, who was one incarnation of holy Vishnu, Rama is always flying about. But he doesn't do it unaided: "When morning dawned, Rama, taking the celestial car…stood ready to depart. Self propelled was that car…. It was large and finely painted. It had two stories and many chambers with windows."

Flying Discs

One group of Sanskrit writings are called *manusa*, and they are differentiated from *diava*, which are myths and stories, because manusa are presented as historical fact. One manusa called the *Samarangana Sutradhara* describes flying discs that could rise vertically in a straight line, maneuver nimbly, hover in place, and travel great distances.

The Moons of Mars

There are many unexpected truths found in manuscripts, books, plays, works of fact and fiction—facts the author could not or should not have known, but that are there nonetheless. In *Gulliver's Travels*, Jonathan Swift describes the discovery of the moons of Mars by the astronomers of Laputa:

> "They have likewise discovered two lesser Stars, or Satellites, which revolve about Mars; whereof the innermost is distant from the

Report from the Field

"Scholars of ancient languages have noted many items which lend themselves readily to interpretation as Unidentified Flying Objects, reported by persons who had to describe them in terms understandable to their contemporaries: Flaming chariots, fiery or glowing shields (which were generally circular, disk-like, with a small 'boss' or domelike center), and of course the glittering lances and other trappings of that distant period."

—Frank Edwards, *Flying Saucers —Serious Business*

Center of the primary Planet exactly three of his Diameters, and the outermost five; the former revolves in the space of ten Hours, and the latter in Twenty-one and an Half; so that the Squares of their periodical Times, are very near in the same Proportion with the Cubes of their Distance from the Center of Mars; which evidently shews them to be governed by the same Law of Gravitation, that influences the other heavenly Bodies."

Swift is a little off in his figures: Phobos, the inner moon actually revolves around Mars in eight hours; and Deimos, the outer moon, takes 30 hours.

Sighting

Gulliver's Travels, actually, *Travels into Several Remote Nations of the World, by Lemuel Gulliver, First a Surgeon, and Then a Captain of Several Ships*, in which Gulliver visits the tiny Lilliputians, the gigantic Brobdingnagians, and several other peoples, is usually thought of today as a children's book. In reality it is a powerful social and political satire.

But the fact that he came that close is remarkable for several reasons: *Gulliver's Travels* is a work of fiction, written in 1726. The moons of Mars were first discovered by astronomer Asaph Hall in 1877, 151 years later!

Was Jonathan Swift prescient? Was he visited by aliens who made a point of telling him of the moons of Mars? Probably not. He was a storyteller, and he made it up. It was just an odd coincidence that his fiction happened to coincide with reality. Such things happen more often than we realize.

The D-Day Puzzle

One of the most closely guarded secrets of World War II was the date and location of D-Day, the day the Allied forces planned to invade Europe. Shortly before that secret date, the crossword puzzle editor of the *New York Times* was startled to be visited by two FBI agents. They wanted to know who the author of a puzzle that had appeared shortly before was, and what the editor knew about him. It wasn't until years later that the editor found out the reason for their interest. Several of the most secret code words for the D-Day invasion had appeared as words in that day's puzzle, including "Utah" and "Omaha," the code words for two of the proposed landing sites on the Normandy coast, and "overlord," the main code word for the entire operation.

After extensive investigation, the FBI concluded that it was just a bizarre coincidence.

And there are other similar cases. Cleve Cartmill wrote a story titled "Deadline" for *Astounding Science Fiction* in 1944, which discussed the atomic bomb—at the time the war's biggest secret—and he and John Campbell Jr., the editor, were seriously studied by the FBI. They managed to convince the authorities that they knew nothing, but were just making it up based on information available to anyone before the war.

The Titan(ic)

One of the most amazing cases of precognition, damn-good guessing, or incredible coincidence that I know of is the similarity between the sinking of the steamship *Titanic* in 1912, the greatest maritime disaster of this century, and the events described in Morgan Robertson's *Futility; or the Wreck of the Titan*, written in 1898.

The correspondences are many and eerily precise. The Titanic was proclaimed by its makers to be unsinkable by virtue of its modern design and construction. So, Robertson wrote 14 years earlier, was the Titan. The Titanic was the biggest ship afloat at the time, weighing 66,000 tons. Robertson had the Titan weighing 70,000 tons. The Titanic was 882.5 feet long; the Titan was 800. The Titanic set sail on its maiden voyage in April, as did the Titan.

The top speed of both the Titan and the Titanic was 25 knots. Both ships could carry 3,000 passengers, but were sailing on their first trip across the Atlantic with only about 2,000. Both had enough lifeboats for less than half of their passengers, not to mention the crew; but neither captain was worried about it because, after all, the Titan/Titanic was unsinkable.

Both ships hit an iceberg on the starboard (right) side, which ripped open the seams below the water line. And both sank, carrying hundreds of passengers to their watery grave.

They say that truth is stranger than fiction, but in this case, fiction, by achieving an uncanny similarity to reality 14 years before the fact, wins the strangeness award.

To compound Morgan Robertson's uncanny knack for foreseeing the unforeseeable, in 1914 he wrote a short story called "Beyond the Spectrum," in which he predicts the Japanese will carry out a sneak attack on the Hawaiian Islands in December. Twenty-seven years later, they did just that. It could have been an incredible coincidence, or Robertson could have had the strange psychic ability to foresee the future; or

Report from the Field

"SHE was the largest craft afloat and the greatest of the works of men....From the bridge, engine room, and a dozen places on her deck the ninety two doors of nineteen water-tight compartments could be closed in half a minute by turning a lever. These doors would also close automatically in the presence of water. With nine compartments flooded the ship would still float, and as no known accident of the sea could possibly fill this many, the steamship Titan was considered practically unsinkable.

Unsinkable, indestructible, she carried as few boats as would satisfy the laws. These, twenty four in number, were securely covered and lashed down to their chocks on the upper deck, and if launched would hold five hundred people. She carried no useless, cumbersome life-rafts; but—because the law required it—each of the three thousand berths in the passengers', officers', and crew's quarters contained a cork jacket, while about twenty circular life buoys were strewn along the rails."

—Morgan Robertson, *Futility; or the Wreck of the Titan*

perhaps the Emperor of Japan had read Robertson's story and thought it was a good idea.

Robertson also describes a bomb that can destroy a whole city, going off with an incredible flash of light that blinds all who look at it.

The Moral of These Stories

There are coincidences so incredible that, were it not that no agency can be thought of to have caused the events that is not substantially more incredible, we would refuse to believe them to be mere coincidences.

A belief in extraterrestrial intelligences will not aid us in explaining Swift's describing the two moons of Mars a century and a half before they were discovered, or Robertson's writing of the sinking of the Titan 16 years before a real ship, that could have been her twin down to the name, did hit an iceberg and go to the bottom.

Sighting

A flipped coin has a 50-50, or 1/2, chance of coming up heads. For two heads in a row, the odds are $1/2 \times 1/2$, or 1/4. For it to come up heads 20 times in a row, the odds are $1/2 \times 1/2 \times 1/2$...and so on for 20 multiplications, which works out to one chance in better than 9 million.

The science of statistics tells us that if you keep flipping an unbiased penny long enough, eventually it will come up heads 20 times in a row. But betting more than a penny on any particular 20 flips is a good way to give some deserving person a share of your fortune. Conversely, if someone offers to bet you that he can flip a penny and have it come up heads 20 times, you'd better examine that penny pretty closely on both sides before taking that bet.

This is the sort of healthy skepticism with which you should view any claim involving the earth having been visited by extraterrestrial life. It could be so, but examine the claim pretty closely on both sides before accepting it.

In that spirit, I offer you the following stories.

Mapping the Unknown

In 1510, a Swiss geographer, mathematician, and poet named Glareanus created a map of America, including the West Coast. But the first one we know of to visit the West Coast of America and map it was Fernando Magellan, and he didn't do that until 1522. How Glareanus knew what to put where on his map is a mystery.

Topkapi

One of the most exciting historical finds of the 20th century was made in the library of the Topkapi Palace Museum in Istanbul. There, in 1929, scholars found a map dated from 1513, signed by an admiral of the Ottoman Empire named Piri Reis.

In 1931, Paul Kahle, a German orientalist, gave a talk to the 18th Congress of Orientalists, describing the map and what he had found out about it. The most exciting thing to his listeners was his describing an annotation in Turkish in one corner of the map: "The coasts and islands on this map are taken from the map of Colombo."

The "Colombo" in question was Christopher Columbus, who had discovered the New World only 21 years before. This map, if really based on that of Columbus, might settle the question of whether Columbus knew where he was going and what he had found. Did he ever realize that he had run smack dab into a great continent that lay between him and Asia, or did he die thinking he had landed on the coast of China?

The signs pointing to the map's authenticity were subtle, and required much study to unravel, but they were there. First there was the history of the map. It was found that Piri Reis's uncle, Kemal Reis, had also been a Turkish naval officer. When, in 1501, Uncle Kemal had captured a Spanish ship, he interviewed one of the sailors on his prize and discovered that the man had sailed with Columbus. And what was more, the man had a map that was drawn by Columbus himself.

During this period, charts of the seas were kept secret, and one ship's captain would be very reluctant to share his information with another—particularly one from another nation. So this map was a great find for Kemal Reis. He passed it on to his nephew Piri, who was determined to combine all the maps he could get a hold of into one great chart of the oceans.

In 1511, Piri Reis began his great project, and kept at it for three years. He had about 20 maps that he considered reliable enough or interesting enough to make a part of his own map. In addition to the Columbus map, there were eight maps of the world dating back to the time of Alexander the Great, which would have made them a thousand years old when he was using them. He also had four Portuguese maps of the Indian Ocean and the coast of China, an Arab map of India, and six more maps that he didn't further identify.

Sighting

For a discussion of the Piri Reis map and others, and what they might mean, get a copy of *Maps of the Ancient Sea Kings* by Charles Hapgood. A trade paperback edition came out in 1977, and should still be available.

When he had finished the map, he added a credit line: "The author of this is the humble Piri ibn Hajji Muhamad, known as the nephew of Kemal Reis, in the town of Gallipoli in the Holy Month of Muharram of the year 919 [1513 A. D.]." He gave the original, which was drawn on gazelle hide, to Sultan Selim, who was so pleased with it that he made Reis an admiral.

The 1513 map of Piri Reis.

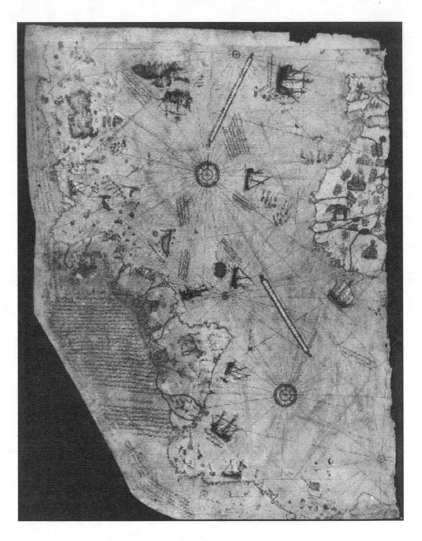

The map is surprisingly accurate, given the extent of 16th-century knowledge of geography. It shows the coast of Brazil, only discovered a few years before, and the island of Hispaniola (Haiti and the Dominican Republic split it between them today), which was probably from Columbus's map (since he discovered it). And, as you might expect, it has a few wild inaccuracies. Hispaniola, for example, is way too big and runs north-south instead of east-west. And Cuba is missing, probably because Columbus didn't realize that Cuba was an island, but thought it connected to the continent.

The map also contains a few surprises. A line of mountains which must be the Andes is indicated in the interior of South America. The major rivers, the Amazon, the Orinoco, and the Rio Plata are also indicated. But the interior of South America hadn't been explored by any Europeans, and the Andes hadn't been discovered.

The major anachronism on the map is at the bottom, where the coastline of what seems to be Antarctica is shown. Some investigators have suggested that it is merely an extension of the coast of South America, turned sideways to fit on the gazelle skin. But if so, it is difficult to explain the inscription: "The nights here are two hours long." True in Antarctica at the right season, not true along the South American coast.

But it would seem impossible for Piri Reis to have known of Antarctica, which was not discovered until, in 1823, James Weddell sailed into the sea which would be named for him. And the Antarctic coast wasn't accurately mapped until the expedition of Lt. Charles Wilkes, U.S.N., in 1840.

The map also has markings in what we're assuming is Antarctica that should be mountains, but in Antarctica today there is nothing but a miles-deep icecap. But sonar studies done this century—450 years after Piri Reis drew his map—show that there are indeed mountains under the ice.

We can only speculate as to how Piri Reis knew about things not discovered until centuries after his death, and I promise to do a bit of that in a moment, but first...

Oronteus Finaeus—His Map

Eighteen years after Piri Reis gave his gift to Sultan Selim, a French cartographer named Oronce Fine—who according to the custom of the time Latinized his name to Oronteus Finaeus—drew his own map. There is no question that this map shows Antarctica; there it is right in the middle of the circular chart. And it looks pretty much like the modern maps of Antarctica, even to the gulf in the middle that James Clark Ross discovered in 1839. (This gulf was subsequently named the Ross Sea in his honor.)

A 1531 map of Antarctica, as drawn by Oronteus Finaeus.

It seems that someone got to Antarctica before Weddell and Ross, and did a pretty accurate job of mapping it. And—sit down for this one—the Oronteus Finaeus map shows Antarctica without the obscuring layer of ice. Instead it shows estuaries and inlets, suggestions that there might have been great rivers on the Antarctic continent before it was put into the deep freeze.

Removing the Impossible

Sherlock Holmes once said that when the impossible is removed, whatever remains, however improbable, must be true. Let us remove the impossible from the Mystery of the Medieval Maps and see what remains.

The Choices

➤ The maps might be forgeries, actually done at a later date.

The Orientalists considered the Piri Reis map pretty carefully, because of the Columbus connection, and they concluded from internal evidence that the map was genuine. As for the maps of Oronteus Finaeus and Glareanus, they were both printed in books at the time—Finaeus's in 1531 and Glareanus's in 1512.

➤ The maps might be based on long-hidden maps from some earlier civilization, since disappeared.

Interesting theory. But the icecap over Antarctica has been there, geologists estimate, for the past 50 million years. The human race isn't 50 million years old. Okay, so the map makers weren't human. That's possible. Maybe intelligent dinosaurs from 65 million years ago. But it would be peculiar if the only artifact that they left behind that has lasted through the millennia is a map.

➤ Extraterrestrial visitors left a map.

Well, I wouldn't go out of my way to believe in extraterrestrials just because some maps can't be explained. But if you're prepared to believe in them for other reasons, then it's a possible explanation for this also.

An overhead spaceship could have used radar imaging to create a map of the planet, and their radar might have penetrated the Antarctic icecap to show the shape of the continent beneath.

And the aliens, for reasons of their own, might have left a map with some human. Perhaps it happened while they were bringing writing down to the ancient Egyptians.

Or perhaps not.

The Least You Need to Know

➤ Ancient myths tell of the gods bringing writing to mankind.

➤ The gods could have been extraterrestrial beings, but the myths could just be myths.

➤ Ancient Hindu scriptures in Sanskrit speak of flying discs.

➤ In *Gulliver's Travels*, Jonathan Swift described the moons of Mars before they had been discovered.

➤ The book *Futility; or the Wreck of the Titan* predicted the sinking of the Titanic in amazing detail 14 years before it happened.

➤ Coincidences, some of them very strange indeed, do happen.

➤ But the Piri Reis map of 1513, and other maps of the period, show details that hadn't yet been discovered, such as the Andes, the West Coast of America, and the continent of Antarctica. It's hard to think of a natural explanation that fits the facts.

Part 2

How Early Were the Astronauts?

Ancient writings, from the Saga of Gilgamesh to the Bible, are full of references to beings that are not human and intelligences other, and perhaps greater, than our own. Structures exist from the dawn of civilization that we would have trouble building today. Drawings on temple walls depict figures that have an eerie resemblance to astronauts suited for space, and vehicles that may be rocket-powered. It's possible that our early ancestors had unearthly assistance building the pyramids and various megaliths and temples; or perhaps they were smarter than we give them credit for.

Part 2 reviews various sightings and happenings with possible extraterrestrial explanations from the dawn of recorded time (about 5,000 years ago) until the middle of the 20th century. We will consider astral apparitions that looked like dragons, angels, balloons, dirigibles, and a few that looked like what we today call flying saucers. Some commentators think the various sky sightings are the aliens' way of preparing us for their eventual arrival. Personally, I've always thought that Big Bird on Sesame Street will turn out to be one of the advance guards of aliens, with our children now brainwashed into seeing him as a friend. But I could be wrong.

Chapter 5

The Pharaoh's Unearthly Friends

> **In This Chapter**
>
> ➤ Secrets of the Great Pyramid
>
> ➤ The Sphinx
>
> ➤ The Mayan Pyramid of Inscriptions
>
> ➤ The Pyramid of Yonaguni-Jima

One of the less-than persuasive arguments for the presence of super-intelligent aliens on earth in the distant past is the belief that our ancestors were too dumb to have built the pyramids, or erected Stonehenge, or worked out an accurate calendar, or transferred technology from one people to another. Human beings have been human beings for the past 50,000 years, and there's no reason to assume that our remote ancestors weren't just as bright as we are.

It is true that steam and internal combustion engines and steel and dynamite have changed the face of our planet, not necessarily for the better, but that doesn't mean that our great, great, great, great (and so on) grandparents had not developed techniques for moving, cutting, and building that worked just about as well for their needs.

But refuting these arguments—by choosing to believe that we are descended from ancestors at least as intelligent as we are who were quite capable of building impressive monuments and transferring techniques of pottery and metalwork from place to place—is not to say that we might not have had intergalactic visitors at some time in our history. It's just that we will have to look for the evidence of it elsewhere.

Report from the Field

"It is a mistake to believe that the ancients were not every bit as intelligent as we. Their technology was more primitive, but their brains were not."

—Isaac Asimov, *Extraterrestrial Civilizations*

And we have been left with tantalizing traces of possible alien presence at many periods in the past. It is an interesting exercise in historical analysis to determine what might be alien intervention and what is probably merely an example of human ingenuity. Let's examine some of these claims of past visitors and see how they hold up.

The Great Pyramid

When the Greek historian Herodotus visited Egypt sometime in the 5th century B.C. the priests of Thebes told him that 341 generations previously (about 11,340 years the way they enumerated a generation) the gods had lived among men, and had shown them how to do great things, but since then the gods had not returned. The obvious inference UFO historians make is that these "gods" were extraterrestrial visitors.

In his 1968 bestseller *Chariots of the Gods*, Erich Von Däniken relates this to the Egyptian custom of mummifying their dead. He suggests that perhaps the "gods," beings from an advanced civilization, could somehow put themselves or their Egyptian hosts into suspended animation for long periods of time.

When the "gods" left, Von Däniken suggests, perhaps the Egyptians attempted to duplicate what they had seen, but without the technological sophistication that would have made the process work. Or perhaps they originally knew how to do it but gradually, as the centuries passed and the machines broke down and the necessarily thin veneer of technology disappeared, what had been a valid technique became a mystical rite.

And so, to follow this through to its logical consequences, the ancient Egyptians continued and perfected the process of mummification. They added details, such as the removal of the brain through the nose, that were certainly not in the original if Von Däniken's theory is true. And perhaps the pyramids are the shape they are because of some faint tribal memory from the distant past of the shape of the "gods" spaceships.

See how easy it is to construct hypotheses about extraterrestrial visitors from the distant past? But you know, maybe I'm on to something there.

Why the Pharaoh?

The question is, why, if a highly advanced alien civilization chose to send a mission to earth—and any civilization that could mount an interstellar mission would be by definition highly advanced—why would they choose to land in the middle of a desert and pass on their advanced technology only to the Pharaoh and his subjects? Why stay in that arid desert instead of going around the world spreading the glad tidings and the scientific advances?

The only possible answer is, why not? As the old joke goes, everybody has to be somewhere. Perhaps deserts were convenient for landing their space-ships. Perhaps they had a mission that had nothing to do with us, and they only used earthlings as the equivalent of day laborers and dish washers.

If I Couldn't Build the Pyramid, Nobody Could

"The Great Pyramid is visible testimony of a technique that has never been understood," according to Von Däniken. He cites a number of reasons why the Great Pyramid of the Pharaoh Khufu (Cheops, as the Greeks called him) has great mystical significance, and why it couldn't have been built by the ancient Egyptians without help from somewhere. He then asks if not aliens, then who? Unfortunately for UFO theorists, both Von Däniken's science and his logic are weak.

According to Von Däniken:

1. No architect today could build a copy of the Great Pyramid, "even if the technical resources of every continent were at his disposal."

Report from the Field

"If we meekly accept the neat package of knowledge that the Egyptologists serve up to us, ancient Egypt appears suddenly and without transition with a fantastic ready-made civilization. Great cities and enormous temples, colossal statues with tremendous expressive power, splendid streets flanked by magnificent sculptures, perfect drainage systems, luxurious tombs carved out of the rock, pyramids of overwhelming size—these and many other wonderful things shot out of the ground, so to speak. Genuine miracles in a country that is suddenly capable of such achievements without recognizable prehistory."

—Erich Von Däniken, *Chariots of the Gods*

2. The stone blocks that made up the pyramid had to be moved. The only way then possible was to put wooden rollers under the blocks. But the Egyptians wouldn't have cut down their few trees—mostly date palms, and they needed the dates—and they couldn't have imported the wood because that would have required a fleet of ships.

3. At the "extraordinary daily piece rate of 10 blocks a day," it would have taken about 250,000 days, which is 685 years. (For some reason, Von Däniken says it's 664 years; perhaps he is innocent of long division.) So it couldn't have been created in the lifetime of any one pharaoh.

4. As Von Däniken put it: "Several hundred thousand workers pushed and pulled blocks weighing twelve tons up a ramp with (nonexistent) ropes on (nonexistent) rollers."

5. There wasn't enough food in all Egypt to feed the workers.

6. There was no place for them to sleep.

Von Däniken also finds some mystical significance in the pyramid, asserting that:

7. The height of the pyramid times a thousand million equals the distance from the earth to the sun.

8. "...a meridian running through the pyramids divides continents and oceans into two exactly equal halves."

9. The area of the pyramid's base divided by twice its height equals 3.14159, which, as any high school student can tell you, is the value of *pi*.

Contact

As you probably know, **pi** is the name given to the ratio of the diameter of a circle to the circumference. It seems to be a basic number that the universe is very fond of, mysteriously showing up in a lot of mathematic and scientific formulae that appear to have nothing to do with circles.

So let's look at these suggestions of Von Däniken's.

There is general agreement among Egyptologists today that building the pyramids was a sort of vast public works project. During the summer the peasants were kept busy doing peasant-type stuff: growing food and flax for clothing and papyrus for paper. During the winter there were thousands of unemployed peasants. So putting them to work on the pyramids was a way to keep them occupied and out of trouble, and have them do something useful for their food.

Not that Khufu and the other pharaohs who ordered pyramids for themselves didn't like the idea of having a monument that would last for centuries as a symbol of their greatness and a home for their *Ka* (spirit). But what made it possible to construct these massive mausoleums was the vast surplus of labor available every winter.

As for specifics:

1. No architect today could build a copy of the Great Pyramid. Any builder of today, given the support and financing of a major government, could re-create the Great Pyramid in a tenth of the time with much less than a tenth of the work force (estimated in the tens of thousands) that Khufu's overseers used. It would be very expensive but by no means impossible.

2. The Egyptians didn't have the ships to import the necessary logs. The pharaoh actually had a fleet capable of transporting thousands of logs. There was a regular trade in, among other things, cedar logs around the Mediterranean. And it has been suggested that the blocks could have been dragged if the smooth sand in front of them was coated with a layer of oil or milk (because of the butterfat) to reduce friction.

3. It would have taken 664 years. Because the base of the Great Pyramid is about three city blocks on a side, there is no reason why two, or even three crews couldn't be working at the same time on each side. And other crews could be moving the blocks to the ready-line as the final work crews were shoving them into place. As Dorothy Parker said when she saw Hearst Castle, "It shows you what God could do, if he had the money." Well the pharaoh had all the money there was.

4. No ropes, no rollers. We have samples of ropes from that time and also pictures of sailing ships, which have nice thick ropes to haul up the sails. And if they wanted rollers, they could have easily made them.

5. Not enough food. The population of Egypt had to be fed, regardless of whether they were building a pyramid. So, as I'm sure the pharaoh thought, they might as well earn their keep and build a tomb worthy of a mighty king.

6. No place to sleep. They could roll up in a blanket and sleep on the sand. Even in winter, it doesn't exactly get cold in Egypt.

Sighting

The Great Pyramid was built around 2530 B.C. as a tomb for the Pharaoh Khufu. It is 755 feet on a side and 480 feet high, and contains 2,300,000 slabs of granite with an average weight of 2.5 tons, which were shipped on barges 600 miles from the quarries up river. It wasn't until some 3,500 years later when other man-made structures—the great cathedrals of Europe—exceeded the height of Khufu's tomb.

7. The height and the area. Nobody knows what the exact original size of the Great Pyramid was, because the cap on top and most of the surfacing stones have been gone for centuries. The locals used the pyramid as a quarry, and built their structures with its stones. The wonder is that most of it is still standing.

8. A meridian running through the pyramids divides continents and oceans into two exactly equal halves. No, it doesn't. It does divide the earth in half, as a meridian drawn anywhere will, and the land masses on each side are approximately equal, but only approximately. Almost any division of the earth along a meridian line will have the same result unless you carefully isolate the Pacific Ocean in the middle of one half.

The Sphinx

We have inherited some genuine mysteries from the past. One of them involves the giant statue in Egypt called the Great Sphinx of Giza (to differentiate it from all the little sphinxes). The conventional wisdom of archeologists dates the Great Sphinx to about 2500 B.C. (about the time the Great Pyramid was built). It is attributed to Khufu (that is, he paid for it), and it is supposed to bear his face. It was carved from a solid block of limestone over 240 feet long and 66 feet high. Presumably the block was found where it is; nobody is suggesting that such a mass of solid stone was moved into place by anyone, extraterrestrial or Egyptian.

Close Encounter

In Egyptian myth, the Sphinx had the head of a man and the body of a lion. The Greeks improved on this, giving their Sphinx the head of a woman, the body of a lion, and the wings of an eagle. The Egyptian Sphinx is taken to be a manifestation of *Ra*, the sun god.

The Greek sphinx roamed about Thebes and challenged all whom she met to solve a riddle. If they failed, she ate them. The hero Oedipus took up the challenge, and the sphinx asked him, "What animal goes on four feet in the morning, at noon on two, and in the evening upon three?" This has become known—you might not be surprised to learn—as the "riddle of the sphinx." Oedipus answered correctly, "Man, who crawls on all fours as a baby, walks upright in manhood, and uses a staff in old age." Upon hearing the right answer to her riddle, the sphinx threw herself off a cliff. As a reward, the people of Thebes appointed Oedipus their king. And then his troubles started.

Strong evidence shows that the Great Sphinx of Giza was already ancient when Khufu was building his pyramid. Robert Schoch, a professor of geology at Boston University, studied the wind- and rain-caused erosion on the body of the Sphinx and compared it with other local statues that could be definitely dated. He found that the Sphinx was much older than had been thought, probably dating to somewhere between 5000 and 10000 B.C.

If it is that old, it predates any known civilization in the Nile Valley, and who built it is anybody's guess. The hunter-gatherer tribes that were around 7,000–12,000 years ago were not supposed to have the sort of tools that would have enabled them to create such a statue out of solid rock. Also they had no agriculture, and therefore no access to the steady, reliable source of food they would need to enable them to stay in one place long enough to create the great monument.

Writer Robert Bauval and his compatriots have suggested that the Sphinx faces in the direction from which the sun rose during the summer solstice approximately 10,500 years ago. All this would suggest a fairly advanced technological civilization, but from where would that knowledge have come?

When the sand was cleared away from between the mighty paws of the Sphinx, a small temple was found. The door to its interior has not been opened for, perhaps, thousands of years. Egyptologists are now trying to get permission of the Egyptian government to investigate the interior of the temple. Perhaps, if they succeed, more than one riddle of the Sphinx will be answered.

The Pyramid of Inscriptions

In his fascinating book *Passport to Magonia* (1969), which examines the flying saucer stories and their relation to the myths of many cultures, Jacques Vallee tells of a 1952 expedition to an ancient Mayan city in the state of Chiapas in Mexico. The four-man expedition, led by archaeologist Alberto Ruz Lhuillier, examined the "Pyramid of Inscriptions," a massive stone structure in the midst of this long-deserted city. They discovered a staircase concealed in the temple that sat atop the pyramid, and followed it down through the pyramid to below ground level.

It ended at a burial chamber containing a great stone sarcophagus. The 12-by-7–foot cover of the sarcophagus was carved from a single stone, and must have weighed at least six tons. The carving on the sarcophagus, done in typical Mayan style, showed a very untypical Mayan scene: a man "…with his knees brought up toward his chest and his back to a complicated mechanism, from which flames are seen to flow." The man seems to be facing some sort of control panel. The whole scene bears an uncanny resemblance to a pilot in an airplane or an astronaut in a space capsule.

A Japanese Pyramid

In 1998, a pyramid was discovered submerged in the sea off the coast of the Japanese island of Yonaguni-Jima, one of the Ryukyu island chain located in the Pacific Ocean between Okinawa and Taiwan. The rectangular *ziggurat* is 75 feet underwater. Scuba divers first spotted it in 1988, but thought it was some sort of natural formation. It was not until ten years later that closer examination suggested that it was artificial.

The structure is 600 feet wide and 90 feet high, and dates back to at least 8000 B.C. This would make it 5,000 years older than the earliest pyramid in Egypt, the Step Pyramid at Saqqara, and about contemporary with the supposed age of the Sphinx.

Robert Schoch, the same professor of geology who helped date the Sphinx, recently did a scuba investigation of the site. He said, "It basically looks like a series of huge steps, each about a meter high. Essentially it's a cliff face like the side of a stepped pyramid. It's a very interesting structure." He

Contact

Ziggurats are step pyramids, which are constructed in a series of sections—each upper section smaller than the one below, like giant square wedding cakes. They are named after the temple-towers of ancient Babylonia and Assyria.

thought that it might be possible that natural water erosion combined with a process of cracked rocks splitting might produce such a structure; but said, "I haven't come across such processes creating a structure such as this."

The probability that the structure is artificial was enhanced when the divers realized that there was what seemed to be a road circling the pyramid, and that nearby there were a group of smaller step pyramids, each about 30 feet wide and six feet high.

"This could be evidence of a new culture," said Professor Masaki Kimura of Ryukyu University in Okinawa, "as there are no records of a people intelligent enough to have built such a monument 10,000 years ago."

We Inherited Their Brains

Professor Kimura makes the usual mistake when speaking of ancient people (at least I assume he does—it might be his translator who did) of confusing intelligence with knowledge. At the rate evolution works, it is almost certain that we are not perceptibly smarter than our ancestors of 10,000 years ago. We do, however, have a much larger knowledge base from which to work.

But there are plausible questions as to whether these ancestors of ours had the proper tools to build such monuments, the ability to stay in one place long enough, and the necessary motivation to take on such an overwhelming project.

With the Egyptian pyramids the answer to all three questions is, Yes. There was a stable agricultural population capable of growing the surplus grain needed, and free to work in the winter; they were settled into one place already, and their pharaoh wanted a tomb that would impress all future generations with his greatness. Well, he got it.

> ## The Least You Need to Know
>
> ➤ Our ancestors were as smart as we are.
>
> ➤ The ancient Egyptian process of mummification, and the construction of the Pyramid of Khufu, might be signs of extraterrestrial visitation.
>
> ➤ But in each case, there is a more mundane explanation.
>
> ➤ The Great Sphinx at Giza is a real mystery, predating any known civilization in the area.
>
> ➤ The ancient Mayan Pyramid of Inscriptions in Mexico has a carving depicting what looks suspiciously like an astronaut.
>
> ➤ A step pyramid dating back 5,000 years has been found submerged off the coast of the Japanese island of Yonaguni-Jima.

Chapter 6

Ezekiel Saw the Wheel in the Sky: UFOs in Religious Texts

In This Chapter

➤ UFOlogists look at the Bible

➤ The Book of Ezekiel interpreted

➤ More revelations from the Book of Revelation

➤ The "Lady of Light"

When (or if) we find life on other worlds, it will have a profound effect on most human religions. Is God's eye, which records the fall of a sparrow, just as jealously watching the implosion of an Aldebaranian Xanthopod? Those religions that preach salvation will have to decide whether an intelligent being who looks like a praying mantis and is certainly not a descendent of Eve can be saved. If dogs don't go to heaven when they die, do little gray aliens? Is there a purgatory for the intelligent slime-molds of Rigel IV? What sorts of sins could be committed by beings who don't have personal property, must practice group sex because there are five sexes, and ritually kill and eat their grandparents?

Close Encounter

Consider the interesting problem presented by extraterrestrial life for those religions that believe in reincarnation. What might you have been before this life, and where in the universe might you have lived? And what are you to become? And, whatever it is, are you traveling up the path or down?

Deus ex UFO

Although most religious authorities would certainly question how relevant the existence of extraterrestrial beings is to earthly spiritual matters, a small minority of believers manage to combine their religious faith with their belief in UFOs in a variety of interesting ways.

Some of the stories in the Bible and other religious works are open to interpretation in a number of ways. UFOlogists see these visions of the prophets as supporting the early presence of extraterrestrials on earth. Ezekiel and others, according to this view, were attempting to describe things they saw and heard with which they had no prior experience and for which they had no proper words. When an angel or the Lord is described as descending on a cloud, that "cloud" may have been a flying saucer or other sort of spacecraft. There are contemporary descriptions of UFOs as looking like clouds or descending from cloud-like objects believed to be disguised "motherships." And when a heavenly being ascends on a "pillar of fire," isn't that just what a rocketship taking off looks like?

Giants Walked the Earth

In Genesis, Chapter 6, the Bible tells us that the "sons of God saw the daughters of men that they were fair; and they took them wives of all which they chose."

The UFO interpretation is that men from the sky bedded women from earth. And further:

> *There were giants in the earth in those days; and also after that, when sons of God came in unto the daughters of men, and they bare children to them, the same became mighty men which were of old, men of renown.*

So, contrary to most of the known laws of genetics, this cross-species mating was fruitful, and produced a superior child. Perhaps a careful study of modern DNA will reveal that some of us are descended from this extraterrestrial miscegenation.

A Pillar of Fire and a Great Noise

In Exodus, the second book of the Bible, it is recorded that "...the Lord went before them by day in a pillar of cloud, to lead them the way; and by night in a pillar of fire, to give them light." Some readers see this as a description of the Lord piloting a UFO. Images of clouds and fire are quite common in contemporary UFO descriptions. This may be pushing the bounds of credibility, but some descriptions in the Bible are not so far-fetched, particularly if we remember that the writers could only describe the phenomenon they observed in images they were familiar with. Nobody could say the object looked like a dirigible or a hovercraft two millennia before these craft were ever dreamed of.

Isaiah, written around 700 B.C., also has a touch of other-worldliness. In Chapter 13, verses 4 and 5:

> 4   *The noise of a multitude in the mountains, like as of a great people; a tumultuous noise of the kingdoms of nations gathered together; the Lord of hosts mustereth the host of the battle.*

> 5   *They come from a far country, from the end of heaven, even the Lord, and the weapons of his indignation, to destroy the whole land.*

Who are these beings that came from "the end of heaven" with such a noise? In reports of sightings these days, UFOs are notable for their complete lack of sound. But in the past 2,700 years, they may have developed a new, improved model saucer.

Close Encounter

The Book of Mormon, holy book of the Church of Jesus Christ of Latter-day Saints, has a few touches of possible extraterrestrial intervention in its descriptions:

From 1 Nephi, Chapter 18:

And it came to pass that they did worship the Lord, and did go forth with me; and we did work timbers of curious workmanship. And the Lord did show me from time to time after what manner should work the timbers of the ship.

Now I, Nephi, did not work the timbers after the manner which was learned by men, neither did I build the ship after the manner of men; but I did build it after the manner which the Lord had shown unto me; wherefore, it was not after the manner of men.

About That Wheel

The Book of Ezekiel can be dated as having been written in about 600 B.C. If Ezekiel saw what we would today call a flying saucer, he would have great trouble describing it; there would be nothing in his experience he could compare it with. But, if it was indeed a UFO that he saw, he did the best he could:

From the Book of Ezekiel, Chapter 1:

4   *And I looked and behold, a whirlwind came out of the north, a great cloud, and a fire infolding itself, and a brightness was about it, and out of the midst thereof, as the colour of amber, out of the midst of the fire.*

5   *Also out of the midst thereof came the likeness of four living creatures. And this was their appearance; they had the likeness of a man.*

6   *And every one had four faces and every one had four wings.*

7   *And their feet were straight feet; and the sole of their feet was like the sole of a calf's foot: and they sparkled like the color of burnished brass.*

8   *And they had the hands of a man under their wings on their four sides; and the four had their faces and their wings.*

9   *Their wings were joined one to another; they turned not when they went; they went every one straight forward.*

Airships from the North

Ezekiel is trying to describe a scene for which his experiences have not prepared him, for which his language has no words. If we could project ourselves back 2,600 years and see through his eyes but with our perception, we might describe it differently. We might have realized we were seeing some sort of airship come from the north, with jet or rocket engines that spurted flame and kicked up a cloud of dust.

And four beings got out of the craft, wearing some sort of brass-colored protective suit with propulsion packs strapped to the back or the shoulders. And they flew in formation.

And...

14   *And the living creatures ran and returned as the appearance of a flash of lightning.*

15   *Now as I beheld the living creatures, behold one wheel upon the earth by the living creatures, with his four faces.*

Report from the Field

The lovely thing about the Bible is its willingness to encompass different viewpoints.

—Hershel Shanks, Editor, *Biblical Archaeology Review*

16   *The appearance of the wheels and their work was like onto the color of a beryl: and they four had one likeness: and their appearance and their work was as if were a wheel in the middle of a wheel....*

19   *And when the living creatures went, the wheels went by them; and when the living creatures were lifted up from the earth, the wheels were lifted up.*

Just What Was It That the Prophet Ezekiel Saw?

He describes a bright object in the sky, with fire coming from it, in the shape of a wheel—or a wheel inside a wheel. Inside the wheel were living creatures that were not human. You don't have to be too dedicated a UFOlogist to see a flying saucer and its extraterrestrial crew in that description. Let's see what else he says.

From the Book of Ezekiel, Chapter 10:

1   *Then I looked and, behold, in the firmament that was above the head of the Cherubims there appeared over them as it were a sapphire stone, as the appearance of the likeness of a throne.*

2   *And he spake unto the man clothed with linen, and said, Go in between the wheels, even under the cherub, and fill thine hand with coals of fire from between the Cherubims, and scatter them over the city. And he went in in my sight.*

3   *Now the Cherubims stood on the right side of the house, when the man went in; and the cloud filled the inner court.*

4   *Then the glory of the Lord went up from the Cherub, and stood over the threshold of the house; and the house was filled with the cloud, and the court was full of the brightness of the Lord's glory.*

5   *And the sound of the Cherubim's wings was heard even to the outer court, as the voice of the Almighty God when he speaketh.*

Contact

Ezekiel had a high opinion of the beings he was dealing with, whoever they actually were. The Hebrew word **Cherubim** signifies "full of knowledge."

6   *And it came to pass that when he had commanded the man clothed with linen, saying, Take fire from between the wheels, from between the Cherubims; then he went in, and stood beside the wheels.*

7   *And one cherub stretched forth his hand from between the Cherubims unto the fire that was between the Cherubims, and took thereof, and put it into the hands of him that was clothed with linen: who took it, and went out.*

Sighting

Ezekiel wasn't the only Old Testament prophet who saw UFOs. The Book of Zechariah relates, "Again I lifted mine eyes and saw, and beheld, a flying roll. The length thereof is twenty cubits and the breadth thereof ten cubits."

Spotlights of God

So the man "clothed in linen" took coals of fire from between the Cherubims, "and the court was full of the brightness of the Lord's glory."

This could be a description of a powerful spotlight held by the man clothed in linen shining its rays about the house, as seen by someone who does not know that such things exist (as indeed in his day it didn't) and therefore has no words for it.

The Book of Revelation

The last book in the Christian Bible, The Revelation of St. John the Divine, also seems to have passages in it that St. John wrote to explain some events he did not understand.

In Chapter 1, John heard a voice behind him "as of a trumpet," and he turned and

> 12 *Saw seven golden candlesticks; And in the midst of the seven candlesticks one like unto the Son of man, clothed with a garment down to the foot, and girt about the paps with a golden girdle.*

> 14 *His head and his hairs were white like wool, as white as snow; and his eyes were as a flame of fire. And his feet like unto fine brass, as if they burned in a furnace, and his voice as the sound of many waters.*

More men in spacesuits?

In Chapter 9, John also tells how he saw in a vision locusts ascending from a bottomless pit. But these were not your ordinary locusts.

> 7 *And the shapes of the locusts were like unto horses prepared unto battle; and on their heads were as it were crowns like gold, and their faces were as the faces of men.*

> 8 *And they had hair as the hair of women and their teeth were as the teeth of lions.*

> 9 *And they had breastplates, as it were breastplates of iron; and the sound of their wings was as the sound of chariots of many horses running to battle.*

> 10 *And they had tails like unto scorpions, and there were stings in their tails: and their power was to hurt men five months.*

Here one could extrapolate long-haired insect creatures, or remote-control vehicles. Perhaps earth rovers controlled from a hovering mothership. Or perhaps not. I offer these possibilities because sincere people have taken them seriously. St. John's visions probably were no more than that—visions, either religiously inspired or caused by too many days of fasting in the desert.

Jesus Astronaut

It has been suggested seriously that Jesus himself was an extraterrestrial come to earth to save humanity. The Aetherius Society, founded by George King in 1954, believes that Jesus is now living on Venus and sending messages to selected people here on earth. (More on the Aetheriuns in Chapter 17.)

Earthlings Beware

It is easy and tempting to get carried away with these interplanetary interpretations of events in the Bible and other ancient texts. Locusts, after all, were a feared scourge; a swarm of locusts could wipe out an entire crop and cause widespread famine. St. John's evocation of supernatural locusts would therefore strike a chord with his readers.

Close Encounter

If you're hunting for signs of extraterrestrial intervention in the religious classics, you don't have to cast your net too wide; they're not difficult to find. Here's a selection from a hymn to Agni, the god of fire, in the Rig-Veda, a Hindu holy work:

He rends the wood and has a blackened pathway, The brightly radiant and divine invoker...The shining thunderer who dwells in lustre, With his unaging, roaring flames, most youthful...Thy steeds, the bright, the pure, O radiant Agni...Let loose, speed on and shave the ground beneath them. Thy whirling flame then widely shines refulgent, The highest ridges of earth's surface reaching.

(translated by A. A. Macdonell)

By now you should have no trouble picking out the UFO symbolism.

The Lady of Light

In the middle of World War I, a series of events—some say they were miracles, some say they were prime examples of mass hypnosis—happened at Cova da Iria, near the town of Fatima in Portugal. I should point out that, although personally I have a hard time believing most miracles, and the closer they happened to the present day the more skeptical I become, still "mass hypnosis" has become a catch-all explanation for any unusual phenomena witnessed by a group of people. There is no proof at all of the existence of the sort of "mass hypnosis" necessary to explain the events at Fatima.

It began on the 13th of May 1917. Three children who had spent the day tending sheep in a meadow came home for dinner and told their parents that a beautiful *"senhorita de luz"*("Lady of Light") had come to them, floating above an oak tree, and told them that she had something to say. She also told them that they should come back in exactly one month.

Their story was doubted. Although the three were known to be good children, they were, after all, children. But on the 13th of June, a small group of townspeople followed the children out to the meadow.

A White Mist

The oldest child, Lucia, began talking to someone the others could not see. As they watched, a strange white mist formed around the group and they could all hear a faint buzzing sound. When Lucia said the Lady was leaving, the branches of the oak tree were seen to bend in the direction she went.

The next month, 13 July, several hundred people showed up, and the event proceeded as before, white mist and all. This time it ended with a loud and unexplainable bang, sharp enough to shake an arch that the townspeople had erected at the spot. Lucia claimed this time that the "Lady" had told her several "secrets."

Boiled in Oil

The next month the local governor had the children arrested and taken to the police station for questioning, trying to get them to admit they were making it all up. In an attempt to win their confidence, he threatened to have them boiled in oil, and told one of the girls, "Your little brother has already been fried."

Meanwhile hundreds of people gathered at the spot, which was rapidly becoming a shrine. When they heard that the children were in custody and would not be coming, they were upset, for surely now no miracle would occur. But at the appointed time, the white mist rose, and a great clap of thunder was heard, followed by a bolt of lightning. Now as everyone knows, thunder follows lightning, not the other way around.

A Glowing Globe

A month later, on 13 September, the children were back, and an estimated 25,000 people crowded around to see what would happen. Many of the observers, but not all, saw a glowing globe appear in the east and cross the sky to the oak tree. "To my great surprise," one witness affirmed, "I saw clearly and distinctly a ball of light sliding slowly and majestically through space....Then suddenly, with the extraordinary light that it let out, this globe disappeared before my eyes, and the priest who was at my side saw it no more either."

At the same time, snowflakes that were not snowflakes "but round and brilliant" fell from the sky, but dissolved when they landed.

The Final Proof

The Lady of Light promised the children that at her next appearance she would do something to prove her existence to those who doubted. On 13 October, between 50,000 and 70,000 people arrived at Cova da Iria. Most expected to see a miracle, but there were enough doubters and skeptics to leaven the crowd.

Black clouds filled the sky, and it was raining heavily as the crowd assembled. Photographs taken then show the assemblage peering out from under thousands of umbrellas. After an hour, Lucia asked those close to her to close their umbrellas, and gradually the umbrellas were furled as word of the request spread through the crowd.

Earthlings Beware

If wise and helpful aliens do land on earth, how easy it would be to mistake an extraterrestrial being whose civilization is 10,000 years ahead of our own for a benevolent god. This could be a costly mistake. As science-fiction writer Damon Knight pointed out many years ago, don't trust an alien just because its book of rules is called *To Serve Man*—it just might be a cookbook.

The Sky Cleared

Around noon the clouds dissipated and the rain stopped and the odd white mist formed around the crowd.

Suddenly Lucia pointed to the sky and called, "Look at the sun!" Forty thousand people turned from the oak tree they had been staring at, and saw the sun. But not the sun they knew: "It was not spherical, it looked like a flat and polished disk which had been cut from the pearl in a shell...and was clearly seen to have a ridged edge like a drawing-board."

And, unlike the sun they were accustomed to, it seemed to many observers to be low in the sky, lower than the clouds.

All at once the "sun" shimmied and shook and began to spin "at an astonishing speed," and it projected rays of colored lights from its rim; green then blue then red. Then it seemed to fall toward the earth, fluttering like a leaf. All at once it flew off and disappeared, and once again the crowd could see the sun that they were accustomed to.

The people had their miracle.

Fluttering Leaf

Several things about this description, attested to by thousands, make it a possible candidate for an extraterrestrial visitor. The spinning disc with colored lights, the flight like a fluttering leaf, the rapid disappearance, are all characteristics of a UFO sighting. And the "secrets" told to the child Lucia also fit the pattern of alien visitations. The visitors have often given words of wisdom, either secret or not, to those they visit. The wisdom often seems true but trite to us: "Give up war," or, "You are harming your environment." But perhaps the saucerians think that we can't handle messages more complex.

Seekers

St. Matthew's injunction "seek, and ye shall find" is, unfortunately, all too true when it comes to biblical interpretation. People can, and have, discovered hidden truths that prove whatever it is they need to prove. But before we take any of it too seriously, perhaps we should heed Saul's admonition: "Behold, I have played the fool, and have erred exceedingly." (1 Samuel)

The Least You Need To Know

➤ Some UFOlogists think that some of the events described in the Bible and other religious works can best be explained by the intervention of alien beings.

➤ A cloud by day and a pillar of fire by night could be the description by an unsophisticated observer of an alien craft.

➤ The Book of Ezekiel is a good candidate for descriptions that could be UFOs.

➤ The Book of Revelation describes giant locusts wearing armor; these could have been aliens in spacesuits.

➤ The bright disc that replaced the sun, seen by thousands in Fatima, Portugal in 1917, may have been a vision from the Virgin Mary, or it may have been a flying saucer.

Chapter 7

What the Monks Saw

In This Chapter

➤ Strange sightings in the pre-Christian era

➤ Sightings in medieval Japan and China

➤ Medieval European sightings

➤ A possible fraud

➤ Odd objects pass in front of the sun

In medieval times, a wise man kept his eyes focused toward the ground. Anything in the sky besides clouds and birds must have been a supernatural apparition, just as likely to be the work of the devil as an angel. Comets and meteor showers were considered portents of great natural disaster, and an eclipse certainly foretold the death of a king or the destruction of an empire.

Those who did look up occasionally, however, saw things that could not be easily explained in terms of anything they knew, real or mythical. Having no other words to describe these celestial happenings, they did the best they could. Where they saw angels or heavenly portents, today we might see flying saucers or other sorts of UFOs. The truth might be just as indistinct to us as it was to them. Who knows what these sightings might be interpreted as in the future.

Report from the Field

The question of all questions for humanity, the problem which lies behind all others and is more interesting than any of them, is that of the determination of man's place in Nature and his relation to the Cosmos.

—T. H. Huxley, *Man's Place in Nature* (1863)

Medieval history is rife with reports of strange objects and happenings that, when peered at carefully by today's UFOlogists, take on the appearance of extraterrestrial origin. The accuracy and truthfulness of many of the medieval accounts cannot be doubted, but what these people actually observed is an open question. The possibilities for more natural explanations, while not limitless, are many: mirages, the Northern Lights, ice crystals, deliberate hoaxes, ball lightning, lenticular clouds (see Chapter 11), hallucinations, or possibly visitors from another planet.

Because such sightings were considered omens, chroniclers of the time kept records of them, along with their interpretations. Many of these records have come down to us—most of them vague, fragmentary references—leaving us to try to interpret what it was that our ancestors actually saw.

Early Sightings

Here are a few examples from various sources of what our ancestors were seeing:

➤ The following was recorded in the Royal Annals of Egyptian Pharaoh Thuthmosis III: "In the year 22 [1479 B.C.], third month of winter, sixth hour of the day…the scribes of the House of Life found it was a circle of fire that was coming in the sky. (Though) it had no head, the breath of its mouth (had) a foul odor. Its body one rod long and one rod large. It had no voice….Now, after some days had passed over these things, Lo! They were more numerous than anything. They were shining in the sky more than the sun….Powerful was the position of the fire circles. The army of the king looked on and His Majesty was in the midst of it. It was after supper. Thereupon, they went up higher directed toward the South."

—*Flying Saucers Have Landed*, by Desmond Leslie and George Adamski (Translation by Boris Rachewiltz)

➤ In 218 B.C., phantom ships appeared in the sky over Italy.

➤ In 214 B.C., the Roman historian Livy records that "An altar appeared in the sky with men in white robes standing around it."

➤ In 100 B.C., the historian Pliny records that "In the consulship of Lucius Valerius and Ganius Valarius a burning shield scattering sparks ran across the sky at sunset from east to west."

Medieval Reports

Some of the medieval reports were more extensive and detailed, and contained some powerful and lovely images. Here are a few for your consideration:

➤ Flying saucer sightings have long been associated with bodies of water; the saucers either dive into them or emerge from them. One of the earliest occurred in China, in approximately 1060. A "great pearl" was seen emerging from a lake or swamp, ascending to the sky in several different locations over several nights. One observer reported that as the pearl hovered over a lake, a door in the pearl opened and a bright light shone from inside. Then the door closed and the pearl flew away. (I am particularly fond of this one; it is a beautiful image.)

➤ In Japan, during the night of 24 September, 1235, lights were seen circling to the south-west of an army camp. The lights continued to circle and swoop until dawn. General Yoritsume ordered his counselors to investigate. They reported that it was a natural phenomenon; the wind was making the stars sway.

Sighting

On 12 September 1271, in Kamakura, Japan, a priest named Nichiren was about to have his head officially removed from his body when a bright object, "like a full moon," suddenly appeared in the sky. The authorities canceled the execution.

➤ The *Annals of Nuremburg* contains the following: "In Nuremburg, April 14, 1561, many men and women saw blood-red or bluish or black balls and circular discs in large numbers in the neighborhood of the rising sun. The spectacle lasted one hour and appeared to fall to the ground as if it was all on fire and everything was consumed amid a great haze.'" (Cited and quoted by C. R. Jung.)

➤ Around the beginning of the 17th century, a long cylindrical craft was seen over an Italian monastery, over a small town in Scotland, and flying along a lake near Flüelen, Switzerland. Each of these sightings was made by many people.

➤ In a reprise of the above item, in 1619, Christopher Scherer, prefect (think "governor") of a canton in Switzerland, wrote to a friend that he had seen, "a fiery shining dragon rise from one of the caves on Mount Pilatus and direct himself rapidly towards Flüelen to the other end of the lake. Enormous in size, his tail was longer and his neck stretched out....In flying he emitted on his way numerous sparks."

➤ In 1645, a bright object was seen in the sky near the planet Venus. It was seen several times over the years, the last report in 1767.

Close Encounter

We'll see in Chapter 10 that many of the UFO sightings are explained away as the planet Venus being mistaken for a nearby object on exceptionally bright nights. When a celestial object is described as being *near* Venus, however, it's safe to assume that Venus is in sight at the same time. Therefore, whatever the object is, it isn't Venus.

➤ In a letter written some 43 years after the event, the Reverend Cotton Mather of Boston reported seeing "ye star below ye body of ye Moon, and within the Horns of it" during the month of November 1668. He was only 5 years old at the time, but he was a precocious child, entering Harvard at the age of 12.

What were all these people seeing and why don't we see them any more? Well, perhaps we do, but we call them UFOs. It's all a matter of conditioning. If you think people would laugh at you if you told them you saw a UFO (although very few people are laughing any more), think what the reaction would be if you told them you saw a dragon.

The Nina, the Pinta, and the UFO

On 11 October 1492, while sailing the ocean blue, Columbus was walking the deck of the *Santa Maria* late in the evening when he saw "a light glimmering at a great distance." Several of the ship's crew also saw the light, which went away and returned several times over the next few hours. Early the next morning, the crew first spotted land. They were still well out to sea, however, when they saw the light, so it could not have been light from the shore. Or so thought Columbus.

Maximam Terrorem

The author of a letter to the (London) *Times,* 9 February 1953, reported finding a manuscript from the year A.D. 1290 at Ampleforth Abbey in York, England. The manuscript refers to happenings at nearby Byland Abbey. One paragraph of the manuscript read:

> Cum autem Henricus abbas gratias redditurus erat, frater quidam Joannes introivit, magnam portentem foris esse referebat. Tum vero omnes ecuccurrerunt, et ecce *res grandis, circumcircularis argentea, disco quodam haud dissimilis*, lente e super eos volans atque maximam terrorem exitans.

Which, of course, you immediately recognize as Latin, and translate to:

> But when Henry the Abbot was about to say grace, John, one of the brethren, came in and said there was a great portent outside. Then they all ran out, and Lo! *a large round silver thing like a disc* flew slowly over them and excited the greatest terror.

Desmond Leslie and George Adamski reported this story in their 1953 bestseller, *Flying Saucers Have Landed*, with the comment: "What probably happened is that a flying saucer did, in fact, pass over Byland Abbey at the close of the thirteenth century...." The story has been picked up by many subsequent flying saucer books. The 1967, *Let's Face the Facts About Flying Saucers*, by Gabriel Green, expanded on the dialog, having the monks shouting "Mother of god!" and "'Tis the end of the world," among other things.

The story, if true, needs no such embellishment. The original story certainly seems to be nothing less than a 13th-century description of a sighting of what we would call a flying saucer. In this case, however, as you will see below, the 13th century might have received a little help.

Samuel Rosenberg, who wrote the chapter "UFOs in History" for the Condon Report (see Chapter 11), asked a friend in London to check the facts of this story for him. The friend cabled back:

> HAVE CHECKED WITH COLLEGE STOP AMPLEFORTH DOCUMENT A HOAX PERPE-TRATED BY TWO SIXTH FORM BOYS IN A LETTER TO THE TIMES (LONDON) REGARDS

Report from the Field

"The Wealth of ancient 'UFOs' is due to a basic fact about man's perception of his contemporary universe. A concentrated glance backward in time quickly reveals that throughout our recorded history (and presumably before that), mankind has always seen UFOs and reported 'sightings' that remained unexplained even after examination by persons believed to be competent. Our earliest ancestors gazed earnestly into terrestrial and outer space to witness an infinite variety of phenomena and—understood virtually none of them. In fact, his entire universe, both 'external' to himself as well as 'internal,' was largely outside of his comprehension. He had only the most rudimentary pragmatic knowledge and was totally unable to explain factually or conceptually whatever he plainly saw. In short, to him *everything was UFO.*"

—Samuel Rosenberg, "UFOs in History" (from *Scientific Study of Unidentified Flying Objects*)

I suppose we must accept this report. It's a shame, however, since it's such a beautiful story, full of the sort of facts that, as W. S. Gilbert put it, "add an air of verisimilitude to an otherwise bald and unconvincing narrative." If it really was a hoax, I certainly must commend the schoolboys for their command of medieval Latin—but British school children were better educated 50 years ago.

Spindles Cross the Sun

As reported in the *Annual Register* for 1762, M. de Rostan, a French astronomer, was observing the sun in Lausanne, Switzerland. On 9 August, he saw "a vast spindle-shaped body, about three of the sun's digits in breadth and nine in length, advancing slowly across the disk of the sun." I'm not sure how big one of the sun's digits is, but it sounds impressive.

At the same time as M. de Rostan made his observation, M. Croste, who was about 50 miles to the north, saw the same thing. But he placed it at a different part of the sun. Another observer in Paris, farther to the north, did not see anything crossing the sun at this time.

This indicates that the object seen was actually between the earth and the sun, and that the *parallax* of the viewers was moving its apparent position about.

Whatever this spindle-shaped (for those of you who haven't seen a spindle recently, think giant cigar) object was, it was somewhere between the earth and the sun, moving slowly across the field of view.

Contact

Parallax is the apparent change in position of an object in relation to its background as the viewer's position changes. Watch a tree as you pass it in a car, and see how it seems to move across the mountains behind it as the car moves.

Close Encounter

If you are wondering why the object was seen only crossing the sun and not elsewhere in the daytime sky, only when the sun was directly behind it would it appear as a dark object. Elsewhere in the sky, the sunlight would have been reflected hither and yon in the earth's atmosphere, and would have effectively shielded any distant object from sight—just as all the stars and planets disappear in the daylight. The moon, which is pretty big and bright at night, is very difficult to see in the daytime except when it passes between the sun and the earth.

In the summer of 1847, Benjamin Scott saw a body that seemed to be the size of Venus crossing the sun. Unwilling to believe his own eyes, he had his five-year-old son look through the telescope. The child saw a "little balloon" crossing the sun. Scott told several people about his sighting, and wrote a letter to the (London) *Times*, without creating much excitement.

These were not the only times an object has been seen passing between the earth and the sun. Similar sightings were made in 1764, 1798, 1818, 1819, 1836, 1837, 1847, 1849, 1865, 1871, 1872, 1873, and 1876. Twice in 1836 and once in 1837, a man named Pastorff reported seeing two round spots of unequal size moving across the sun at the same time but taking different paths.

Vulcan or Not Vulcan? That Is the Question

In 1845, French astronomer Urbain-Jean-Joseph Leverrier, who was studying the planet Mercury, announced that at *perihelion* the planet moved just a little faster in its orbit than it should. It was as though the gravitational effects of another planet, one closer to the sun, were pulling it along.

Leverrier decided that there must be a planet closer to the sun, named this presumptive new planet that was influencing Mercury "Vulcan," after the Roman god of fire, and suggested that other astronomers start looking for it.

A year later, after Leverrier discovered the planet Neptune because of its gravitational effects on the planet Uranus, his reputation as a predictor of planetary position increased and many astronomers began the search for Vulcan.

Contact

The orbits of planets around the sun are not perfectly round, but slightly elliptical (shaped like a racetrack). The point in their orbit where they are closest to the sun is their **perihelion**.

A Planet Crosses the Sun...

On 26 March 1859, a French amateur astronomer named Dr. Lescarbault spotted an object "of planetary size" crossing the sun. He wrote to Leverrier to tell him of his discovery. Leverrier hurried to Dr. Lescarbault's house and quizzed him about what he had seen. After giving Lescarbault a tough time for a few hours, Leverrier satisfied himself that the good doctor was an honest man and a good observer, and announced that Vulcan had been found.

Basing his calculations on Lescarbault's sighting, and that of five others, Leverrier computed the orbit of Vulcan. The figures worked out to give Vulcan a "year" of about 20 days, which was reasonable for an object in such a close orbit. An editorial in the June 1859 edition of *Nature* magazine said it would be difficult to explain how six observers, unknown to each other, could have come up with data that matched so precisely unless there was something there to be seen.

On the basis of Leverrier's figures, he calculated where and when his newly discovered planet would be easiest to spot from the earth. If astronomers would aim their telescopes at a certain spot in the sky next to the sun on 22 March 1877, he announced, the discovery of Vulcan would be confirmed.

...and Disappears

Astronomers in the United States, Chili, England, Scotland, Madras, Melbourne, Sydney, New Zealand, Japan, and Siberia prepared for the big event. They trained their telescopes at the exact position in the sky, made the necessary provisions for observing that close to the sun, and saw nothing.

Leverrier computed other dates when Vulcan should be visible, but it again failed to appear. Had the planet been eaten by the sun? And what of the odd orbit of Mercury?

Einstein to the Rescue

It wasn't until 1916, when Albert Einstein released his general theory of relativity, that the behavior of Mercury in its orbit was explained, eliminating the need for Vulcan. Einstein's new theory predicted a change in the behavior of gravity from the laws Sir Isaac Newton had postulated in 1687, but only a slight change and only in special circumstances. One of those circumstances was when Mercury was whirling about in its orbit around the massive sun. The slight speed up at perihelion that Leverrier had noticed back in 1845 was exactly the effect predicted by Einstein.

In their relief at having the mystery of Mercury's orbit successfully explained, the astronomers and physicists never paused to wonder just what it was that had been seen by M. de Rostan, M. Croste, Dr. Lescarbault, and all the other astronomers, professional and amateur, who had been gazing at the sun since 1762 and reported spots before their eyes.

I suppose the spots could have been comets passing in front of the sun, although one would think they'd be visible at night as they headed toward or away from the sun. Perhaps the spots were some sort of disturbance in the earth's atmosphere.

Or perhaps the spots were a shift change of the flying saucers, or competing groups of aliens arriving and departing from earth at different times.

The Least You Need to Know

➤ There are many records of strange sightings through the ages.

➤ In 1479 B.C., the Pharaoh Thuthmosis III saw a "circle of fire" in the sky.

➤ In China, in about 1610, a "great pearl" emerged from a lake and flew away.

➤ Throughout the Middle Ages many people saw many strange things in the sky, among them blood-red balls, circular discs, dragons, and distant lights.

➤ A manuscript, purportedly from the year 1290, tells of monks seeing a large silver disc in the sky. The report is probably a hoax, however.

➤ Many daylight observations have been made of strange objects crossing in front of the sun.

The 19th-Century Sky: Full of Silver Cigars

The newspapers our great-grandparents read were full of reports of UFOs from all over the world. They didn't call them UFOs back in the 19th century, though. They didn't know what to call them.

Thousands of people, among them many reputable "solid citizens," including statesmen, scientists, and clergymen, saw these apparitions in the sky.

The temptation of the readers of these accounts was to pass them off as drunken hallucinations, apparently a common complaint a century ago. But for many of these observers, that explanation would not hold. As a reporter for the *Chicago Tribune* put it, these ladies and gentlemen "did not touch the wine when t'was red nor the corn when t'was liquid."

These 19th-century UFOs came in a variety of shapes and sizes, some in the now-familiar saucer shape as well as triangles, dumbbells, globes, and eggs. There were also reports of soaring serpents, dragons, angels, and other creatures from the bestiary of conjecture. But most of the witnesses described flying silver cigars, and many were reported to be balloons or airships (*dirigibles*) with gondolas suspended beneath. Some had bright searchlights on the nose or the bottom, with which they peered about the countryside at night.

Contact

A **dirigible** is a lighter-than-air craft that has a rigid frame and is capable of powered flight and is steerable. Most of them looked a lot like the Goodyear blimp, which is not actually a true dirigible because it does not have a rigid frame, but deflates like a balloon.

Well, you might say, what of that? After all, the balloon was known of in the 19th century. The first man-carrying balloon was invented by Joseph and Etienne Montgolfier back in 1783. They went aloft in a basket suspended below a large silk bag filled with hot air, which they heated by burning straw.

Yes, but, although the principles for dirigibles were understood by the mid-19th century, and diagrams and drawings of all sorts of possible lighter-than-air craft appeared in newspapers, books, and magazines, none that were steerable and could stay aloft for any length of time were actually built until 1898, when Count Ferdinand von Zeppelin in Germany and Alberto Santos-Dumont in France reached the construction stage in their experimenting. And the mysterious craft we're talking about were seen years before and in places where no dirigibles were known to fly.

But the shape that lighter-than-air airships were to take was known. The numerous articles in the popular press had prepared the public for the coming of cigar-shaped craft with suspended gondolas sometime in the near future.

Close Encounters

In earlier times when people looked to the skies and saw strange objects, they described what they saw as dragons, angels, chariots, or sailing ships. By the 19th century, it was mostly balloons and dirigibles. Countless psychological experiments have shown that people tend to see what they expect to see. If the only airborne artifacts that could plausibly exist are cigar-shaped dirigibles, then that's what will be seen. This is one explanation for the changing descriptions of just what was seen in these sightings. Another possibility is that extraterrestrial visitors with a peculiar sense of humor designed their craft to look like dragons and chariots in the Middle Ages and balloons and dirigibles in the 19th century.

Look—Up in the Sky!

Let's look over some of these accounts as they appeared at the time and try to decide what it was that these people saw, or thought they were seeing.

Serpents Take to the Air

On 6 July 1873, the *New York Times* carried an account of a group of field workers in Bonham, Texas who saw a "giant serpent" fly over their farm. Whatever it was, it was on the move. The next day, the *Times* reported that in Fort Scott, Kansas, "About half way above the horizon, the form of a huge serpent, apparently perfect in form, was plainly seen."

The serpent was next reported on 30 May 1888, when it passed over Darlington County, South Carolina, moving with a hissing sound, "but no visible means of propulsion."

Angels We Have Seen on High

The Reverend W. Read and two members of his family saw "a host of self-luminous bodies" passing through the field of view of his telescope on 4 September 1851. Most were going from east to west, but some moved from north to south. He wrote a letter about it which was printed in the *Monthly Notices of the Royal Academy of Science*.

On 18 September 1877, according to the *New York Sun* of the 20th, W. H. Smith saw a "winged human form" passing over Brooklyn.

Silver Cigars and Flying Ships

On 20 August 1880, a respected member of the French Academy, M. Trecul, saw a great silver cigar high in the sky. He noted a small circular-shape craft leave the cigar shaped "mothership" (as it would now be called) and fly off.

The Floating Triangle

The *London Times* for 29 September 1886 printed a report from Bermuda that about two weeks earlier—it took news longer to travel back then—several people had seen, "a strange object in the clouds, coming from the north." The object was shaped like a triangle, and seemed to have "chains" dangling from it. It descended as it crossed the land, but then went over the sea again and rose out of sight. Letters to the *Times* from learned gentlemen suggested that the object was a large balloon, perhaps a deflating balloon, to account for the triangular shape. But there were no large balloons being flown from Bermuda, and none were reported launched and lost at that time anywhere else in the world. And besides, a deflating balloon does not rise out of sight; it sinks.

Say Cheese

The first known photographs of UFOs were taken over 100 years ago by Mexican astronomer José A. Y. Bonilla, who was working at the observatory in Zacatecas, a town in Central Mexico about 200 miles northwest of Mexico City. Bonilla was doing a study of the sun at eight o'clock in the morning on 12 August 1883, when he saw a flight of strange objects crossing the sun's disc. He kept watch during that day and the next and spotted several hundred such crossings. Bonilla recorded them as looking variously disc-shaped, cigar-shaped, and spindle-shaped. He took pictures in which blurred formations of discs, cigars, and spindles can be seen; what these shapes actually are cannot be made out. One of his photographs was published in *L'Astronomie*. It shows, according to Charles Forte, "a long body surrounded by indefinite structures, or by the haze of wings or planes in motion." Some UFO critics have suggested that Bonilla took fuzzy pictures of flights of migrating geese, fooled by their distance and the effect of sunlight; but geese do not usually migrate in mid-summer.

The "Great Circular Disc"

On the night of 17 November 1882, E. Walter Maunder, an astronomer at the Royal Observatory, Greenwich, was one of the many people who spotted something strange in the sky. Among the other witnesses was Pieter Zeeman of Holland, who 20 years later would win the Nobel Prize for Physics.

Maunder records that he was outside near the observatory that night, watching an auroral display, which cast rose-colored rays across the northern sky, when the unexpected happened:

> Then, when the display seemed to be quieting down, a great circular disc of greenish light suddenly appeared low down in the E.N.E., as though it had just risen, and moved across the sky, as smoothly and steadily as the Sun, Moon, stars and planets move, but nearly a thousand times as quickly.

A little further on, he says:

> …various observers spoke of it as 'cigar-shaped,' 'like a torpedo,' or 'a spindle' or 'shuttle.'

Maunder considers the possibility that it might have been a meteor and decides against it. Obviously not a man to leave a celestial event unexplained, he decided that what he and so many others had seen was the visible result of a magnetic disturbance on the earth, and somehow connected to the "disturbances in the Sun," by which I assume he means *sunspots*.

Now we know that sunspots do cause magnetic disturbances here on earth and interfere with radio transmission. But their ability to cause flying "spindles" is unproven.

Contact

Sunspots are dark patches on the surface of the sun believed to be caused by the upwelling of hot gasses from the sun's interior. The number of spots increases and decreases in an 11-year cycle. When at their greatest, they have been known to cause disruption of radio transmission on earth.

The Winged Cigar

On Saturday, 21 November 1896, a "winged cigar" with a brilliant searchlight in its nose appeared over the streets of Oakland, California. According to stories the next day in the *Oakland Tribune* and the *San Francisco Call*, the aerial cigar, "moved rapidly, going at least 20 miles an hour. It shot across the sky in the Northwest, then turned quickly and disappeared in the direction of Hayward." (Hayward is to the southeast of Oakland.) The sightings continued around northern California for the next few days and provoked much excitement.

The Cigar Moves East

A wave of sightings slowly crossed the country, from west to east, over the next few months. On 2 February 1897, an airship was reported over Hastings, Nebraska. Two weeks later a bright light, believed to be the powerful searchlight carried by the mysterious airship, swept over south Omaha at a height of about 500 feet. The chief witness of this event interviewed by the *Omaha Bee* was one Thomas Hazel, who "holds a responsible position with the Hammond Packing Company and is considered trustworthy in every respect."

The Cigar Is Explained—And Explained

Shortly after the Hastings sighting, a local kite-flier named McLean was accused of sending his kites a half mile into the air with lights attached to them. If so, that might have explained the Hastings events, but McLean was nowhere near Omaha or other places where airships or lights were seen.

An alternate explanation of the light over Omaha was published by the *New York Sun* of 11 April 1897. The *Sun*'s reporters had discovered a pair of practical jokers, Roy Arnold and Jack Rogers, who claimed the light was a burning wicker basket suspended from a balloon they had sent up on the night in question. Whether Rogers and Arnold were fooling the citizens of Omaha or the reporter from the *Sun* is not known.

Another explanation for the sightings, which will become a common refrain with UFO sightings after World War II, was that the witnesses had mistaken the planet Venus for an airship.

The Silver Cigar Passes Chicago

After several sightings in the Chicago suburbs of Rock Island and Evanston, the craft was first seen over Chicago on 9 April 1897.

"At several points the moving wonder was observed by persons equipped with small telescopes or powerful field glasses, and these persons claim to have described the outlines of a structure bearing the lights" according to the *Chicago Times Herald*.

Sighting

Professor G. W. Hough of the Dearborn Observatory in Evanston debunked the notion that the witnesses had seen an airship and equally derided the "Venus" theory. His idea was that they had seen "a fixed star in the constellation Orion. Alpha Orionis is its scientific name, it being a star of the first magnitude." The professor admitted that he had not seen the object himself.

"The consensus of judgment...is that the main body of the night flier was about seventy feet in length, of slender proportions and fragile construction. To this body, it is reported, were attached the movable headlight and the other lights described."

Some of the observers reported seeing short wings or sails protruding from the sides of the object.

Close Encounter

The passage of the airship, or whatever it was, caused a flood of newspaper stories and letters, and some bad verse. This, for example, was printed in the *Chicago Record*:

Twinkle, twinkle, little star,　　　　And the traveler in the dark,
How I wonder what you are;　　　　Sees your eighteen-karat spark;
Comet on your nightly trip,　　　　Tells of it next morning—then
Or some stray aerial ship.　　　　Listeners murmur, "Drunk Again."

When the evening sun is gone
Like an overcoat in dawn,
Then it is your brilliant speck,
Causes men to rubberneck.

Alexander Hamilton Loses a Cow

On Friday, 23 April 1897, in the staid state of Kansas, a local farmer named Alexander Hamilton had a run-in with a strange flying object. Hamilton was 65 years old at the time, successful and well respected and not given to seeing things. An account of his story appeared in the weekly *Yates Center Farmer's Advocate*, and was promptly picked up by papers all over the country.

A Noise Among the Cattle

According to Hamilton, he and his son Wallace and a tenant named Gid Heslip had been awakened at about 10:30 on the previous Monday night by "a noise among the cattle." When he went to look, he saw "that an airship was slowly descending upon my cow lot, about forty rods (600 feet) from the house." Gathering their courage and a couple of axes, the three men ran to the corral. When they got there, the ship was no more than 30 feet off the ground, and Hamilton got a good look. He described what he saw for the paper:

> It consisted of a great cigar-shaped portion, possibly three hundred feet long, with a carriage underneath. The carriage was made of glass or some other transparent substance alternating with a narrow strip of some material. It was brightly lighted within and everything was plainly visible—it was occupied by six of the strangest beings I ever saw. They were jabbering together but we could not understand a word they said.

> Every part of the vessel which was not transparent was of a dark reddish color. We stood mute with wonder and fright. Then some noise attracted their attention and they turned a light directly upon us. Immediately on catching sight of us they turned on some unknown power, and a great turbine wheel, about thirty feet in diameter, which was revolving slowly below the craft, began to buzz and the vessel rose lightly as a bird.

The Airship Grabs a Cow

Hamilton reported that the airship had looped a rope of some sort around a two-year old heifer and was trying to lift it off the ground, but the animal had become tangled in a wire fence. When the men found that they couldn't cut the rope, they cut the wire fence and the mysterious airship flew off dangling the heifer below. A farmer some miles away found the hide, legs, and head of the unfortunate cow lying in his field the next day.

"I don't know whether they are devils or angels or what," Hamilton finished his story, "but we all saw them, and my whole family saw the ship, and I don't want any more to do with them."

A dozen local citizens, including the sheriff, the doctor, the town banker, and the local justice of the peace all signed and swore to an affidavit stating that "we have known Alexander Hamilton from one to 30 years and that for truth and veracity we have never heard his word questioned and that we do verily believe his statement to be true and correct."

Sighting

The story of Alexander Hamilton and the airship was pretty much forgotten until Frank Edwards rediscovered it and put it in his 1966 bestseller *Flying Saucers—Serious Business.* After that, it became a staple in the UFO literature, retold time after time in books and magazines and reenacted for the television tabloids.

The Liars Club

A convincing case, wouldn't you say? You should have one additional bit of information before you make a decision as to whether aliens filleted Mr. Hamilton's cow. Hamilton was a member of a local liars club. The members would get together on Saturday afternoon and swap tall stories, the taller the better.

These clubs (the one in Yates Center was called the Ananias Club) were common in late 19th-century America. They were regarded as a harmless form of entertainment in those unfortunate days before the invention of television.

The art of the lie, as practiced in these clubs, was to tell your story completely seriously and to defend it against all doubters. This presents us doubters of a century in the future with an interesting problem. If Alexander Hamilton's story was a tall tale, it was a good one and he deserves whatever prize was handed out for the best story of the week. On the other hand, perhaps strangers in a strange airship did float by and fillet the cow. Your guess is as good as mine.

Close Encounter

In the Book of Acts, Ananias and his wife Sapphira were struck dead for lying about the price of a piece of land, even though they intended to give the proceeds to the church. Many of these liars clubs were called Ananias clubs in honor of this biblical prevaricator.

From Mars to Texas

The *Dallas Morning News* carried a story on 19 April 1897 about a strange airship that had collided with a windmill near the town of Aurora, Texas. The pilot of the ship, apparently the only one on board, was killed in the crash, and his body was buried in the town cemetery. What raises the story above the run-of-the-mill airship story is the following: "Mr. T. J. Weems, the U.S. Signal Service officer at this place and an authority on astronomy, gives it as his opinion that he [the pilot] was a native of the planet Mars. Papers found on his person —evidently the records of his travels—are written in some unknown hieroglyphics and cannot be deciphered."

What characteristics of the corpse placed its origin as the planet Mars is not stated. Attempts to find the body—or even the headstone—in the Aurora cemetery have met with no luck. Residents of the town who were interviewed in the 1970s, and who were small children at the putative date of the crash, do not remember the event. They do not even remember the existence of a windmill. Perhaps there was a branch liars club in Aurora at the time.

A Few Odd Reports

Charles Fort, who collected stories of odd happenings, recorded a vast number of incidents that could be attributed to extraterrestrial interference. A few of them are as follows:

➤ **4 February 1821:** A bright point of light was seen shining on the moon—in the crater Aristarchus, which was otherwise in the dark at the time. The light returned on the 5th and 7th. A similar light was seen 45 years later, on 10 June 1866.

➤ **15 July 1822:** A large number of "little round seeds" fell from the sky at Marienwerder, Germany. The locals tried to cook the seeds, but boiling water had no noticeable effect on them.

➤ **23 October 1822:** Two dark objects were seen to cross the face of the sun by an astronomer named Pastorff.

➤ **20 October 1824:** At five in the morning, once again a light was seen in the dark part of the moon. It kept up an irregular blinking until 5:30, when the light of the rising sun became bright enough to obscure it.

➤ **17 February 1841:** An oily red material fell from the sky at Genoa, Italy. More fell on the 19th.

➤ **27 June 1870:** According to a report of Captain Banner of the bark *Lady of the Lake*, his ship was off the coast of Brazil (5? 47' North Latitude, 27? 52' West Longitude, as reported by the ship's log) when he and his crew saw "a remarkable object." It looked like a cloud, except that it was perfectly circular, "with an included semicircle divided into four parts, the central dividing shaft beginning at the center of the circle and extending far outward, and then curving backward." Although cloud color, "it was much lower than the other clouds." And, here's the kicker, it was traveling *against the wind*.

Captain Banner drew a diagram of the object that looked like this:

Report from the Field

"By far the most usual way of handling phenomena so novel that they make for a serious rearrangement of our preconceptions is to ignore them altogether, or to abuse those who bear witness to them."

—William James, *Pragmatism* (1907)

*This is the "cloud" that
Captain Banner saw.*

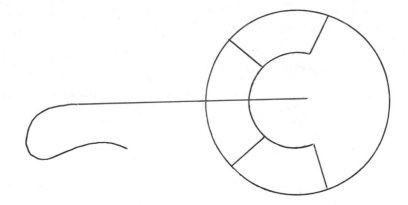

➤ **11 June 1881:** The two young sons of the Prince of Wales, both of whom were destined to become kings of England (Edward VII and George V), were on the steamship *Bacchante* somewhere between Melbourne and Sydney. At four in the morning, the ship's lookout reported seeing "a strange light, as if of a phantom vessel all aglow." The young princes and 12 other crew members came out to observe the unexplained lights.

What Did They See?

The interesting thing about these visions, or visitations if you prefer, is that most of them are so similar. The witnesses saw what they might be expected to see in the mid- to late-19th century: They saw gondolas suspended from cigar-shaped gas bags. At the time, these sightings were not attributed to alien beings, but usually to earthly inventors who were said to be conducting secret experiments. The 19th century was a time of great inventive ferment, and people expected continuous wonders from their inventors. Extraterrestrial explanations were not necessary.

If we analyze what was seen, there are a number of possible explanations with varying degrees of probability. And, since there were many sightings, it is possible that several of the explanations are true. One, of course, is that a rash of inventors were indeed floating their experimental airships all about the country. But if so, there is no record of the ships ever coming to earth. What could have happened to them?

Another is that there were more liars clubs around than we realize, and thousands of people practiced telling whopping great lies with perfectly straight faces. But, aside from Mr. Hamilton, whose children recalled him being a member of Ananias, and his dozen character witness, who presumably were fellow members of the club, there are no records of any of the other thousands of witnesses being amateur liars.

And there is the ever-popular sighting of the planet Venus or an especially bright star. How it managed to travel from north to south across the sky, shining a bright searchlight on the ground, is not recorded.

Then there is the possibility that observers from outer space chose to disguise their vehicles as dirigibles, which would create excitement but not the sort of panic (we assume) that a full-fledged flying saucer would have caused in 1897.

All these explanations are unsatisfactory in one way or another. The only thing we can be sure of is that unusual sightings were made by usually reliable people who, in most cases, were not particularly suggestible, had not been drinking, and had no known reason to lie. The royal princes, for example, had no reason to seek a notoriety beyond that which followed them about in their everyday life.

In the next chapter we'll look at more recent examples of oddities around the world that might have some mundane explanation that we just haven't figured out yet, or that might be signs left by visitors from a distant planet.

The Least You Need to Know

➤ People tend to see what they expect to see, and in the 19th century, people expected to see dirigibles.

➤ The first known photograph of an unidentified flying object was taken by a Mexican astronomer in 1885.

➤ Thousands of people saw a 400-foot-long "silver cigar" as it sailed leisurely from the West Coast to the East.

➤ There are many possible explanations for the dozens of sightings, but no one explanation will cover all the facts.

Chapter 9

Oddities from Outer Space and Elsewhere

In This Chapter

➤ A healthy skepticism is advised

➤ Geoglyphs around the world

➤ The Nasca Lines

➤ Giants at the Golan Heights

➤ The collector of Ambroses

➤ The Norfolk Regiment

If our alien friends *did* come to visit us in the past, recent or distant, and interacted with one or more groups of humans, they didn't leave any positive signs that one could point to and say, "There! On that spot, next to the glittering thousand-meter spire of an unknown metal, did the beings from the fifth planet circling a distant star they call Squambash make themselves known to our ancestors and give us the cure for all diseases and the recipe for a really good fruit punch!"

This chapter recounts a scattering of historical events and oddities around the world, and tries to see why some people think there is a possible extraterrestrial connection.

Extraordinary Claims

The doubters wonder why, if we have been visited by intelligent extraterrestrial life forms, these alien visitors would leave no tangible record. They downplay what

Report from the Field

"We have to understand how to handle uncertainty. How does something move from being almost certainly false to being almost certainly true? How do you handle the changes of your certainty with experience?"

—Richard Feynman

evidence there is of alien encounters because it is all indirect and circumstantial, and they have a point. As astronomer Carl Sagan once said, "Extraordinary claims require extraordinary proofs."

On the other hand, the supporters say that, even though the evidence for extraterrestrial visitors is circumstantial, fragmentary, and anecdotal, the sheer volume of it indicates that there could well be some basic germ of truth to the story. Somewhere in all that smoke, they would have it, there must be a fire.

The Importance of Evaluation

My opinion is, and I'm so glad you asked, that as long as you're just listening to and reading about the evidence for UFOs, collecting and evaluating anecdotes, and enjoying the stories for the fascinating vistas of possibility they open up, it's a good idea to have an open mind and a well-developed sense of wonder. But there *is* such a thing as objective reality, and beliefs that are in conflict with reality have a habit of rising up to bite you in a painful place when you least expect it.

Stories about UFOs need this sort of careful evaluation. There are numerous tales of human contact with extraterrestrial visitors, many of which are mutually exclusive. That is, if one of them is true, then another probably is not true. If the UFOs are round, they are probably not triangular; if the visitors are short and grey, they are probably not tall and blonde.

If you ever have to make a decision based on any person's particular view about the existence or nonexistence of extraterrestrial visitors, it would be a good idea to back up and sit down and think hard about what you're doing.

There were a passel of people in the 1940s and 1950s who claimed that they had met and talked with alien visitors, and these visitors had told them they were from Mars or Venus and had a message for the people of earth. There was George Hunt Williamson, who communicated telepathically with "Nah-9 of Solar X Group," on the planet Masar (Mars) by using a Ouija board on his dining room table. There was George Adamski, who "felt like a little child in the presence of one with great wisdom and much love," when he met a saucer man from Venus in the California desert. (See Chapter 17 for more about Mr. Adamski.)

But the discussions with aliens from Mars and Venus tapered off over the next 20 years as we sent our own spacecraft to these two planets and found that Venus was too hot for life, and that if there is life on Mars, it's microscopic and probably can't communicate telepathically.

Peering Through the Smoke

There probably are extraterrestrial life-forms out there in the galaxy, as we'll discuss in Part 4, and they well may have visited us in the past or be with us still; but the story any individual expert or guru is trying to sell you might not be the true goods, and his or her motives might be less than pure.

Earthlings Beware

For a view of some of the dangers of too easy an acceptance of one person's belief in alien beings and what they intend for us, see Chapter 17.

Geoglyphs

In various spots throughout the world, clusters of ancient *geoglyphs* seem designed for nothing except to be viewed from the air. Good examples are found in the United States (California and the Southeast, mostly), Malta, Egypt, and various South American countries.

Har Karkom

In the desert of Sinai, where the tribes of Israel wandered after their Biblical flight from Egypt, are the caves and altars of Har Karkom. Along with a great deal of rock art from periods dating back over 30,000 years and continuing until biblical times, are some sizable geoglyphs. There are animals and humans, some over 90 feet long, and some representations of beings that might be misshapen humans—or something, or someone, else.

Contact

Geoglyphs (from the Greek for earth-writing) are figures drawn on the ground. They are not necessarily cut very deeply into the earth; they might just have the top layer of dirt removed to reveal a different colored clay or rock underneath, or they may be created from pebbles or stones. Many of them are very large and seem to have been created to be seen from above.

The Nasca Lines

The most impressive geoglyphs are to be found in Nasca, a province of Peru about 320 miles south of Lima, the capital. Known as the Nasca Lines, they were first discovered by people not native to the area in the 1930s. They are spread about an area of about 300 square miles of vast treeless plains at the foot of the Andes Mountains that the natives call pampas, although they are a stark version of the pampas grasslands of the lowland plains.

The Nasca Lines look like the sort of drawings a child might make in the sand with a pointed stick, if the child were a couple of hundred feet tall. Some of them are so large that they cannot be interpreted from the ground at all, but only from a thousand feet or higher in the air. But the area is a plain, and the nearest natural high points, the Andes Mountains, are miles away.

Close Encounter

Whenever any ancient artifact is discovered and its use is not immediately obvious to the archaeologists, they assign it a religious or ritualistic purpose. If, as author Randall Garrett has pointed out, our civilization were to disappear tomorrow, all signs of it would wither away within 10,000 years or so except for tens of thousands of ceramic toilet bowls. And some archaeologist from the far future would write a learned monograph explaining how these were altars to our household gods.

So it is no surprise that many of the learned investigators of the Nasca Lines have decided that they had a ritualistic significance.

The area is a hodgepodge of drawings, geometric figures, crude animals, great V-shapes, and straight lines that extend for distances of up to five miles. These are not roads or walls or ditches, and if they were it would still be as much of a puzzle because they run from nowhere straight as a taut string to nowhere else.

Among the animal figures on the pampas at Nasca are a monkey over 150 feet long, a spider over 130 feet long, a lizard over 500 feet long, and the great pelican, which extends for over 850 feet. What they signify, and just who put them there is not known. It is hard to see how they could even have been designed from the ground, particularly for an ancient people without surveying instruments.

But here I am falling into the Von Däniken trap of assuming that our ancestors weren't all that bright (see Chapter 5). Two sticks tied at right angles with a peg in the middle can be used as a surveyor's transit, and, with a knotted rope for measuring distance, fairly accurate ground surveying can be done. The Nasca animals and geometric figures aren't that precise anyway.

The question that remains, however, is why would anyone, any group, any tribe, any culture, want to construct giant drawings that can only be seen from the air at a time when no device existed for humans to fly. And of that we are fairly sure. So, if not humans, who was flying around up there?

The monkey, as seen from above.

Of What Use Could They Be?

Among the other possibilities that have been discussed are the following:

➤ An astronomical site, with the figures lining up with objects in the night sky.

➤ Each symbol or series of symbols was sacred to a particular clan, which held, possibly, coming-of-age rites connected with the figure.

➤ An airport or spaceport.

➤ A set of instructions or suggestions for passing flying gods or aliens.

The archaeologists who have examined the site came up with several of these suggestions. The first, and still popular, notion was that the figures had an astronomical significance. The National Geographic Society looked into that in 1968 and decided that some of the figures did line up with the position of the sun, the moon, and certain prominent stars as they were 2,000 years ago, but that most of the figures didn't line up with anything in particular.

Sighting

It was Von Däniken, in *Chariots of the Gods*, who suggested that the lines and triangles remind him of an airfield, and indeed there is a certain similarity. The problem with that theory is that the pebbles that make up the geoglyphs would make a lousy surface for anything to land on or drive across, and there is no indication that anything ever did.

In his article, "Desert Ground Drawings in the Lower Santa Valley, North Coast of Peru," (*American Antiquity*, 1988), David J. Wilson wrote: "As is well known, several studies have been conducted that involved mapping and computer analysis of the Nasca lines to examine the hypothesis that they were related to astronomical phenomena. This theory is now discounted, at least as it applies to the great majority of the lines which do not appear to have been oriented toward the sky."

I'm not sure I follow this reasoning, since the sky is, after all, straight up, and who can tell what part of the anatomy of these figures was intended to point to what part of the heavens.

And the idea that I modestly throw out for your consideration: Let us assume that the gods, or beings that the Nasca dwellers thought of as gods—call them extraterrestrial visitors if you like—flew regularly past your village.

Come to think of it, it doesn't have to be all that regularly; if a god flies by, you would probably remember it for a long time.

So you and your villagers want to attract the gods' attention, or show your humility, or avert their wrath. What do you do? Six hundred years ago our ancestors (if you're of European descent), built the great cathedrals, the largest structures in the world at that time, to show respect for their God.

And the Nascans, poor subsistence dirt farmers, did what they could do: They drew giant pictures on the ground of things they thought would interest the gods passing overhead.

I wonder whether they got a response.

Gilgal Refaim

On the Golan Heights, for the moment the property of Israel, sits an ancient stone monument called in Hebrew *Gilgal Refaim*—the Circle of Refaim. It is made up of five stone rings, one outside the other, and the whole structure is about 475 feet across. The outer ring, which is in the best shape, is a circle of stones six feet high and 10 feet thick.

There are two large entrances into the structure, one facing northeast and the other southeast. Carbon dating of potsherds found at the site show that it existed 5,000 years ago, a period known as the Early Bronze Age, and is therefore older than the pyramids. Some of the stones in it weigh 20 tons, and the whole is estimated to weigh 37,000 tons. In the center of the circles is a 60-foot-wide mound, probably a burial mound.

The Worlds Largest, Heaviest Calendar

Professors Yonathan Mizrahi of Harvard and Anthony Aveni of Colgate discovered in 1968 that, 5,000 years ago, the *summer solstice* of each year would find the first rays of the rising sun shining directly through the northeast entrance, and the star Sirius would be peering in through the southeast entrance. On the basis of this, speculation is that the structure was an astronomical observatory, or a sort of calendar. It could be, but moving 37,000 tons of stone seems a lot of trouble to go through just to spot the summer solstice. And why the solstice would be of such great significance to the tribes of nomadic herders who are believed to have been the inhabitants of the area is beyond speculation.

But let's speculate anyway.

In the general area of Gilgal Refaim are hundreds of dolmens, megalithic (Stone Age) structures made of two upright stones with a capping stone, like a doorway with no house. Many of these are grave markers, but not all. The largest of them have stones that are over 20 feet tall and weigh over 50 tons.

It Stands Alone

One of the interesting things about the site is that it is unique in the Middle East. Whatever tribe or fraternal organization built it did not get the idea from any other local tribe, and no other group in the area seems to have taken it up.

Both the ring structure and the dolmens are similar to ones found in northern Britain and France. But how the nomadic shepherds of the Middle East could have come into contact with a people living so immeasurably far from them, in Stone Age terms, is not known. And if the local shepherds didn't construct the great stone ring, who did?

By piecing together biblical stories and myth, we can arrive at the following explanation: A people called the Anakim or the Refaim lived around what is now the Golan Heights. They were a great and powerful tribe, descended from the Nefilim, a race of gods who fell from the heavens. Their king, Og, of Bashan, lost a war with the tribes of Israel. His bed was captured and taken to Rabbah. It was made of iron and was 13 1/2 feet long and 6 feet wide.

Contact

The **summer solstice** is the moment when the earth reaches that place in its orbit around the sun that the sun appears at its farthest northern point in the sky for that year. This is caused by the fact that the axis of the earth is tilted, so that at one point in its orbit the North Pole leans toward the sun and at the opposite point it leans away from the sun.

Close Encounter

On Salisbury Plain, eight miles north of the city of Salisbury in England, rests the great prehistoric monument called Stonehenge. Like Gilgal Refaim, it is constructed of a circle of giant stones, and recent excavations and radiocarbon dating place its age also at about 5,000 years. Until recently it was believed to have been a druid temple, but the druids came to England no more than 2,500 years ago; so Stonehenge was already ancient when they arrived.

One legend about the creation of Stonehenge says that it was erected by the magician Merlin, who brought the stones from the "Giant's Dance" in Killaraus, Ireland, where they had originally been transported from Africa by a race of giants who had great powers.

So in Gilgal Refaim we have a massive artifact that might have been built by a tribe descended from gods who fell from the heavens. If I were the sort of UFOlogist who sees alien visitations in every odd historical fact, that would be pretty convincing. But I like to think I'm cool and rational.

Nonetheless, it might be very interesting to excavate that mound in the center of the stone rings and see what lies within.

Appearing and Disappearing Men

In southern England on 3 October 1843, a man named Charles Cooper heard a rumbling sound in the sky. He looked up and saw three men flying toward him at treetop level. They appeared to be completely white, and wafted through the air side by side without apparent motion of their own. Cooper and several other observers took these apparitions to be angels. He did note that they were all wearing belts, and if he could see the belts from his distance they must have been fairly large.

Perhaps it was the belts that were doing the flying.

The Collector of Ambroses

Sometime around 1914, noted writer Ambrose Bierce disappeared somewhere between Texas and Mexico, while supposedly going off to interview the Mexican bandit or revolutionary (depending on your point of view) Pancho Villa. The word in some quarters was that Villa had him murdered and hid the body; but this is unlikely as Villa knew the value of American journalists for building support and had one named John Reed traveling around with him for years.

Five years later, a businessman named Ambrose Small of Toronto, Canada, disappeared from his office in the Toronto Grand Opera House in the middle of the business day, while his outer office was full of people who would have seen him leave. They didn't. He left behind over a million dollars worth of securities.

While investigating the disappearance, the authorities discovered that Small's secretary, John Doughty, had subsequently taken over $100,000 and disappeared himself. Doughty was found living in Oregon under the name of Cooper. Small was never found.

Charles Fort, who wrote the two incidents up in his book, *Wild Talents*, suggested that perhaps somebody or something was collecting Ambroses.

The Norfolk Regiment

In an article in *The People's Almanac Presents the Twentieth Century*, T.A. Waters relates the story of the Norfolk Regiment. This happened during World War I, when British and Turkish forces spent most of the year 1915 hammering at each other at Gallipoli.

On the evening of August 12, the six regiments that made up the British 163rd Brigade began an advance against the fortified Turkish positions. Most of the Allied force was soon pinned down and unable to move forward, but the Fifth Norfolk managed to advance into a wooded area. And all 267 men promptly disappeared.

In the words of Sir Ian Hamilton, who reported on this to Commander in Chief Lord Kitchener, "Nothing more was seen or heard of any of them. They charged into the forest and were lost to sight and sound. None of them ever came back."

Fifty years later, three New Zealanders who had been soldiers at that battle, but luckily in a different regiment, wrote out and signed a statement of what they had seen during the advance. According to their statement, odd, dense clouds, "shaped like loaves of bread," had settled in front of the advancing Fifth Norfolk. The troops had marched into the cloud that was directly in front, and as soon as the last of them had disappeared into the mist the cloud rose up and moved away—*against the wind*.

Skeptics have pointed out that, while a low-lying mist was covering the area that day, no clouds were reported, that the three New Zealanders wrote that it was the Fourth

Report from the Field

If there have ever been instances of teleportations of human beings from somewhere else to this earth, an examination of inmates of infirmaries and workhouses and asylums might lead to some marvelous astronomical disclosures....Suppose any human being ever should be translated from somewhere else to this earth, and should tell about it. Just about what chance would he have for some publicity? I neglected to note the date, but early in the year 1928, a man did appear in a town in New Jersey, and did tell that he had come from the planet Mars. Wherever he came from, everybody knows where he went, after telling that.

—Charles Fort, *Lo!*

Norfolk instead of the Fifth, and that the New Zealanders couldn't possibly have seen what they said they saw. But if the "cloud" had come in just to pick up the Fifth Norfolk and then sailed away again, few people would have noticed it in the heat of battle, and again in the heat of battle it is easy to get the name of a nearby regiment wrong. As for them seeing what they claim to have seen, well, I wasn't there and you weren't there and they held their peace about this incredible event for 50 years, probably because it *was* incredible, and grown men who have just fought a war don't like being laughed it.

The Least You Need to Know

➤ If extraterrestrials were here in the past, they left subtle signs.

➤ Several ancient peoples drew gigantic geoglyphs on the ground that could best be seen from the air—and we don't know why.

➤ The Nasca Lines in southwest Peru are among the most impressive geoglyphs yet found.

➤ Gilgal Refaim on the Golan Heights is an ancient structure in the shape of concentric stone rings.

➤ It is the only structure of this sort in the entire Middle East, but it resembles some found in France and Britain.

➤ Men clad all in white were seen flying about wearing large belts in 1843. Perhaps they were angels.

➤ People named Ambrose had a tendency to disappear during the first quarter of this century.

➤ During World War I, an entire regiment of British troops marched into a low-lying cloud and disappeared forever.

Part 3
Weather Balloons of the Gods

The present fascination with what we call "flying saucers" began in 1947 when a formation of strange craft was sighted flying among the Cascade Mountains in the state of Washington. Since then, we have seen the number of sightings grow into the tens of thousands, the number of people who profess to believe in "flying saucers" grow into the millions, and the stories surrounding the events grow stranger and stranger.

But for some reason our alien visitors, if they are out there, choose to remain shy and elusive. Some of our fellow earthlings claim to have talked to extraterrestrial beings, to have taken trips in their craft, to have been poked, prodded, and, in some cases, violated by these beings; others claim to have indulged in consensual sex with the unearthly visitors. Yet no convincing close-up photographs have been shown, no alleged parts of alien spacecraft have proved to be of unearthly genesis when analyzed, no hybrid babies have been produced (the aliens evidently steal them from the mothers' wombs), and no alien being has stepped, hopped, or slithered forward to explain his or her—or its—behavior.

And yet...

Chapter 10

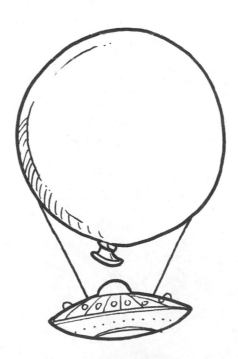

Skipping Saucers: The Term "Flying Saucer" Is Invented

In This Chapter

➤ Kenneth Arnold sees strange flying objects

➤ Flying saucers get their name

➤ The first casualty

➤ The explanations begin

After the rash of silver cigar-shaped dirigible sightings in the late 19th century, UFO reports slowed down for a while. The newspapers of the first third of the 20th century were quiescent with regard to unidentified objects flying about our skies.

But all this changed in 1947, two years after the end of World War II. Over a three month period, sightings of unidentifiable flying objects became commonplace. Military pilots on training flights and commercial airline pilots reported seeing strange craft of unknown design darting around in the sky at unbelievable speeds, and it was hard to doubt either the pilots' ability as observers or their sincerity. Official interest—and public fascination—quickly mounted.

Close Encounter

During World War II, strange flying objects that came to be called "Foo Fighters" or occasionally "fireball fighters" were seen by our fighter and bomber pilots. Usually described as glowing balls of light, or sometimes as small (a foot or so in diameter), shiny metallic discs, they would follow a plane, or occasionally perch on a wingtip for a while and then scoot off. They appeared often enough for the Allied air forces to worry that they were an enemy secret weapon. It wasn't until after the war that German and Japanese military records showed that the same phenomena appeared to their pilots, and they had no explanation for them either.

The first few people to view these craft, whatever they were, did not suggest that they might be from outer space. Some thought they were military airplanes being secretly tested. As the Cold War developed, the fear grew that they were secret Soviet reconnaissance aircraft. Even the U.S. Air Force became alarmed enough to investigate the sightings. But both the way these craft were said to maneuver and their estimated top speed put their technology way beyond anything that any group on earth was known to be capable of developing.

One obvious possibility, considered by those who believed that UFOs existed at all, was that these craft were artifacts of an alien civilization. But where that civilization might be located was an open question. Ray Palmer, the editor and founder of *Fate* magazine insisted that the saucers were piloted by a race of dwarfs and came from a hole in the earth located somewhere around Mount Ranier in Washington State. But his was a minority view.

Some who wrote about the sightings, like George Adamski (see Chapter 17), suggested that they were from outer space, from the planet Venus or Mars. A few, like Donald Kehoe (see the section "Observers from Another Planet" later in this chapter) and J. Allen Hyneck (see Chapter 11) suggested that they were visitors from a planet circling some distant star. Some thought they were from an alternate earth, or a different dimension, or that they were time travelers from the far future. But, whatever they were, they were not from around here.

The First Flying Saucers

The term "flying saucer" originated in 1947 with private pilot Kenneth Arnold, who reported seeing a flight of them. His story was the first of what became a flood of "saucer" sightings that ebbed for a while and then came back stronger than ever.

Twice the Speed of Sound

It was Tuesday, 24 June 1947, and Kenneth Arnold, a 32-year-old married man with two daughters, who owned his own business, was flying his private plane through the Cascade mountain range, from Chehalis to Yakima, two towns in Washington State. His route passed over an area where a missing Marine C-54 transport plane was believed to have crashed, so he had been asked to keep an eye out for the wreckage. Early in the afternoon, he was at an altitude of 9,200 feet and about 20 miles west of Mount Rainier when he saw a bright blue-white flash out the window to his right. He looked out and saw, "a chain of nine peculiar looking aircraft flying from north to south at approximately 9,500 feet elevation."

The craft, whatever they were, weaved in and out among the mountain peaks at high speed and with amazing dexterity. Arnold timed them with his wristwatch as they traveled from the southern edge of Mount Rainier to Mount Adams: It took them 102 seconds. He checked the distance between these two points on a map when he landed, and found that they were 47 miles apart. A simple calculation showed that the nine "aircraft" had been traveling at about 1,660 miles an hour.

Back in 1947, the speed of sound had been exceeded a few times by military fighter aircraft in power dives, but no plane yet was capable of breaking that barrier in normal flight. The idea of a craft that could travel more than twice the speed of sound in level flight was in the realm of science

Sighting

The first known description of a UFO as a "flying saucer" was by a Denison, Texas farmer named John Martin. He reported to the *Denison, Texas News* that he had seen an object pass over his head that "was about the size of a large saucer and was evidently at a great height." The date was 25 January 1878.

fiction. Also the ships Arnold saw were like nothing then known to be flying. He described them as being mirror-bright and sort of boomerang-shaped. It was the sun glinting off the shiny bodies of the craft as they banked and turned among the mountain peaks that had caused the flashes that first drew his attention to them. He estimated them to be 45 to 50 feet long, not quite that wide, and about three feet thick.

The Newspaper Picks Up the Story

Later that day, Arnold told his story to Nolan Skiff, an editor at the *East Oregonian* newspaper. He described the way the craft flew as, "like a saucer would if you skipped it across the water." Skiff put the story on the AP news wire, and "flying saucers" were born.

That day the Associated Press issued its first "flying saucer" story:

> PENDLETON, Ore. June 25 (AP)—Nine bright saucer-like objects flying at "incredible speed" at 10,000 feet altitude were reported here today by Kenneth Arnold, a Boise, Idaho pilot who said he could not hazard a guess as to what they were.

Arnold, a United States Forest Service employee engaged in searching for a missing plane, said he sighted the mysterious objects yesterday at three p.m. They were flying between Mount Rainier and Mount Adams, in Washington State, he said, and appeared to weave in and out of formation, Arnold said that he clocked and estimated their speed at 1,200 miles an hour.

Notice that the AP report got Arnold's job wrong and lowered the object's estimated speed, perhaps to keep it believable. Also Arnold described the objects as flying "like a saucer would," he didn't say they looked like saucers.

Earthlings Beware

The power of suggestion is very strong. If you ask a witness, "which way was the green car going?" you may well change the color of a car to green in the witness's memory, whatever it may have been in reality. So it could be that the reports of flying saucers are all based on what the witness expects to see due to the misunderstanding of what Arnold saw.

On the same day as Arnold had his experience, there were over a dozen other reported sightings of strange objects in the skies over Washington and Oregon. Within the next week, there were more than 25 sightings.

Newspapers all over the country carried the Arnold story, calling the objects variously "flying platters," "mystery discs," and "flying pancakes," but "flying saucers" was the favorite, and it quickly carried the day. For the next few weeks, everybody and his uncle were seeing strange objects in the sky and reporting them to the local papers. There was a particularly heavy rash of sightings around Portland, Oregon on 4 July 1947, the same day that the Army Air Force (it didn't become just the "Air Force" until later in 1947) came out with a denial that the saucers were some homegrown secret weapon.

After spending much of his time over the next three years telling and retelling his story, Arnold wrote it down. In 1950, he produced a 16-page pamphlet called "The Flying Saucer as I Saw It." In 1952, he collaborated with Ray Palmer on *The Coming of the Saucers: A Documentary Report on Sky Objects That Have Mystified the World.*

Close Encounter

Ray Palmer, then the editor of *Fate* magazine, wrote a series of articles with writer Richard Shaver claiming that the UFOs were piloted by short beings called the Abandondero ("dero" for short) who inhabited the land of Lemuria, which was located inside the earth with a secret entrance somewhere around Mount Ranier. This became known as the "Shaver Mystery (see Chapter 16)."

In September 1947, after hundreds of flying saucer sightings had been reported in the newspapers, General Twining, the Army Chief of Staff, authorized *Project Sign*, the first official study of UFOs. It was conducted by the Air Technical Intelligence Center (ATIC) at Wright Patterson Air Force Base outside of Dayton, Ohio.

It was around then that the term *UFO* for Unidentified Flying Object was coined by ATIC chief Edward J. Ruppelt, who needed a more official-sounding term for what they were researching than "flying saucer."

The Mantell Case

The first known death caused by interaction with a UFO was that of Captain Thomas Mantell of the United States Air National Guard. Captain Mantell was the leader of a group of four F-51 Mustang fighter planes that arrived at Godman Air Force Base, just outside of Louisville, Kentucky, at 1:45 p.m. on the afternoon of Wednesday, January 7, 1948.

About half an hour earlier, the Kentucky State Highway Patrol began getting calls from people in several different towns who were watching a strange saucer-like object somewhere between 200 and 300 feet in diameter heading west across the state. The Patrol called Godman AFB to ask if the Air Force knew anything about the object, and Godman said no.

The Air Force Sees a UFO

By this time, the object was visible to the tower operators in Godman's control tower. They called the base commander, Colonel Hix, and he came over to take a look. There it was in the distance, large and round and silver colored.

Hix told the tower radio operator to call the flight of Mustangs that was just coming in, and ask them if they had enough fuel to take a look at whatever-it-was. Captain Mantell, the flight leader, and two of his wingmen agreed to see what they could see. The fourth pilot, who was running low on fuel, landed his plane.

At first the three pilots couldn't find the object, and had to be guided toward it by the control tower operators. They had climbed to an altitude of 10,000 feet before Mantell, who was in the lead, finally spotted the thing and headed for it. "I see something above and ahead of me, and I'm still climbing," he radioed to the tower. The other two pilots broke off the chase, since none of the planes was equipped with oxygen and going much over 12,000 feet without oxygen was dangerous.

Moments later Mantell radioed, "It's above me and I'm gaining on it. I'm going to 20,000 feet." That was Captain Mantell's last transmission. At 4:00 p.m. the report came in that his Mustang had crashed. The investigation of the crash showed that the canopy lock on Mantell's cockpit was still in place, showing that he didn't try to parachute from the plane during its more than three mile drop to the ground.

Explanation or Cover-Up?

The official explanation of Mantell's crash was that he had been chasing the planet Venus, which was then 33 degrees above the southern horizon and unusually bright in the sky, and had climbed too high and lost consciousness from lack of oxygen. The Air Technical Intelligence Center's report then continues:

Earthlings Beware

Those of us who live in cities find it hard to believe that the planet Venus can ever be mistaken for a UFO. But on a clear night away from city lights, with Venus low on the horizon shortly after sunset, it is by far the brightest object in the sky and can easily be mistaken for a strange object hovering not too far away. But whether an experienced pilot would make such a mistake, I cannot say.

"...the aircraft being trimmed continued to climb until increasing altitude caused a sufficient loss of power for it to level out. The aircraft then began a turn to the left due to torque and as the wing drooped so did the nose until the aircraft was in a tight diving spiral. The uncontrolled descent resulted in excessive speed causing the aircraft to disintegrate. It is believed that Captain Mantell never regained consciousness."

But Mantell's friends described him as a very cautious pilot who would never climb past his oxygen limit, and who would certainly never chase the planet Venus. Besides, although Venus was certainly bright that evening, Mantell crashed in late afternoon, when the planet would not yet have been all that visible.

The Balloon Chase

It wasn't until four years later that an alternate explanation was advanced that was more credible to those who

A skyhook balloon being inflated in the 1950s.

doubted the Venus story. In 1952, Edward Ruppelt who had been the director of the Air Force's Project Blue Book, researched the Mantell case for his book *Report on Unidentified Flying Objects*. He had some information not available to the original investigators. At the time of the incident, the Navy was secretly lofting giant "skyhook" balloons as part of a classified research project.

One of the launch points was Clinton County Airport in Ohio. The prevailing winds would have taken a skyhook balloon, at an altitude of about 60,000 feet, right along the path of the sightings in Kentucky. At that altitude, the balloon would have expanded into a globe several hundred feet across, and would have been highly reflective. Because of its height and the lack of perspective, it would have looked closer than it was, and Captain Mantell might well have thought it was within range. If so the theory that he climbed until he lost consciousness because of insufficient oxygen is a good one. Believing the balloon was closer, he would not have been aware of how fast or how high he was climbing.

The problem with this theory is that there is no record of a skyhook balloon being launched on January 7, 1948. Not all the records have been located, however, and the people who have been questioned have no reason to remember a launch on a specific date. So the question of what all those people saw, and of what actually happened to Captain Mantell is probably solved; but there is still the possibility that a future investigation will discover that there was no skyhook balloon launched on that date. In that case, we will have to reconsider what it was that Captain Mantell was chasing on that Wednesday afternoon.

Report from the Field

"The most probable explanation is that Captain Mantell did, indeed, confront a skyhook [balloon] launched from Camp Riley, Minnesota, early on the morning that Captain Mantell was killed."

—David R. Saunders and R. Roger Harkins, *UFOS? Yes!: Where the Condon Committee Went Wrong*

Lieutenant Gorman Chases a Disc

Almost a year later, at about 8:30 in the evening of 1 October 1948, Second Lieutenant George Gorman of the North Dakota Air National Guard was approaching the Fargo, North Dakota, airport in his F-51 Mustang, completing the last leg of a cross-country trip. He radioed the Fargo tower for permission to land and was told that he could come in right after a Piper Cub that was making its approach. He looked down and spotted the Piper below him, and then began circling to give the small plane a chance to land.

Suddenly Gorman spotted a light passing him on the right side of his plane. Taking it for the tail light of another aircraft, he called the tower to complain that they hadn't informed him about this other plane. The tower told him that there were no planes flying in the area except his Mustang and the Piper Cub. This, whatever it was, was not the Piper Cub.

Angry over the dangerous behavior of this strange craft, Gorman turned his F-51 toward the light, to find out what it was. When he was about 1,000 yards from the light, he found, much to his surprise, that the light was a bright disc, about eight inches across, which seemed to be pulsating. There was no plane attached, just the disc, which seemed to have a life of its own.

In Gorman's report, he stated:

> "It was from six to eight inches in diameter, clear white and completely round, with a sort of fuzz at the edges. It was blinking on and off. As I approached, however, the light suddenly became steady and pulled into a sharp left bank. I thought that it was making a pass at the Tower.
>
> I dived after it…but I couldn't catch up with the thing. It started gaining altitude and again made a left bank.
>
> I put my 51 into a sharp turn and tried to cut the light off in its turn. By then we were at about 7,000 feet. Suddenly it made a sharp right turn, and we headed straight at each other. Just when we were about to collide, I guess I got scared.
>
> I went into a dive and the light passed over my canopy at about 500 feet. Then it made a left circle about 1,000 feet above, and I gave chase again."
>
> (as quoted in *Flying Saucers* by Donald H. Menzel)

Gorman's dogfight with the disc continued for some time, but he never caught it or even came close. The disc broke off contact by starting to climb rapidly, and then disappearing. Gorman later said that he was convinced that the object, whatever it was, was controlled by an intelligence, although it was too small for there to have been anyone inside of it. He also noted that it turned at angles and speeds impossible for a human pilot—he blacked out temporarily when he tried to follow too closely.

A Whirlpool of Air

The Air Force concluded that Gorman had been chasing a lighted weather balloon. But study of the balloon's track shows that it was not close enough and that it was moving in the wrong direction.

Professor Donald H. Menzel, who debunked as many of the saucer sightings as he could in his 1953 book *Flying Saucers*, decided that Gorman had been chasing, "light reflected from a distance source by a whirlpool of air over one wing of the plane." Menzel dismissed the other sightings of the time as mirages, weather balloons, sightings of the planet Venus, refracted ice crystals, or outright frauds.

Close Encounter

Donald Howard Menzel (1901–1976) was a professor of Astronomy at Harvard University and the director of the Harvard Observatory. He saw UFOs himself while driving in New Mexico in 1949: two large fuzzy white objects in the distance, parallel with the horizon, that did not move for some minutes and then suddenly disappeared. By the time he wrote *Flying Saucers* in 1953 and embarked on his avocation of debunking UFOs, he had decided that what he saw was "merely a reflection of the moon."

Some of the sightings undoubtedly were fraudulent, and a few weather balloons were chased by puzzled pilots, but "the planet Venus" was never a reasonable explanation for sightings by experienced pilots who reported large objects making erratic zigs and zags through the sky.

Observers from Another Planet

The experiences of Mantell and Gorman, among others, caused Donald E. Kehoe to reach an entirely different conclusion. Kehoe, an aviation expert who had been an aide to both Admiral Richard E. Byrd and Charles Lindbergh, and had served as an instructor with the Naval Aviation Training Division during World War II, had recently retired from the Marines as a major. In 1949, *True* magazine asked Kehoe, who had written several articles on aviation for them, to look into the flying saucer stories that were then going around.

Kehoe investigated for some months and concluded that there was something real happening. In January 1950, *True* published his article, "The Flying Saucers Are Real" (later expanded into a book with the same name). In the article, Kehoe concluded the following:

1. For the past 175 years, the planet earth has been under systematic close-range observation by living, intelligent observers from another planet.

2. The intensity of this observation, and the frequency of the visits to the earth's atmosphere by which it is being conducted have increased markedly during the past two years.

3. The vehicles used for this observation and for interplanetary transport by the explorers have been identified and categorized as follows:

➤ **Type I:** A small nonpiloted, disc-shaped aircraft equipped with some form of television or impulse transmitter.

➤ **Type II:** A very large (up to 250 feet in diameter) metallic, disc-shaped aircraft operating on the helicopter principle.

➤ **Type III:** A dirigible-shaped, wingless aircraft which, in the earth's atmosphere, operates in conformance with the *Prandtl* theory of lift.

4. The discernible pattern of observation and exploration shown by the so-called flying discs varies in no important particular from well-developed American plans for the exploration of space expected to come to fruition within the next 50 years. There is reason to believe, however, that some other race of thinking beings is a matter of two and a quarter centuries ahead of us.

Contact

Ludwig **Prandtl** (1875–1953), considered the father of aerodynamic theory, developed mathematic models for how air flows over the surfaces of a wing at various speeds.

Earthlings Beware

Some people just naturally like tricking their friends and neighbors. Others enjoy the limelight and will say anything to get it. The first thing a UFOlogist must do in evaluating a "sighting" is establish as well as possible the credibility of the observer.

The hardest UFO sightings to "debunk" are ones by otherwise successful people—military and airline pilots who are experienced with the sort of things one might find flying about, and policemen, ministers, and other professional people who do not seek notoriety and have nothing to gain from telling their story (particularly when several people who don't know each other or are only casual acquaintances report seeing the same thing).

Many of these people have had to put up with the disbelief of the authorities and the ridicule of their friends. Most of them must have had a good idea of how their story would be greeted, and it must have taken a good bit of courage and stubbornness for them to come forward. It makes me wonder how many people have seen strange and unexplainable objects in the heavens, but have chosen not to come forward.

The Least You Need to Know

➤ Modern flying saucer sightings began in 1947.

➤ Kenneth Arnold reported seeing a flight of "peculiar looking" flying objects while flying his private plane through the Cascade Mountains in Washington State.

➤ His description of the craft flying "like a saucer would if you skipped it across the water," gave birth to the name "flying saucers."

➤ In 1948, Air National Guard Captain Thomas Mantell was killed while chasing a UFO in his Mustang fighter.

➤ Lieutenant Gorman of the Air National Guard chased a small disc in late 1948 but couldn't catch it.

➤ By the early 1950s, a number of books had been written explaining flying saucers, the explanations ranging from sightings of the moon and the planet Venus to craft piloted by little men from beneath the earth.

➤ Among those who believe in the existence of UFOs, the explanation that these craft are from another planet begins to be favored over the previous idea that they are a secret Soviet weapon.

UFOs Come of Age

On 24 July 1948 at 2:45 in the morning of a bright, moonlit night, Captain Clarence S. Chiles and his copilot, John B. Whitted, were flying their Eastern Airlines DC-3 near Montgomery, Alabama when they saw "a bright glow" and watched as a "long rocket-like ship" flew passed them. They described it as a "wingless aircraft, 100 feet long, cigar-shaped and about twice the diameter of a B-29, with no protruding surfaces, and two rows of square windows….From the sides of the craft came an intense, fairly dark blue glow…like a fluorescent factory light." They said the ship, whatever it was, "pulled up with tremendous burst of flame from the rear and zoomed into the clouds at about 800 miles an hour." Their DC-3 was shaken with its "prop or jet wash." One of the passengers, who happened to be awake, also saw the strange craft. And investigators turned up a ground maintenance crewman at Robins Air Force Base in Georgia who had seen the same thing an hour earlier.

This was one of the many sightings by skilled observers—pilots are trained and accustomed to locate and evaluate other objects in the sky around them, for safety reasons if

Report from the Field

"UFO researchers are caught in a classic 'Catch-22' situation: When they seek funds and projects to collect quantitative evidence, critics point to the absence of supporting data. For example, NASA, in rejecting President Carter's request that it undertake an examination of the UFO question, stated in effect that it would do so only if presented with 'hard' data."

—J. Allen Hynek, "The UFO Phenomenon: Laugh, Laugh, Study, Study," from *Technology Review*, July, 1981

Report from the Field

"The phenomenon reported is something real and not visionary or fictitious....It is recommended that...Headquarters, Army Air Forces issue a directive assigning a priority, security classification, and Code Name for a detailed study of this matter."

—General Nathan F. Twining, Commanding Officer, Air Material Command, 1947

nothing else—who had nothing to gain and possibly much to lose by perpetrating a hoax. It became a matter of some concern to the U.S. military to determine what these people were seeing.

Project Sign

Shortly after the first wave of flying saucer sightings, the Air Force—which had good reason to be concerned about stories of strange unidentified craft flying about in U.S. airspace—decided to take the reports seriously. In an operation called Project Sign, the Technical Intelligence Division of Air Material Command at Wright Patterson Air Force Base in Dayton, Ohio collected and analyzed the reports. Most of them could be dismissed as hoaxes, or misidentification of commercial or military aircraft, but a few defied analysis.

The officers assigned to Project Sign created a standard questionnaire for sightings to be reported on (see Appendix B). The information was then evaluated, and if the case seemed important or promising enough, case officers would fly to the scene to interview and investigate.

Sign's first job was to make sure that what was being seen couldn't be secret Soviet aircraft of some sort. That was seriously considered, but quickly ruled out. The maneuvering capability of the craft observed showed that they were too far ahead technically of anything we could do for them to have been produced by any country on earth. Either the incidents were all hoaxes, or some strange meteorological phenomena, or we were dealing with something truly unearthly.

By the end of 1948, Project Sign turned in a Top Secret Estimate, endorsed by its director, Captain Robert R. Sneider, which concluded that there was credible reason to believe that we were being visited by extraterrestrial beings.

When the Chief of Staff of the Air Force, General Hoyt S. Vandenberg, read the report, he rejected it because it had failed to come up with positive proof of any of its extraterrestrial contentions, and ordered it destroyed. All copies were supposedly burned.

Project Grudge

As a result of General Vandenberg's displeasure, it was not considered a way to further your Air Force career to conclude that extraterrestrials might be involved in any future UFO sightings. Project Sign was disbanded, and a new operation, code-named Project Grudge, was established to handle future reports of UFO sightings. Whether the grudge was against the idea of flying saucers, the civilians who were making the reports, or the General, is not known.

Earthlings Beware

The information about Project Sign's Top Secret Estimate is all second-hand. No actual copy of the document has ever been released, although several are reported to have escaped the burning.

Don't Believe It

In August 1949, Project Grudge compiled Technical Report #102-AC 49/15-100, classified Secret, a 600-page document that examined 244 UFO reports covering Europe and the United States for the past three and a half years. Although the report admitted that 56 cases, or 23 percent of those examined, had not been satisfactorily explained, it attributed them to "psychological explanations." In other words, if you saw flying saucers, you were crazy.

For the next few years, Project Grudge was down-graded, and its personnel were assigned to other duties, until the entire staff consisted of one lieutenant.

Crazy or Not, They're Here

But then, in 1952, a new wave of sightings—many of them of the sort that couldn't be ignored—were observed by commercial pilots or trained Air Force pilots or observers. Fighter pilots fighting in Korea reported seeing silver discs in the air, and radar in Japan, Okinawa, and Korea tracked objects that were not airplanes.

During the year, 1,501 UFO sightings were reported to Project Grudge, including one of the most famous, the flight of seven UFOs over the White House.

Sighting

In the words of Captain Edward J. Ruppelt, who became the last director of Project Grudge and the first of its successor, Project Blue Book, Project Grudge had an institutional bias: Reports were to be evaluated, "on the premise that UFOs couldn't exist. No matter what you see or hear, don't believe it."

Seven Blips

It began at 11:40 the night of Saturday, 19 July 1952, when seven blips appeared on the air traffic control radar screen at Washington National Airport. Edward Nugent,

one of the controllers, watched the blips as they moved at about 100 miles an hour toward Washington, D.C. from the south-southwest.

Nugent called his supervisor, Harry G. Barnes, over to look at the strange blips, which were not where any airplanes ought to be.

Barnes had the radar set checked out; it was working perfectly. Then he called Tower Central, Washington National Airport's final approach radar center, and was told that they, too, had the objects onscreen. And they could actually see one of the objects, "a bright orange light," from the tower window.

A UFO Plague over Washington, D.C.

During the course of that night, there were continuous sightings from all over the Washington, D.C. area:

➤ An "orange ball of fire trailing a tail" was seen to the south of the tower. After being observed for a short time, it "took off at an unbelievable speed" and disappeared.

➤ Seconds later, a second orange ball appeared, circled around, and then disappeared.

Report from the Field

"We knew immediately that a very strange situation existed....Their movements were completely radical compared to those of ordinary aircraft. They followed no set course...were not in any formation, and we only seemed to be able to track them for about three miles at a time, the individual pip would seem to disappear from the scope at intervals. Later I realized that if these objects had made any sudden burst of extremely high speed, that would account for them disappearing from the scope temporarily."

—Senior Air Traffic Controller Harry G. Barnes

➤ Capitol Airlines pilot S.C. Pierman watched from the cockpit of his DC-4 as a fiery, blue-white object flashed across the horizon in front of him. Shortly after this, the radar tower radioed him that a cluster of unidentified objects showed on the screen as being about nine miles away from his plane and approaching fast. Shortly after that he saw a total of six white, tailless objects scoot by him at impressive speeds over a 14-minute period. The objects also showed up on the radarscopes.

➤ Seven white discs were seen in the sky passing over the White House and the Capitol building.

➤ The two civilian radar towers and the tower at nearby Andrews AFB all fixed on an object hovering over the Riverdale radio beacon. After watching it for 30 seconds, all three had it disappear from their screens at the same instant.

Unfortunately the runways at Andrews Air Force Base were closed for repairs, so no interceptors could take off from there. By the time intercept aircraft arrived from Newcastle Air Force Base in Delaware at around three in the morning, the mysterious intruders were gone.

They're Back!

One week later at about 8:15 in the evening, the radar screens at Washington National Airport and Andrews AFB both lit up with unidentified tracks. About a dozen UFOs were moving around the Washington, D.C. skies at a leisurely 100 miles an hour.

Unidentified flying lights of various colors—red, orange-white, white, and green—were seen by people all over Washington. F-94 Interceptor jets were called out, and the pilot of one of them reported that four "white glows" circled around his plane, stayed for a few moments, and then shot away.

On Tuesday, 29 July, the Air Force held a press conference at the Pentagon where they did their best to dismiss the sightings as *temperature inversions* or other anomalies. In general, the newspapers went along with this theory, the *Washington Post* headlining, "AIR FORCE LAYS SAUCER BLIPS TO HEAT."

Contact

A **temperature inversion** happens when a layer of cold air comes in on top of a layer of warm air. Usually, since heat rises, the warm air is on top. Because the two different temperatures of air refract light at slightly different angles, a temperature inversion can have a magnifying effect, causing a far-away object to look much closer than it is.

Project Blue Book

But the Air Force was not convinced by its own explanation, and brought in Captain Edward J. Ruppelt to head a new team at Project Grudge and resuscitate the investigation. He immediately began devising ways to gather more and more accurate information, and to verify the reports. As to the Air Forces' "inversion" theory, Captain Ruppelt noted, "Hardly a night passed in June, July and August, in 1952 that there wasn't an inversion in Washington, yet the slow-moving, 'solid' radar targets appeared on only a few nights."

In 1952, Project Grudge was renamed Project Blue Book, with Captain Ruppelt still in charge. Air Force personnel reported UFO contacts and were taken seriously, and the staff of Blue Book investigated. But this didn't last.

The Robertson Panel

On Wednesday, 14 January 1953, a five-man panel of scientists was assembled by the CIA to consider the UFO question. The panel was headed by H.P. Robertson, head of the Weapon System Evaluation Group at the Defense Department. For four days, the panel reviewed and evaluated the material on UFOs and the arguments for and against the possibility that the mysterious craft were visitors from another planet—or that they existed at all.

But the deck was stacked on the "against" side. All the panelists were skeptical of the UFO cases, and two were known to be actively antagonistic. The results were predictable. Because most of the sightings could be explained as hoaxes, cases of mistaken

Report from the Field

"National security agencies [should] take immediate steps to strip the Unidentified Flying Objects of the special status they have been given and the aura of mystery they have unfortunately acquired."

—from the Robertson Panel report

identity, or natural phenomena, the panel decided that the rest must be the same and that it wasn't worth expending the resources necessary to prove the point.

Moreover, the panel declared that the mass of UFO reports coming in to Air Force and other military channels might overload these channels with "material quite irrelevant to hostile objects that might some day appear." In other words, in looking at UFOs, we might miss Soviet bombers or missiles.

Project Blue Book, the panel recommended, should immediately start doing everything it could to debunk these UFO reports. Explanations should be found for all the reports that could be explained, and the rest should be ignored—all this in an effort to lessen "public gullibility."

The Air Force came out with Regulation 200-2 (see Appendix B), which told Air Force officers how to report UFO sightings. In addition to a listing of the information required, and in what form it should be given, was the instruction that only UFO

An artist's rendition of some of the types of flying saucers that observers have reported seeing.

reports that could be considered solved could be discussed with the public or the press; unsolved cases were classified and passed on to higher authority. This was a response to the Robertson Panel's suggestion that UFO sightings should be debunked whenever possible. UFOlogists saw, and see, this as a cover-up, but the Air Force's view was that it was taking steps to defuse situations that could result in mass hysteria.

When Captain Ruppelt left Project Blue Book in August 1953, a sergeant was left in charge, an indication of the little importance the government was now giving to UFO sightings. But the sightings wouldn't stop. Eventually an officer was put back in charge, but now it was clear that the function of Blue Book was to debunk any reports that came its way and to defuse whatever public interest it could manage to defuse.

Menzel Debunks Flying Saucers

In 1953, Professor Donald H. Menzel published a book called *Flying Saucers*, in which he explained copiously and in great detail how they didn't exist. Menzel, a professor of astrophysics at Harvard, opined that all the reports could be explained away as having been caused by one or another of a variety of natural causes, mostly meteorological; and those that couldn't be so explained away should be.

The saucers, according to Menzel, those that were not outright hoaxes, were all balloons, the planet Venus or Jupiter, reflections and refractions due to atmospheric conditions, ice crystals in the atmosphere, *sundogs,* or *lenticular clouds.*

Menzel was the first prominent scientist to come out with an opinion on UFOs, and the devastating negativity of his opinion convinced many people that there was nothing to the stories—that they all had reasonable explanations outside the extraterrestrial-visitor hypothesis.

But Menzel's skepticism had its skeptics. Physicist James E. McDonald commented in a 1967 lecture:

Contact

Sundogs are apparitions of the sun, like mirages, that occur when atmospheric inversions cause the image of the sun to be refracted to a different position. Sometimes two or more sun dogs are visible on both sides of the real sun.

Lenticular clouds are clouds that form in the shape of ovals or circles. They can have distinct edges and look convincingly like solid objects.

> Dr. Menzel's background in physics and astronomy is well attested by his authorship of a number of texts and references in those areas. Despite that background, when he comes to analyzing UFO reports, he seems to calmly cast aside well known scientific principles almost with abandon, in an all-out effort to be sure that no UFO report survives his attack. Refraction processes are quite well understood in optics, and the refracting properties of the atmosphere are surely as familiar in astronomy as in meteorology, if not more so. Yet in explanation after explanation in his books, Menzel rides roughshod over

elementary optical considerations governing such things as mirages and light reflections.

Doctor Condon Reports

A wave of UFO sightings occurred through 1965 and 1966, including several prominent ones in southern Michigan. These prompted Project Blue Book science advisor J. Allen Hynek to make the unfortunate suggestion that they might be caused by "marsh gas." These sightings caused Air Force Secretary Harold Brown and Hynek himself to suggest to the House Armed Services Committee that "a civilian panel of physical and social scientists" be convened to look at the UFO question. The committee thought that might be a good idea.

On 31 August 1966, the Deputy Executive Director of the Air Force Office of Scientific Research proposed to the University of Colorado that a scientific study of the UFO phenomenon conducted by a neutral, unbiased body of researchers picked by the university should be conducted. The Air Force found itself in an uncomfortable position, one that it was not used to. It was being attacked on one side by the growing body of believers in UFOs for not taking the reports and other evidence of extraterrestrial visitation seriously, and on the other side by the skeptics of UFO reports for paying any attention to them at all, and thus taking time and resources away from more serious pursuits.

The university agreed to do the study and picked Dr. Edward U. Condon, about as eminent a scientist as they could find, to head the project. After three years, they produced a massive document called the "Scientific Study of Unidentified Flying Objects," or more popularly known as the Condon Report.

So That's a UFO

Dr. Condon began by defining what they were talking about:

> An unidentified flying object (UFO, pronounced OOFO) is here defined as the stimulus for a report made by one or more individuals of something seen in the sky (or an object thought to be capable of flight but seen when landed on the earth) which the observer could not identify as having an ordinary natural origin, and which seemed to him sufficiently puzzling that he undertook to make a report of it to police, to government officials, to the press, or perhaps to a representative of a private organization devoted to the study of such objects.

The Condon investigators did their best not to blame the people who saw the UFOs for making up or exaggerating the phenomena. The report concludes the following:

> In our experience, the persons making reports seem in nearly all cases to be normal, responsible individuals. In most cases, they are quite calm, at least by the

time they make a report. They are simply puzzled about what they saw and hope that they can be helped to a better understanding of it. Only a very few are obviously quite emotionally disturbed, their minds being filled with pseudo-scientific, pseudo-religious or other fantasies.

But the fairness of the project with regard to whether UFOs were a real phenomena was compromised at the start. The university, concerned about its image in the academic world if it espoused the notion of extraterrestrial visitations, ensured that no such espousing would occur.

In a private memo from Assistant Dean Robert J. Low to several other university officials, written as the project was getting started, he gave the game away:

Report from the Field

"If, as many people suspect, our planet is being visited clandestinely by spacecraft, manned or controlled by intelligent creatures from another world, it is the most momentous development in human history."

—Walter Sullivan (from the introduction to the Condon Report)

> Our study would be conducted almost exclusively by nonbelievers who, although they couldn't possibly *prove* a negative result, could and probably would add an impressive body of evidence that there is no reality to the observations. The trick would be, I think, to describe the project so that, to the pubic, it would appear a totally objective study but, to the scientific community, would present the image of a group of non-believers trying their best to be objective but having an almost zero expectation of finding a saucer.

As expected, the massive (1,485 pages in the Government Printing Office edition) report found no extraterrestrials and no persuasive evidence that there were or ever had been extraterrestrials visiting earth. Considering the bias of the investigation, no other finding was possible.

Bye, Bye, Blue Book

In 1969, Project Blue Book was officially disbanded, having come to the official conclusions:

1. No unidentified flying object has ever posed a threat to national security.
2. No evidence has been submitted to indicate that unidentified sightings represent technological developments beyond the range of our scientific knowledge.
3. There is no evidence that the sighted objects are of an extraterrestrial nature.

And so it goes.

The Least You Need to Know

➤ In response to repeated sightings of UFOs, the Air Force started Project Sign.

➤ Air Force Chief of Staff General Vandenberg refused to believe in flying saucers.

➤ Project Sign turned into Project Grudge, which reported and explained, but didn't believe.

➤ Project Grudge gave way to Project Blue Book, which investigated honestly briefly, but then ignored what it could not explain away.

➤ Waves of flying saucers seen over the capital frightened the public but did not convince the unconvinced.

➤ The massive and supposedly unbiased Condon Report changed no one's mind on either side of the extraterrestrial visitor debate.

Chapter 12

Roswell and Alien Autopsies

In This Chapter

➤ A flying disc crashes outside of Roswell, New Mexico

➤ The Air Force claims it's a weather balloon

➤ The story improves with each retelling

➤ Alien bodies found with the wreckage

More than 20,000 recorded sightings of UFOs have been reported since the end of World War II. Many of them can be eliminated, as Dr. Condon discovered (see Chapter 11), with a minimum of investigation, but some persist despite all attempts to explain them away. One of these, which has attracted more believers and debunkers than any other, occurred in southern New Mexico in mid-1947.

This is the most famous of all the UFO cases, the one that has created the most discussion and controversy as well as a few dozen books and magazine articles. It has become known as the "Roswell Incident," or sometimes, "the Incident at Corona."

Curiously, for three decades after the Roswell Incident occurred, it was not considered important at all. After a brief flurry of reporting that lasted a little over a week, UFO investigators lost interest in the events at Roswell. The story was not mentioned again for 30 years, except perhaps for a passing—albeit strident—paragraph in an occasional UFO book.

The story began in June 1947 with claims of a downed spaceship. By July, the spaceship had been explained away by the Air Force as a weather balloon, and the story died. It wasn't until 1979, 32 years later, that a new, expanded version of the incident came to light. Fresh interviews were conducted with people who had been on the scene and who were still alive and could be located. These interviews and a reexamination of the existing evidence brought doubts about those weather balloons and the conviction that there had been a great cover up to conceal one of the most important stories of the century.

After this initial rediscovery of the Roswell story, the tale has grown larger and stranger with each retelling. To date in this on-going story, there have been charges that:

➤ The U.S. Air Force, FBI, and CIA have been deliberately fabricating evidence to conceal what really happened.

➤ Dead humanoid aliens have been found at the site of a crashed flying saucer.

➤ An autopsy was performed on at least one of the alien bodies.

➤ At least one of the aliens was found alive.

And that all this has been hushed up because of fear of overreaction by the public as well as a desire by the military to secretly learn everything they can from the advanced technology in the alien's spacecraft.

How It Was

It is difficult to separate the facts from the extensive myth that has grown around the events, but I will do my best. The simplest version of the original story went something like this:

A Field of Debris

On 14 June 1947, a ranch foreman named William W. "Mac" Brazel, with his eight-year-old son Vernon along for company, was making his regular rounds on the J.B. Foster ranch, a large spread in southern New Mexico. A bit over seven miles away from the ranch house, they came across a scattering of debris spread over an area about 100 yards wide and maybe 1,000 yards long. There wasn't much of it, and what there was seemed to be made up of "rubber strips, tinfoil, a rather tough paper, and sticks."

Brazel didn't bother with the debris then, but he told his wife about it, and a couple of weeks later they went back to the spot to collect some samples of the stuff to take into the nearby town of Corona to see whether anyone knew what it was or where it came from. Nobody in the small town of Corona had any more idea of what the stuff was than Brazel himself. It wasn't from a conventional weather balloon. Weather balloons were regularly lofted from the nearby Air Force base, and Brazel had previously come across the debris from several of them on the ranch property. This stuff was somehow different.

It was on 24 June 1947, ten days after Brazel's initial discovery of the debris field, when Kenneth Arnold sighted his skipping saucers in Washington State (as we saw in Chapter 10), and for the next few weeks "flying saucers" were making head-lines in all the newspapers. Brazel thought that maybe what he had was debris from one of these flying saucers. The next Monday, 7 July, when he was in Roswell, he told Sheriff George Wilcox about it.

The Air Force Takes a Hand

Wilcox called Roswell Army Air Field and told the people there about it, and they sent two officers, Major Jesse A. Marcel, the intelligence officer of the 509th Bomb Group, and counter-intelligence officer Captain Sheridan Cavitt, to accompany Brazel back to the ranch and see what there was to be seen.

While they were waiting for the officers, Sheriff Wilcox told Frank Joyce, a reporter from the local Roswell paper, about the "flying disc," and Joyce had a brief interview with Brazel. The paper had a real scoop the next day, with the headline: RAAF Captures Flying Saucer on Ranch in Roswell Region.

When they arrived at the ranch it was already getting dark, so the two officers stayed the night. The next morning, Brazel took them out to the debris field, and they spent some time gathering up what they could. Marcel tried to reconstruct the object from its debris. The closest he could come to anything was a large kite, and that didn't seem right. He took the stuff back to Roswell Army Air Field.

Report from the Field

"We have, indeed, been contacted by extraterrestrial beings, and the U.S. government, in collusion with the other national powers of the earth, is determined to keep this information from the general public. The purpose of the international conspiracy is to maintain a workable stability among the nations of the world and for them, in turn, to retain institutional control over their respective populations."

—Victor Marchetti, former CIA official, in *Second Look* magazine (May 1979)

Sighting

It was reported in the *Roswell Daily Record*, as part of the original flying saucer story of 8 July 1947, that in the evening of the previous Wednesday, 2 July, Mr. And Mrs. Dan Wilmot of Roswell had seen a craft shaped "like two inverted saucers facing mouth-to-mouth," passing over their house headed toward the northwest.

The Roswell Daily Record *has a scoop.*

The base public relations officer knew a good story when it ran by his nose. The next morning, he issued a press release that has haunted the Air Force ever since. In part it said:

> The many rumors regarding the flying disc became a reality yesterday when the intelligence office of the 509th Bomb Group...was fortunate enough to gain possession of a disc through the cooperation of one of the local ranchers and the sheriff's office of Chaves County.

Oops!

In the meantime, the debris had been flown in a B-29 to Eighth Army Air Force Headquarters at Carswell Air Force Base near Fort Worth, where Brigadier General Roger M. Ramey, commanding officer of the Eighth, and the base weather officer, Warrant Officer Irving Newton, quickly set about refuting the Roswell press release.

Warrant Officer Newton said that he recognized the debris as being from a large radar reflector that is attached to certain weather balloons when you want to be able to trace their movements through the atmosphere. On the evening of Tuesday, 8 July, General Ramey held a press conference and said the first "flying disc" release was too hasty. The debris was actually from a weather balloon with a radar reflector. "The wreckage is in my office now," he told the reporters, "and as far as I can see there is nothing to get excited about."

Close Encounter

Nine years after the event, Frank Edward's 1966 book, *Flying Saucers—Serious Business*, dredged out the Roswell case and recapitulated it:

"There are such difficult cases as the rancher near Roswell, New Mexico, who phoned the Sheriff that a blazing disc-shaped object had passed over his house at low altitude and had crashed and burned on a hillside within view of the house. The Sheriff called the military; the military came on the double quick. Newsmen were not permitted in the area. A week later, however, the government released a photograph of a service man holding a box kite with an aluminum disc about the size of a large pie pan dangling from the bottom of the kite...."

In this sort of gross distortion, we can see why the military, civil authorities, and most serious scientists stay as far away from flying saucer reports as they can get.

Flying Disc Explained

The next day, Mac Brazel gave an interview at the office of the *Roswell Daily Record*. He did his part to defuse the excitement. He claimed that the debris he had found was mostly of a gray rubber material, along with some Scotch tape and some other tape with flowers printed on it. But he still insisted that it didn't look like any weather balloon he had ever seen.

That afternoon Brazel gave a radio interview, where his story had shifted even more. Now he said that it probably was a weather balloon that had come down on his ranch. Frank Joyce, the local reporter, noted that Brazel's story had changed since he (Brazel) had had several long talks with some officers from the Army airfield who were accompanying him.

But the newspapers were satisfied that the story went no deeper, and after looking over the "wreckage" in General Ramey's office, the reporters wrote stories with headlines like "Flying Disc Explained." The excitement died down, and the story was quickly forgotten. The UFO sightings did not let up, however, and over the next few years a spate of

Report from the Field

Where the flying saucers had gone, no one knew last week and few cared. Saucer-eyed scientists blamed the whirling phenomena on (1) optical illusions followed by (2) mass suggestion. As quickly as they had arrived, the saucers disappeared into the limbo of all good hot-weather headlines.

—*Newsweek*, 21 July 1947

flying saucers books came out, but few of them even mentioned the events at the J.B. Foster ranch. And none that did treated it as any more interesting than the scores of other saucer sightings that came in and were continuing to come in to the various people who kept track of such things.

Roswell Rekindled

In 1979, Jesse Marcel, the Air Force intelligence officer who had first interviewed Mac Brazel and examined bits of the debris, started giving interviews to UFOlogists and reporters from the tabloids. His Air Force days were long over, and apparently he had subsequently become interested in flying saucers. In a story printed in the *National Enquirer*, Marcel revealed that the debris he had examined that day 32 years before, "was nothing that came from earth." According to Marcel's new recollections, the thin aluminum foil bits were so strong that they couldn't be dented with a sledge hammer. Why he decided to take a sledge hammer to bits of aluminum foil, he didn't say.

In 1980, William Moore and Charles Berlitz published a book called *The Roswell Incident*, based on interviews of Marcel and some 60 other people in a variety of places. In it, they related a story which, if it could be shown to be true, would have a profound effect on everyone and everything on earth, and change the way we think of ourselves as a species and the way we view the universe.

The story they pieced together, the way they tell it, went something like this:

An extraterrestrial spaceship was hit by lightning during the night of Wednesday, 2 July 1947, shortly after passing over the town of Roswell, New Mexico. Some bits of the craft fell onto the J.B. Foster ranch. Although severely damaged, it continued onward, finally crashing about 150 miles farther west, in an area in New Mexico called the Plains of San Agustin.

The next morning a soil conservation engineer named Grady L. Barnett, who was working near the Plains of San Agustin crash site, as well as some archeologists who happened to be in the area, came across the wreckage of a saucer-shaped ship and the bodies of some human-looking aliens about four feet tall. The military soon arrived from White Sands Missile Test Range and chased the civilians away.

As soon as the military realized what it had, it clamped down on all the news, succeeding so well that the story soon disappeared from the newspapers, and no reporters got so much as a hint of the alien bodies.

The material gathered from the two crash sites, according to this version of the story, contained samples of a metal lighter and harder than any known on earth, and some light, slender I-beams imprinted with hieroglyphic-like symbols in some alien language.

Sighting

On 29 June 1947, Dr. C.J. Zohn, a naval rocket expert who was working at White Sands, reported seeing a silver disc he could not identify in the sky overhead.

Wait, There's More!

In May 1987, a document surfaced that was supposedly a secret report that had been prepared for President-Elect Eisenhower on 18 November 1952. It was on a roll of 35mm film sent anonymously to television producer Jaime H. Shandera.

Majestic-12

The document was in the form of a top-secret, seven-page memorandum detailing a secret operation code-named "Majestic-12," or "MJ-12," that was, according to the document, set up by President Truman on 24 September 1947 in direct response to the Roswell Incident. The document asserts that an alien spaceship had crashed and exploded in the New Mexico desert. And that "four human-like beings had apparently ejected from the craft at some point before it exploded. ...All four were dead and badly decomposed due to action by predators and exposure to the elements during the approximately one week period which had elapsed before their discovery." The figure on the following page shows the first page of the FBI copy of MJ-12.

The bodies of the aliens were "removed for study," and the wreckage of the craft was distributed to several different locations for examination. It was determined that the vehicle was probably "a short-range reconnaissance craft," and the beings, "although...human-like in appearance, the biological and evolutionary processes responsible for their development has apparently been quite different from those observed or postulated in homo-sapiens." The examiners suggested the term "Extra-terrestrial Biological Entities," or "EBEs" be used as a name for the little dead aliens until a better name came along.

MJ-12 also detailed a second extraterrestrial wreck, this one along the Texas-Mexican border on 6 December 1950. There wasn't enough left of this one after the crash to be of much use.

Bogus Indeed

Stories about the discovery of the MJ-12 Report appeared, among other places, in the *Washington Post* and the *New York Times*. This gave the report, the Roswell stories, and UFO research in general a certain amount of respectability for a while. But the coverage didn't last long. It soon became clear to all but the most hardened UFO buff that Majestic-12 was almost certainly a phony. That's what I think after studying the story, and, as you have noticed by now, I am never wrong.

A whole collection of little things about the documents make the various document experts who have studied them carefully begin to doubt their

Sighting

If you want to check out the complete MJ-12 document for yourself, the FBI has released their copy, as well as a mess of other documents on UFO subjects, on their Freedom of Information Act Web page, the FBI FOIA Electronic Reading Room: www.fbi.gov/foipa/foipa.htm.

The first page of document MJ-12 from FBI files. The word "BOGUS" has been overlaid by the FBI.

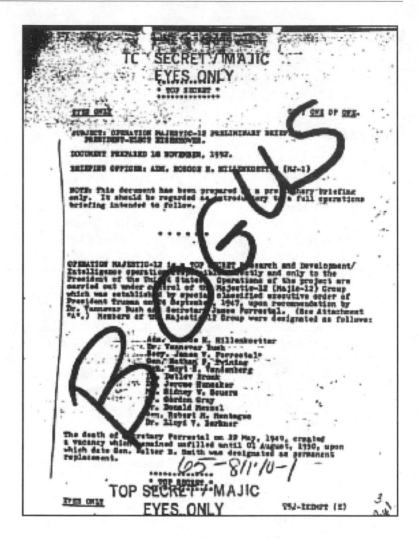

reality. But the clincher, I think, was the discovery that the signature of President Truman that was on one of the appended letters was a forgery.

It's not completely cut and dried yet—there is still a controversy about the document. Although as time passes, the consensus among UFOlogists is swinging around to the opinion that the thing is a forgery. The document was well done and has that air of verisimilitude that prevents it from easily being spotted as a bald and unconvincing narrative. For one thing, several of those mentioned on the committee of 12 appointed to oversee "Majestic-12" were important and well known people. Among them are Vannevar Bush, who was President Truman's chief science advisor; James Forrestal, who was Secretary of Defense; and General Hoyt Vandenberg, who, as you saw in Chapter 11, was the Air Force Chief of Staff. And you couldn't just go up to one of them and ask about Majestic-12. He would have to deny knowing anything about it, wouldn't he? After all, it was top secret!

NYU Flight #4

In a book called *UFO Crash at Roswell* by Benson Saler, Charles A. Ziegler, and Charles B. Moore (Smithsonian Press, 1997), Mr. Moore writes in convincing detail of a probable explanation for the Roswell Incident. At this time (early 1947), the New York University (NYU) Constant Level Balloon Group was flying balloons out of the Alamogordo Army Air Field in New Mexico.

This was part of a secret program code-named Project Mogul to develop balloons that would carry instruments aloft to predetermined altitudes to detect and gather information on Soviet atomic tests. What crashlanded at Roswell, they feel, was probably NYU balloon flight #4.

It wasn't until 1990 that UFOlogists discovered the existence of Project Mogul and offered that as a probable explanation of the events at and around the Foster ranch. But now the Roswell story took on a new, and much stranger, dimension.

UFO investigators Kevin D. Randle and Donald R. Schmitt, in their 1994 book, *The Truth About the UFO Crash at Roswell*, pretty much ignored the implications of Project Mogul and revealed that a saucer did touch down briefly at the Foster ranch, perhaps to try to repair some mechanical problem, but then it went on. The problem, whatever it was, was not fixed, because the craft soon crashed at the base of a cliff, spewing debris and little alien bodies about the landscape.

The military soon arrived and threatened the few observers of the crash with dire consequences if they told anyone what they had seen, then took away the wreckage, and the bodies, and cleaned up the area, leaving only some scorched earth as a sign that anything had happened.

Later in 1994 in an article in a UFO periodical, Karl T. Pflock stirred the Project Mogul balloon into the mix. In his version, the UFO hit the balloon, causing both to crash. Then the Army came and took the spaceship, the balloon fragments, and the dead aliens away, and did God knows what with them.

This version gives the military a double reason for covering up the Roswell Incident every way they could: to hide the existence of Project Mogul and to keep secret the discovery of little dead aliens and their craft.

Report from the Field

"If we ever establish contact with extraterrestrial life, it will reveal to us our true place in the universe, and with that comes the beginning of wisdom."

—Isaac Asimov

Alien Autopsy

And then, in 1995, came the clincher—or the best fake around. A film surfaced that was supposedly taken by an Air Force cameraman in 1947 showing the autopsy of one of the downed, and dead, extraterrestrial visitors.

The footage was used in a Fox TV special called, naturally, "Alien Autopsy," and it is very convincing. But then *Star Wars* is very convincing, and the techniques of fooling people with film get better and cheaper every day.

An alien on the autopsy table awaiting the knife.

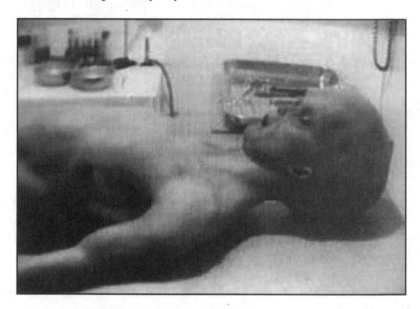

Experts at Kodak have said they could date the film if they were allowed to examine it, but the film's owners have refused to allow this. If the film proved to date back to 1947, that would go a long way to establishing its authenticity, because the odds are slight that someone could have prepared a fake this good back then or would have gone to the trouble and expense.

Therefore, because it would be so easy to add credibility to the film, and because the purveyors of the film are refusing to do so, we must regretfully conclude that it just isn't real.

Also it seems to me that finding real aliens, even real dead aliens, would be such an exciting and important story that it couldn't have been kept secret all these years. Look at all the lesser secrets that have come out in the past: Project Mogul, the U-2, the Nixon White House tapes, Iran-Contra, the secret life of J. Edgar Hoover, the Houdini trunk escape. If alien bodies were being kept hidden by the military—or anyone else—surely some security guard or politician or retired officer would have spilled all by now. I would like to think that there are alien bodies in a vault somewhere, or even little gray aliens working at some secret base, but it doesn't seem likely.

The Least You Need to Know

➤ The Roswell Incident is the most famous, most written-about UFO sighting.

➤ In 1947, a New Mexico ranch foreman found some debris on his ranch and thought it might be from a flying saucer.

➤ The Air Force investigation decided it was a weather balloon—but this was a cover up.

➤ Project Mogul, which secretly monitored Soviet atomic tests by balloon-launched instrument packages, was being tested in the area, and the downed balloon was probably one of theirs.

➤ Recent books, written more than four and five decades after the event, have claimed that a downed saucer, possibly with its alien crew, was found and spirited away by the Air Force.

➤ A movie of a supposed alien autopsy from this period has shown up, but it is probably a phony.

Chapter 13

Close Encounters, Crop Circles, and Conspiracies

In This Chapter

➤ The Extraterrestrial Hypothesis and Charles Fort

➤ Astronaut Frank Borman, Gemini 7, and the UFO

➤ Close encounters of all kinds

➤ Flying saucers seen

➤ Sex and the saucer people

➤ Crop circles

➤ Conspiracies in fact and myth

There are a variety of ways in which whatever extraterrestrial visitors there may be are said to interact with earthlings. They include mere contact and, as you will see later in this chapter, four degrees of close encounters. They also may be connected in some fashion to the crop circle phenomenon and other bizarre events that do not yield to more mundane explanations.

Our nature is to worry over problems, devise theories to fit them, and then promptly discard the theories when some new fact makes them unsupportable. Finally, usually, the truth, or some close approximation of it, is revealed.

Well, UFOlogists have theories, many of them, and await the new facts that will reveal which of them, if any, approximates the truth. Until then, your guess is as good as mine.

ETH: The Extraterrestrial Hypothesis

The theory that UFOs are spacecraft from another planet, possibly one circling a star other than our sun, is known as the *Extraterrestrial Hypothesis*, abbreviated by those who know and love it as the ETH. The first proponent of the ETH was Charles Fort, who you will see mentioned here and there in this book.

Fort catalogued the strange events that happen all about us here on earth, not so much to solve them as to keep reminding us that we don't know everything. His particular bugaboo was scientific complacency. The trouble with scientists, Fort believed, was that they don't know what they don't know. He found accounts of sightings of strange objects, human disappearances and reappearances, rains of frogs, fish and stones, lights seen moving about in the sky or on the moon, and many other miracles that challenged science to explain them.

It is not clear what Fort actually believed himself, as he offered explanations for the various events he catalogued more to make the reader think than as actual solutions. But the possibility of extraterrestrial visitation gets more than its share of mentions in his books, which were published between 1919 and 1932.

If you accept the ETH, you are accepting the following as probably true:

1. There is life on other worlds (see Chapter 22).
2. On some of these worlds, intelligent life has developed.
3. This intelligent life has devised a way to travel across the immense distances of interstellar space (see Chapter 24).
4. We have somehow attracted the interest of such a spacefaring race.
5. Members of this race have come to visit.
6. They prefer not to announce themselves in a very public way.
7. Their goals, motives, and methods are unknown to us, although we occasionally see glimpses of the results.

Some UFOlogists take this several steps further:

8. For their own inscrutable reasons, they occasionally kidnap individual humans.
9. Although these abductions may cause great fear, pain, and residual severe psychological problems, the aliens mean us nothing but good.
10. They are preparing us for something, perhaps knowledge of their presence, perhaps something else.

Earthlings Beware

The history of technologically advanced cultures interacting with less-advanced cultures here on earth is not a good one. The Arab slave traders in Africa, the English and French in North America, the Spaniards in South America; all took advantage of their technological superiority to destroy the society, and in some cases the people, they were dealing with. A voyage of discovery for one people often meant the end of civilization for another.

Gemini Spots a Bogey

Some reports of strange objects cannot be discounted as hoaxes or misunderstandings, and surely an account by an astronaut reporting live from his space capsule should rank high on that list.

The Gemini 7 space capsule was launched from Cape Canaveral on 4 December 1965 with astronauts Frank Borman and James Lovell on board. In looking out the space capsule's small window while the craft was in orbit above the earth, Borman could make out the rocket booster, floating free of the capsule, and some small specks that twinkled like fireflies, and...something else. He reported to Houston control:

Gemini 7:	Gemini 7 here, Houston how do you read?
Capcom:	Loud and clear, 7. Go ahead.
Gemini 7:	*Bogey* at ten o'clock high.
Capcom:	This is Houston. Say again 7.
Gemini 7:	Said we have a bogey at ten o'clock high.
Capcom:	Roger, Gemini 7. Is that the booster or is that an actual sighting?
Gemini 7:	We have several, looks like debris up here. Actual sighting.
Capcom:	You have any more information? Estimate distance or size?
Gemini 7:	We also have the booster in sight.
Capcom:	Understand you also have the booster in sight. Roger.

Even the Condon Report (see Chapter 11) admitted that they had no satisfactory explanation for just what it was that astronaut Borman saw that day as he and Lovell were circling the earth.

Close Encounter of All Kinds

A standard reporting code has been developed for "close encounters," dividing them into four kinds. Obviously there will be many cases that do not fit cleanly into one of these categories, or that straddle two of them, but this is a useful handle for most of the reported cases. The divisions are as follows:

Close Encounters of the First Kind

When UFOs are seen at close range, and possibly heard, but you don't touch them and they don't

Contact

For those of you not up on your NASA terminology, **capcom** is the capsule communicator—the man on the ground who is responsible for keeping in touch with Gemini 7 in orbit. Originally, a **bogey** was World War II slang for an enemy plane; now a bogey is merely an approaching unidentified craft.

touch you. And they depart without leaving behind any sign of their presence. This sort of experience may leave you with disturbing memories, despite the lack of physical contact.

Close Encounters of the Second Kind

Like the Close Encounter of the First Kind with the addition of physical indications of their presence. Some common possibilities are scorched ground where the UFO landed, flattened vegetation, or broken tree limbs. Car engines or radios may suddenly stop, and electronic devices may not work while the UFO is present. Usually these effects end when the UFO leaves.

Close Encounters of the Third Kind

These involve the observer seeing intelligent alien beings in or around a (usually landed) UFO. The possibilities of a third-kind encounter range from merely watching the beings to speaking with them (usually telepathically) or having some other interaction.

Close Encounters of the Fourth Kind

Also called alien abduction, these are cases where aliens will take you aboard their craft against your will to examine you physically and/or mentally and possibly talk with you (again usually telepathically) before returning you whence you came. These experiences are often accompanied by loss of memory for specific periods of time, and powerful psychological reactions (see the "Ten Signs of Alien Abduction" in Chapter 15).

Earthlings Beware

Claims that you have taken trips around the world or to other planets aboard the alien ship, or that an alien kidnapped you to have sex with you, or that the aliens told you that you have been chosen to save the world, will probably be discounted these days by even the most fervent UFO believer. I'll give you several examples of this sort of thing later in this chapter.

Daniel Fry Takes a Saucer Ride

On the evening of 4 July 1950, surely a great date for an adventure, Dr. Daniel Fry, one of your proverbial rocket scientists (at the time he was working for the Aerojet General Corporation), took a walk in the desert at White Sands Proving Ground in New Mexico.

Suddenly, Dr. Fry reported, a large oblate spheroid (science talk for "flattened ball," or in other words, a saucer shape) settled to the ground in front of him. He walked over to it and reached his hand out, when suddenly a voice, seeming to come from the air at his side, called out, "Better not touch that hull, pal, it's still hot!"

Fry was, as you or I might be, startled. "Take it easy, pal," the voice reassured him, "you're among friends." Eventually the saucerian, who said his name was A-Lan, but that Fry could call him Alan, took Fry for a ride in his saucer and asked him to write a book about it. Fry obliged with *The White Sands Incident*, published in 1954. In it, A-Lan warns us about the evils of nuclear war.

George Van Tassel Talks to the Space Patrol

In 1947, George Van Tassel got a 99-year lease on a six-story high boulder and a patch of land surrounding it in the middle of the California desert. He, his wife, and three children moved to the area, called appropriately, "Giant Rock," and set up housekeeping. The previous resident had turned a dry lake nearby into a landing strip, but he had blown himself up a few years before in an altercation with the county sheriff. George improved on the runway and opened a café next door, calling the complex the Giant Rock Airport.

The Yucca Valley Mentalphysics center, a home for New Age research, was nearby, and George went to meetings and took up chanting and meditation.

On 6 January 1952, George reportedly found himself in telepathic communication with "Lutbunn, senior in command first wave, planet patrol, realms of Schare (rhymes with pear-bee)," a Space Patrol commander from the planet Mars. He subsequently was contacted by a number of space beings; among them were Astar, Clatu, Clota, Elcar, Hulda, Kerrull, Lata, Latamarx, Leektow, Locktopar, Luu, Noma, Oblow, Singba, and Totalmon. They brought him messages from the Council of Seven Lights on the planet Sanchea. The main message was that we earthlings should raise our "vibratory attunement" to achieve peace and harmony and avoid atomic war.

In the 1950s, Van Tassel founded the Church of Universal Wisdom and the College of Universal Wisdom, which passed on the messages being given to George by his extraterrestrial friends. An annual flying saucer convention was held at Giant Rock which, at its height in the 1960s, attracted 18,000 people. Many notables in the UFO field, such as George Adamski, Daniel Fry, and Howard Menger attended the conventions regularly.

George Van Tassel died of a heart attack in 1978, and with him died both the Church and College of Universal Wisdom, and the Giant Rock flying saucer conventions.

Sighting

Since he first revealed himself to George Van Tassel, Astar (or occasionally Ashtar), commandant of Quadra Sector, Patrol Section Schare, has been in telepathic, or possibly psychic, contact with several other mortals, including Beti King and Tuella (Thelma B. Terrell). Astar's fleet, according to Tuella, is in orbit 72,000 miles above the earth, a part of the Confederation of Planets for Peace.

Sex and the Single Extraterrestrial

Among the many reports of contacts with extraterrestrials are some claims of contact of a much more intimate nature. In his book *Intruders*, Budd Hopkins claimed that

135

human-alien sex was "a central purpose behind the UFO abduction phenomenon." Here are the stories of some who claim it happened to them.

Villas-Boas Has Alien Intercourse

A 26-year old Brazilian named Antonio Villas-Boas of Brazil claimed several encounters with UFOs, the third of which was definitely of the third kind. At one in the morning of 16 October 1957, he was driving his tractor through his field when he noticed a big, red glowing object approaching and his tractor engine stalled. The flattened dome-shaped object landed on three extended legs, and humanoids emerged and took him aboard the craft. They were dressed in form-fitting white clothes, white shoes, thick gloves, and helmets with wide eye-slits. Once in the ship they took his clothes off, took a blood sample, sponged a thick, odorless liquid all over his body, and left him alone in a room.

A little while later, a short woman with whitish-blonde hair entered the room. Villas-Boas reports that, aside from an overly pointed chin and long, slanted eyes, she looked completely human. And, since she was also naked, he could tell. Without speaking to him or kissing him, she indicated that she wanted to have sex, and he obliged twice. After the second time, she collected a semen sample. The woman pointed to her stomach and then to the ceiling, indicating to Villas-Boas that their baby would be born on another planet. After he left the ship, he never saw her again.

Report from the Field

"It definitely seems to me, though, that what they're doing is for their purposes, not for ours. The hidden religious hopes that I think everyone has would connect with the idea that they're coming here to help us...the paranoid fears that many people have are they're coming here to take us over. I don't see a sign of either one of those being true. They seem to be here for their own purposes. Now, they could take what they need. Our DNA, our genetics, they could create their hybrids to solve some particular evolutionary problem that they may be facing. Who knows? And they could just simply leave and then leave us alone again, which would be quite wonderful."

—Budd Hopkins interview on *Nova*

Men Are from Saturn

Back in 1932, at the age of 10, Howard Menger met a beautiful long-haired blond Venusian woman in the woods in New Jersey. He met a second Venusian, this one dark-haired, while in the Army in Hawaii during World War II. The "Space People" contacted him while he was in the desert in the Southwest, and told him that they had helped many earlier earth civilizations, including the Aztecs.

Menger met his original blonde, long-haired contact when he returned to New Jersey in 1946, and was told that he had a mission to save earth from itself, that he would meet the alien lady's sister, now in her "earthly incarnation" at a future time, and that he would know her when he saw her.

Ten years later, Menger met Connie Weber in the audience while George van Tassel was lecturing about UFOs. He immediately knew that she was the one and that they had been lovers in a previous life, when he had been Sol da Naro, a guru from Saturn, and she a Venusian.

Recognizing the futility of fighting fate, Connie and Howard became lovers and eventually married. She wrote a book about it under the pen-name of Marla Baxter. The book, *My Saturnian Lover* (1958), told of a love that was certainly not earthly:

> Alyn [Menger's *nom d'amour*] bent down to kiss my brow. I felt the undulating tremors of his body again, and then began a strange and fascinating transformation, right before my eyes. Alyn began to grind his teeth, and turn and twist and stretch. He appeared to be getting taller and stronger. He breathed in deeply, and I felt his chest expand greatly. It seemed as if he had grown a head taller. Not only did he grow taller and stronger, but his facial contour changed. His face seemed to get longer and triangular in shape, and his eyes grew larger and deeper. Even his voice was different—deeper and lower. He had ceased to be Alyn and had become a Saturnian.

These reports contain many unanswered questions, if we are to take them seriously, like why beings from another planet would look enough like us for sex to even seem possible, or why they would procreate in a manner so similar to ours, or why an alien from a superior civilization would find one of us poor earthlings sexually desirable.

One theory that has been advanced is that the aliens are from a dying civilization and need to begat children with human genes to bring youth and vitality to their dying world. This makes about as much sense to me as for a sheep to decide to mate with a buffalo to improve the genes of sheepkind, but maybe I'm just a cynic. Perhaps someday soon a flock of young, beautiful beings will land on a spaceship and tell us, "We are your children, sort of." But until that happy day, I will continue to believe that no extraterrestrial could, or would want to, mate with any of us. I picture her (usually, but not always, it's an alien woman) looking over what's available here on earth and saying to herself what so many earth women say every evening as they leave the bar alone: "I could do better."

Crop Circles

The phenomena known as "crop circles" have a variety of possible explanations besides the obvious one that they are all done by pranksters, but they seem inevitably to be associated in the public mind with UFOs. They certainly share some of the characteristics of UFOs; they are mysterious and unpredictable, nobody understands their purpose, and they look as if they were created by an intelligent being possessing powers, or at least techniques, that we do not understand.

The major difference is that crop circles possess a physical reality and remain where they are. They can be inspected and examined and photographed, and there is no disputing their existence. Some experts hold that they are all hoaxes, create by two or more men dragging a wooden plank behind them as they circle a field. And indeed some were

Report from the Field

"And, a very interesting example of this [lack of rigorous application of scientific skepticism] is the so-called crop circles in England in which wheat and rye and other grains—these beautiful immense circles appeared and then more and more complex geometries. And there were lots of people who said that these were made by UFOs that were landing and that it was too complex or too highly mathematical to be a hoax.

And it turns out that two blokes in Southern England, at their regular bar one night, thought it would be a good idea to make a kind of hoax to see if they could lure in UFO enthusiasts. And they succeeded every time—every time an explanation was proffered: A peculiar kind of wind. They then made another one which contradicted that hypothesis. And they were very pleased when it was said that no human intelligence could do this. That gave them great satisfaction. And for 15 years, they succeeded in these nocturnal expeditions using rope and board—all the technology they needed. And in their 60s, they finally confessed to the press with a demonstration of how it was done. And, of course, the confession received very little play in the media."

—Carl Sagan, interview with *Nova* television program

created that way. Others seem too intricate, too precise, and were created too quickly to be thus explained.

The earliest of the modern crop of crop circles that we know of occurred outside of Warminster, England, in 1972. Two men, Arthur Shuttlewood and Bryce Bond, were sitting on a local incline called Star Hill one evening when they saw in the moonlight a large circle forming by itself in the crops on the meadow below them.

Since then, there have been over 9,000 reported crop circles, mostly in Britain, but some in various European countries, the United States, and Canada.

The "circles" range in complexity from simple circles or other geometric designs to very complex and organized patterns involving dozens of interrelated figures. Many of them are said to have been created in less than half a minute, and the creation is often associated with strange light effects on or around the field that hosts the circle.

The circles look deceptively easy to create, if we discount the testimony of those who claim to have seen them created. Indeed, many people have come forward to "admit" that they were responsible for the patterns. In a 1992 TV documentary, two men named "Doug and Dave" claimed to have made all the circles in the Hampshire area. That would still leave many thousands of circles unaccounted for.

Researchers claim to be able to distinguish the hoax circles, of which there are quite a few, from the genuine not-made-by-human-hands variety, of which there are many more. In the man-made circles, the affected plants are broken off at the base by the wooden board or whatever is used to flatten the area. In the genuine circles the stems are bent parallel with the ground, usually about an inch up, but not broken. Nobody seems to know how to replicate this effect.

There are other differences in the affected plants; the seeds have been disturbed and will not germinate, and the plants seem to have been subjected to intense brief bursts of extreme heat. Also, the plants crushed by the hoaxers die, but the plants affected by genuine crop circle events continue to grow, bent over though they are.

There are several theories to account for these effects. Since some people have seen lights and what they think

A complex crop circle in England.

are craft of some sort above the circles when they are forming, they could be either a deliberate message of some sort from our extraterrestrial visitors or an artifact of their propulsion system, which may be a form of magnetic force or antigravity. An alternate, and more natural theory is that the circles are the result of electromagnetic meteorological (weather-related) effects related to the northern lights.

If you're interested in learning more about the research into crop circles and related phenomena, see the listing for Nancy Talbott of the BLT Research Team in Appendix C.

Conspiracies in Fact and Myth

Something about the UFO mythos, whether it is based on fact or is entirely fanciful, seems to provoke conspiratorial behavior or the fear of conspiratorial behavior in many of those involved in studying it. The whole UFO field could be used as a training ground for conspiracy theorists. For the past half century, it has been rife with conspiracies, real and imagined. Sometimes the same event will be layered in a real conspiracy or two and a half-dozen or more imaginary conspiracies.

The literature of UFO conspiracy in fact and theory is vast, but most of it shares a similar belief system: The government is hiding from us the existence of aliens, living or dead, for our own good or for some sinister purpose of its own. Much of this material centers around the Roswell Incident (see Chapter 12).

Roswell Redux

The Roswell saga itself is a good example of the mix. The Air Force did begin a conspiracy to hide the truth, but the truth they were hiding was Project Mogul, a secret high-altitude balloon operation to detect Soviet atomic blasts. And then some people, we can't be sure who, created the MJ-12 papers, thus engaging in a conspiracy to create

139

a disinformation campaign accusing the government of a conspiracy to hide the existence of a crashed saucer and some alien bodies. And this is just the beginning.

The Cooper Files

As an example of the sort of story touched off by Roswell, let me tell you about Milton William Cooper.

Beginning in late 1988, Cooper began producing and publicizing stories of the incredible facts he had learned while involved with an "intelligence team" in the Navy. The military, according to Cooper, had for some time been dealing with extraterrestrial beings, which were called "ALFs" for Alien Life Forms. A group within the military and the CIA are the "secret government," which actually runs the country and most of the world with alien help.

The aliens, from a dying planet circling the star Betelgeuse, signed a treaty with President Eisenhower, who went to Edwards Air Force Base in California to meet them. This treaty allows them to abduct an occasional human if they return him or her unharmed. Eventually all the aliens will emigrate to earth and occupy secret underground caverns which are now being prepared in the southwestern United States. The aliens are responsible for the assassination of JFK, the career of George Bush, and the massive increase in drug use in America (they needed to raise money).

There's a lot more, including secret bases on the moon and Mars, time machines, and the Second Coming.

If you have noticed a similarity between the Cooper view of the world and one of the major subplots of *The X Files*, you know too much and must be silenced!

The Least You Need to Know

➤ The theory that UFOs are from another planet is known as the Extraterrestrial Hypothesis.

➤ Even astronauts have seen UFOs.

➤ The UFO experiences, called "close encounters," come in four kinds.

➤ Some accounts of interaction with UFOs are more plausible than others.

➤ Some contactees claim to have had closer encounters than most, including alien sex.

➤ Crop circles have been related to UFOs. Although some of them are certainly hoaxes, many cannot be so easily explained.

➤ The UFO phenomenon for some reason lends itself to conspiracy theories, and there have been many of them.

Chapter 14

From Close Encounters to Abductions

In This Chapter

➤ The 5-5-5 scale

➤ Alien abduction stories

➤ The river otter's tale

➤ Appearances and disappearances

➤ The strange adventure of Betty and Barney Hill

There is a story about a young boy who desperately wanted a pony for his birthday. His excessively cruel father dumped a great pile of horse manure on the front lawn the night before and, when the child woke up, told him that was his present.

Instead of being upset, the boy grabbed a shovel and started digging into the pile. "What are you doing?" his father asked.

"Somewhere under all this manure, there's got to be a pony!" the boy told him.

I don't know whether the boy got his pony, but we who are interested in UFOs face a similar pile of manure. We have the problem of deciding how to determine which accounts, out of the tens of thousands of UFO sightings and alien abductions that have been reported, are concealing the pony of truth.

The 5-5-5 Scale

Intelligence agencies use a reliability scale to estimate the validity and value of information received. I have freely adapted that scale, which I call the *5-5-5 scale*, to our present needs in discussing UFO sightings and encounters.

The 5-5-5 scale consists of the following three parts:

➤ The credibility of the observer

➤ The credibility of the observation

➤ The clarity of the observation

Each of these is rated from 5 (the most reliable) to 1 (the least reliable). My version of the scale looks like this:

The Credibility of the Observer

5. The observer is a bishop, judge, or someone with status in the community who is known for his or her veracity—someone who has no reason to lie and probably would just as soon not tell the story at all.

4. The observer is a professional pilot or military or police officer, trained to know what he or she is looking at and with no reason to lie.

3. The observer is a random civilian with nothing to gain from reporting the observation.

2. The observer has seen many flying saucers, written about them, and is on a mission to save the world.

1. The observer is Geraldo Rivera.

The Credibility of the Observation

5. The observation was made by multiple observers who were at different locations and don't know each other.

4. The observation was made by several observers at the same location who don't know each other.

3. The observation was made by a small group of observers at the same location who are friends.

2. The observation was made by a single random observer whose background can be checked.

1. The observation was given by an observer who refused to be identified, or it was phoned in anonymously.

The Clarity of the Observation

5. The alien craft landed close enough to touch and left behind an artifact, or the observer was able to take clear pictures.

4. The alien craft landed close and left behind indentations of the landing gear, broken tree limbs, or the like, or the observer took fuzzy, out-of-focus pictures.

3. The craft flew by low and slowly, and close enough for markings, if any, to be made out.

2. The craft flew high but still low enough for its shape to be made out; it maneuvered in an unearthly way.

1. The observer just got a glimpse of a high-flying craft.

Ideally, we're looking for a 5-5-5 score: a bishop with pictures of the spacecraft he saw at a gathering of his fellow bishops, who also saw the craft and who were mostly strangers to him. But, failing that, we'll have to get by with what we can as we decide the credibility of each case.

Abduction Claims

The reliability of alien abduction claims is much harder to judge. They tend to happen to one person or a closely related group at a time when there are no witnesses, and the evidence they leave behind—scars, burn marks, psychological trauma—is subject to a variety of interpretations.

Tens of thousands of people in the United States and elsewhere profess to believe they have been abducted by aliens. Many of these people tell similar stories, although they don't know each other and many of them claim to have never read or heard anything about alien abductions before it happened to them.

On the other hand, some of the researchers in this field are so zealous in their search for victims of alien abductions that their very enthusiasm must make their findings subject to careful scrutiny. Much of the testimony of the abductees is obtained under hypnotic regression, and unfortunately such testimony is known to be unreliable. Hypnotized subjects will tell the questioner what they think he or she wants to hear. Although the bias of the questioner can be very subtle or even unconscious, the subject may still pick it up and respond to it.

Sighting

A Roper poll commissioned in 1992 seems to indicate that a large number of Americans, perhaps as many as three million, have experienced some of the symptoms that indicate to some researchers (notice how carefully I'm hedging) that they have had an abduction experience. As I write this book, the preliminary data from a second poll seems to show pretty much the same results.

I tend to be very skeptical about abduction stories, however obtained. My main problem with them is that I can't figure out any possible reason why the aliens, wherever they might be from, might want to kidnap human beings, poke and prod them for a while, and then return them, as the song says, to from whence they came. I must admit, however, that it very well could be that the aliens are working from a set of needs and goals of which we are unaware and wouldn't understand if they tried to explain them to us. As a matter of fact, several abductees claim they have asked their alien abductors something like, "Why are you doing this?" and have received answers like, "It's for your own good, but you wouldn't understand."

My doubts, however, have recently been tempered with the knowledge that we humans are not entirely innocent of the sort of behavior attributed to the aliens. A friend recently told me the following story. (Thank you, Morgan.)

The River Otter's Tale

A group of biologists in southeast Alaska are studying the habits of river otters, a subgroup of otters that spend their time—you guessed it—in rivers. They (the otters, not the scientists) dig burrows in the river bank where they set up housekeeping and sleep snug, safe, and warm.

The biologists periodically dig into the side of the riverbank, penetrate the burrows, and remove an otter to weigh it, take a blood sample, occasionally pull a tooth, and perform various tests. This is all for the eventual good of otters everywhere, but it must puzzle the hell out of the otter it happens to.

I have an image of one otter telling another, "And then this strange being came right through the wall into my burrow, grabbed me, stuck me with needles, pulled out one of my teeth, and poked me with rods. I swear, Percival, that's what happened."

Percival Otter looks at his friend with pity and pats him on the fur. "There, there, Sigismund. Perhaps you should keep away from those fermented clams from now on."

Every once in a while, however, another river otter looks relieved upon hearing Sigismund's tale. It also had happened to him, but he was afraid to tell anyone. The scorn of your fellow otters must be hard to bear.

I don't mean to imply that because river otters suffer such indignities at the hands of people that it necessarily follows that people are similarly handled by extraterrestrial biologists. But it would be an interesting resolution of the abduction question and perhaps a salutary experience for the human ego if someday we discover we are some alien college student's thesis experiment.

The Disappearing Larch and Others

Report from the Field

"I have records of six persons, who, between 14 January 1920 and 9 December 1923, were found wandering in or near the small town of Romford, Essex, England, unable to tell how they got there or anything else about themselves. If human beings ever have been teleported, and, if some mysterious appearances of human beings be considered otherwise unaccountable, an effect of the experience is an effacement of memory."

—Charles Fort, *Lo!* (1931)

Otto Binder, in his book *Unsolved Mysteries of the Past*, tells of Oliver Larch, an 11-year-old Indiana boy who left his family's house on Christmas Eve, 1889, to get a pail of water from the well. Suddenly, the family and their Christmas guests inside the house heard the boy screaming, "Help! Help! They've got me!" They ran outside. The lad's footprints in the fresh snow ended abruptly some feet from the house. Oliver could be heard still screaming for help, but he could not be seen. His voice appeared to be coming from somewhere over their heads, grew more distant, and finally disappeared.

On 6 January 1914, a man suddenly appeared on High Street, Chatham (which is in Kent, England). He claimed to have no idea who he was or where he had come from. Despite the weather, which the *Chatham News* described as being "bitterly cold," the man was devoid of clothing, naked. The area was searched, but no clothing was found. The authorities decided the man was insane, and he might well have been. But about how he arrived in the midst of a busy street, where he had come from, and what happened to his clothes, the authorities expressed no opinion.

The London *Daily Chronicle* of 29 September 1920 reported that a young man named Leonard Wadham had been found by a constable wandering along a road near Dunstable looking puzzled and frightened. Twenty minutes before, Wadham told the police, he had been walking down a street in South London, 30 miles away. Suddenly the houses of London seemed to melt away, and country fields appeared. Apparently, he had traveled 30 miles in 20 minutes with no memory of the trip or how it had been accomplished.

These events and the many more accounts from past newspapers, mostly gathered by Charles Fort in one of his eclectic books, can be interpreted as you please—as hoaxes, mystical events, cases of transient amnesia, transdimensional transfers, or the practical jokes of an alien race. But all the stories have one or more similarities to what we have come to identify today as the alien abduction phenomenon. It raises the interesting possibility that they are all somehow related, precursors to the events that overtook Betty and Barney Hill and those who came after them—and that our possible interaction with extraterrestrial beings does go back to the past. Perhaps someday we will discover just how far back these visitations go.

Within the past half a century, the sort of happening we call an alien abduction has been, we might say, standardized. The reports of people who believe they have been abducted mostly contain common elements that indicate they are all part of the same meta-event, just as soldiers on different battlefields facing different enemy troops are all part of the same war.

Betty and Barney Hill

One of the earliest of what we might call the modern wave of alien abduction events to come to light happened to a New Hampshire couple named Betty and Barney Hill. It was the evening of Tuesday, 19 September 1961. They were driving home through New Hampshire's White Mountains from a holiday in Canada. Somewhere south of Lancaster they noticed that a very bright star near the moon seemed to be getting bigger and brighter as they drove. Barney decided the star was actually a satellite crossing the sky and, after watching it through a pair of binoculars for a few minutes, stopped the car to get a better look.

The object was moving too erratically to be a satellite; Barney decided it must be an airplane. Betty had her doubts but didn't have anything better to suggest. They drove on.

After a few minutes they realized the object was headed in the same direction they were traveling and at about the same speed. Whether it was following them or just pacing them by happenstance, they couldn't tell. It was close enough now that they could see it was a circular disc, "as wide in diameter as the distance between three telephone poles," as Barney described later. It had a row of windows around it and two fins sticking out with red lights on the end.

They stopped the car when the disc halted and hovered about 50 feet above a field by the road. Barney got out to take a closer look. As he approached the huge disc, he could make out human-looking beings inside the windows staring out at him. When he was about 75 feet away, some sort of door in the craft opened. Barney was overcome suddenly with the feeling he was about to be captured, so he raced back to the car. Barney started the car and headed down the highway, and the disc—or whatever it was—disappeared.

A short time later, both Betty and Barney heard a strange beeping noise and felt as though they were being enveloped in a sort of haze. When they came out of it, again to a beeping sound, they realized some time had passed but that the car was still moving and Barney was still driving it.

They arrived home feeling confused and somehow unclean. The next day Betty decided to phone the local Air Force base to tell them about the experience. Barney would just as soon have forgotten about the whole thing but agreed to speak to the Air Force officer on the phone.

Their story was written up for Project Blue Book, but the Air Force evaluation added up to "insufficient data," since the Hills could not give information regarding the object's location or maneuverability. For some reason, probably fear of being laughed at, Barney chose not to tell the investigator about the beings he had seen in the alien craft.

While discussing the event with a few UFO investigators, the Hills came to realize that two hours during the course of that evening were unaccounted for. They drove over the route again and again, trying to determine where they had gone, but several landmarks, including a diner they thought they had pulled up to, had unaccountably disappeared.

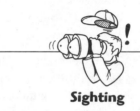

Sighting

What the Hills didn't know at the time was that there had been an unidentified contact by the radar at nearby Pease Air Force Base at the same time as their sighting.

Two years later, after long periods of nightmares—mostly by Betty and many involving alien abduction—and inexplicable fears affecting both of them, the Hills decided to seek psychiatric help. They went to see several doctors, finally settling on a Dr. Benjamin Simon, a respected Boston psychiatrist. Dr. Simon gave each of them a course of hypnotic therapy, during which repressed memories of being taken aboard the alien ship and examined were released.

Dr. Simon was not overly interested in UFOs as such; his interest in the one with which the Hills had interacted was not in its objective reality, but in how the experience, however it was arrived at, had affected the Hills and how best to help them. Over a period of six months, he slowly drew from them, under deep hypnotic trance, the story of the missing two hours. If the hypnotic induction was working properly, however, the Hills could not have compared stories, since each was told to forget the details during the course of therapy and only remember the whole story when the therapy ended. The stories told by Barney and Betty Hill corresponded in great detail.

The Hills probably would not have come forward with their story if parts of it had not appeared in a mangled and inaccurate form in a local newspaper. They decided it would be better if the true story were told their way, and so they told their story to author John G. Fuller, authorizing him to listen to the tapes of their hypnotic sessions with Dr. Simon. The result was the book, *The Interrupted Journey*, which tells one of the fullest and most detailed accounts of an alien abduction available.

The Hills' Own Story

Here is a composite of the story from the point where they found themselves fleeing in their car, as revealed by the hypnosis of Barney and Betty Hill.

> Barney, who was driving the car, felt compelled to leave Route 3, the main road, and take a side road that led deep into the woods. Six men stepped in front of the car, and Barney stopped. Three men came to take him out of the car and three to take Betty. Barney felt a compulsion to keep his eyes closed during most of what followed, and he did so with some relief; it was somehow less scary with his eyes

closed. He did not attempt to speak with his abductors. Betty kept her eyes opened and conversed with her captors.

They were taken inside the ship, which was of the traditional saucer shape, and led to different rooms where each of them was examined. The aliens put Betty on an examining table and took her shoes off to examine her feet. They also looked at the skin of her arm, behind her neck, and in her ear. At one point they had her take off her dress and stuck a needle into her navel—the only part of the procedure that was actually painful. When she cried out in pain, the alien she thought of as the leader put his hand over her eyes and told her that it would stop hurting, which it did. She was told that the needle was for a "pregnancy test."

She was then allowed to get up but had to wait because they weren't finished examining Barney yet. When she asked the leader where the aliens were from, he pulled a star map from a drawer and showed her. The pattern, however, made little sense to her. As she described it, "...there were all these dots on it. And they were scattered all over it. Some were little, just pin points. And others were as big as a nickel. And there were lines, they were on some of the dots, there were curved lines going from one dot to another. And there was one big circle, and it had a lot of lines coming out from it. A lot of lines going to another circle quite close, but not as big."

The leader told her that the heavy lines on the map represented the trade routes among the stars, the solid lines were places they went occasionally, and the broken lines were expeditions. Betty later drew what she could remember of the map.

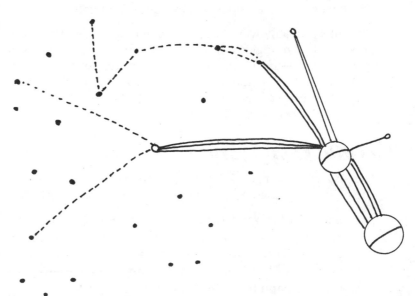

An artist's copy of the map Betty Hill drew from memory showing the trade routes the aliens use among the stars.

Close Encounter

The star map Betty drew was reproduced in Fuller's book, *The UFO Incident*, and in the movie that was made from the book. In 1968, Marjorie Fish, an Ohio schoolteacher, tried to correlate the map with the local star field around us, assuming that our sun was one of the stars on the map. She created a three-dimensional star field of the stars within 50 or so light years that were like our sun and which presumably might have planets that could sustain life.

Fish concluded that she had found a pattern that corresponded to Betty Hill's star map. Whether or not she is right is a question still being debated. An article in *Astronomy* magazine described what she had done and solicited comments. Some astronomers agreed with Fish, and some, such as Cornell University's Carl Sagan, thought the apparent correspondence was pure chance. If Fish is right, the stars Zeta 1 Reticuli and Zeta 2 Reticuli are the centers of an interstellar trading empire.

Black and White

For some reason, those who have told the tale of Betty and Barney Hill have made a big deal of the fact that they were an interracial couple; Barney was African-American, Betty was Caucasian. It didn't seem to bother them; they loved each other very much. I don't see why it should bother us. But in case you can deduce something relevant to their experience from that fact, I'm throwing it in here.

Dr. Simon, who chose not to believe in UFOs, thought that Barney had picked up on his wife's nightmares and unconsciously created an abduction fantasy. Since the Hill case, however, many people have come forward with similar stories, often also retrieved from the unconscious mind by hypnotic therapy.

Barney died of a sudden cerebral hemorrhage in 1969. He was 46 years old. Betty, not surprisingly, developed a profound interest in UFOs and talked to UFO groups about her and Barney's experience.

As the years passed the abduction claims grew ever more frequent and ever more complex. (We will examine some of these later abductions in the next chapter.) Betty Hill grew more disillusioned with the current crop of researchers and therapists who find abductees wherever they look. Very few of these experiences, Betty feels, are real; most are hoaxes or the result of incompetent therapists using inadequate hypnotic techniques. People under hypnosis, Betty explains, are extremely suggestible and will believe what you want them to believe. Dr. Simon took all sorts of precautions to make sure this didn't happen, but most hypnotic practitioners don't know what they're doing.

As Betty explained in an interview for the *Fortean Times*, "…the investigators are directing [the abductees] to have these fantasies. They're suggesting them to them. They're very, very destructive people. They don't care who they hurt to make people buy a book to make some money."

Betty has written a book, *A Common Sense Approach to UFOs*, in which she explains how to tell the real abduction phenomena from what she calls the "me too people."

The Least You Need to Know

➤ The 5–5–5 scale is useful in analyzing UFO sighting reports.

➤ Alien abduction reports are more difficult to assess.

➤ Stories of mysterious disappearances and appearances are reported many times a year, and have been for many years.

➤ The story of Betty and Barney Hill is one of the best documented and most reliable cases of alien abduction.

➤ Betty's experience may have provided us with a map of the nearby stars, showing which ones are occupied by intelligent alien beings.

➤ Betty Hill herself warns us about accepting abduction stories without careful consideration.

Chapter 15

The Abduction Parade

In This Chapter

➤ Contactees versus abductees

➤ Ten signs of possible abduction

➤ Many similarities in abduction tales

➤ Abductees are normal people

➤ Abduction stories and hypnotic regression

The continuing saga of UFOs and their alien crews has grown tremendously since Betty and Barney Hill had their journey interrupted. It now includes people who have contacted them, been contacted by them, been instructed by them, been abducted by them, been studied by them, and been examined by them. Still others claim to have been sexually molested by them, been impregnated by them, been operated on by them, have received physical implants from them, or otherwise participated willingly or unwillingly in unworldly experiences.

Abduction Versus Contact

UFOlogists make a noteworthy distinction between abductees and contactees. *Abductees*, by and large, have had an experience that is beyond their control, against their will, and unpleasant. Their basic feeling of the experience is that they were guinea pigs in someone else's experiment. They are not trying to profit from the experience (most of the books written about abductions have been written by someone not involved) and would just as soon be left alone.

Contactees, on the other hand, claim that they were singled out by their "space broth-ers" for contact and that they were given a message of some importance for the human race. The message usually is some variant of "Don't fight, play nice!" Contactees write books about their experiences, go on talk shows, and give lectures.

The Abduction Experience

Some of the multitude of stories told by the abductees are very serious, causing us to carefully reconsider our ideas about the earth and its relationship to the universe. Some stories are frightening, causing us to seriously consider spending the night in a bedroom with no windows, with the lights on, and the blankets pulled over our heads. And some stories are very silly. Whether this is because some silly people have made up stories or because some aliens are behaving in a silly manner is a worthy question.

That extraterrestrial visitors are said to behave in a ridiculous and inexplicable manner does not, of itself, prove the story is not true. After all, aliens are alien. They, we assume, are not human and cannot be expected to act like humans. When the first aliens reveal themselves so completely that there is no doubt they are here and are alien, I'm willing to bet they will be doing things that we find incomprehensible.

Close Encounter

The following ten signs are said by investigators to be reliable indicators that a subject has been abducted by aliens:

➤ Missing periods of time
➤ Frequent nightmares about aliens and UFOs
➤ Sleep disorders
➤ Unusual body sensations upon awaking
➤ Unexplained marks or scars on the body
➤ A feeling of being watched
➤ Repeated sightings of UFOs
➤ Partial memories of alien encounters
➤ Sudden unexplained healing of a long-term illness or affliction
➤ Phobic reaction to discussions about UFOs or extraterrestrials

Who Gets Taken?

Since the story of the Hill's abduction (see Chapter 14) was published in 1966, well over 1,000 people have come forward, willingly or hesitantly, to report that they have been abducted by aliens. Some of these are conscious memories, easily recalled; many more are memories buried deep in the unconscious, recalled only by hypnotic regression over a period of time.

In some cases, the abductions started at an early age—four or five years old or even younger—and continued periodically ever since. The people who have come forward represent only a small percent of the people who believe that they have been involved in an alien abduction experience. The surprising results of surveys taken recently would seem to indicate that there have been tens of thousands, perhaps hundreds of thousands, of people in the world today who have been, or think they have been, abducted by aliens.

Allowing for the repeat abductions, this would be a rate of between 10 and a 100 abductions a day for the past 30 years and would certainly show that the aliens have an extensive and ongoing need to poke, prod, scrape, pierce, examine, and inseminate human beings. Therefore, the number of UFO reportings is no longer surprising, but rather, it is surprising how few of the fleet of saucers that must be skittering about picking up and delivering abductees have been seen.

There doesn't seem to be any preference among the aliens about what sort of human they choose to monitor and experiment on. David M. Jacobs, Ph.D., in his book Secret Life, recounts the results of more than 325 hypnosis sessions he conducted with more than 60 abductees. He describes the abductees as, "by and large, average citizens who did not desire publicity, who were not trying to commit a hoax, and who, with one exception, were not mentally disturbed. They were Protestant, Catholic, Jewish, white, black, male, female, younger, older, professional, nonprofessional, married, single, divorced, employed, unemployed, articulate, and inarticulate."

Your Eyelids Are Getting Heavy

The problem with stories obtained by hypnosis is that they are known to be unreliable. The subject has a desire to say what he or she thinks the hypnotist wants to hear. This is almost universally

Report from the Field

"There is a tendency, sometimes called *role expectancy*, on the part of many hypnotic subjects to comply with what they perceive as the expectations of the hypnotist. This can occur even when the hypnotist has no conscious investment in the outcome, and is of course even more likely to occur when the hypnotist does have such an investment. This is more the rule than the exception in hypnosis."

—Michael B. Conant, Ph.D., Director of The Institute for Bioenergetics and Gestalt true, as people who do not trust the hypnotist will not allow themselves to be hypnotized. Therefore, when dealing with an unusual and traumatic event such as a possible alien abduction, a hypnotist must be very careful not to suggest in any way that there is a preferred outcome to the session, a story that he or she would like to hear, or even a direction that he or she thinks the session should go in.

The separation of the hypnotist's desired result from the result obtained by the hypnotic regression is not easy. Most of us are much better than we realize at picking up the slightest cues from those around us, particularly those we're impressed by, trying to impress, or afraid of. The relationship of the subject to the hypnotist embraces a bit of all three of these feelings.

The Basic Story

There is a great deal of similarity among the tales told by abductees. Some of the individual cases present events shared by no other, of course, but there is a great overlap. It's possible to compile an "average" abduction scenario that corresponds to most of the details in most of the stories. Because different students of the phenomena tend to focus on different details, depending on their own interests and conceits, my rendition will not be the same as another, but it will be close. Lets look at an "average" abduction, along with some of the more common variants.

Sighting

Harry Houdini used to do a trick in which he would seem to walk through a brick wall that had been constructed onstage in full view of the audience. Houdini would be on one side of the wall, a curtain would be raised briefly and dropped, and he would be on the other side. Sir Arthur Conan Doyle is said to have congratulated Houdini on his ability to dematerialize, but Houdini assured Sir Arthur that it was just a trick. And so it was.

The Average Abduction Begins

My average abductee couple, let's call them John and Marcia, are driving down a deserted stretch of highway when they notice bright lights overhead. (Single abductions are more common, but dual abductions do happen. We'll follow a pair of abductees so that we can show the experiences of both men and women, which differ in some intimate details.) The lights follow the vehicle for a while and, at first, they think it's a helicopter. But then they realize—or see—it is nothing that was made on earth. Perhaps the driver turned down this road without knowing why, as though moved by some external impulse.

Or perhaps our abductees are in bed when they notice a strange, powerful light outside the window. They lose conscious control of their bodies, unable to move by themselves or, in some cases, think coherently. Then a coterie of little people come through the window and remove the victims.

These beings appear, in some cases, to be able to come through the window without bothering to open it. They even materialize through a solid wall occasionally. Even more astounding, they are able to take their victims out the same way, without harming the window or wall.

The Saucer

John and Marcia are carried or led to a large saucer—perhaps the size of a one-family house, perhaps as big as a football field—that has landed at a convenient spot nearby, or is hovering close to the ground. Usually the area is deserted of other humans, but occasionally there are others around. If so, they are in a state of suspended animation, are frozen in place, and have no knowledge of what is happening around them. When they come to, they have no idea that any time has passed.

Sighting

The saucer shape is not mandatory; sometimes the craft is cigar-shaped, triangular, or shaped like an egg.

John and Marcia are taken up a ramp into the ship, floated up to the ship, or mystically pass through the ship's walls. At this point in the adventure, the two are probably frightened (as would you or I) and feeling helpless and vulnerable. This may pass and be replaced by a feeling of ecstasy and awe, which also may pass after the abduction and be replaced by an intense anger.

The Examination

John and Marcia are taken down a hallway to examination rooms, usually separate rooms where they are alone with their captors. Some abductees, however, have reported seeing other people on examination tables in the same room.

The examination rooms are usually circular, white or metallic in color, and contain no furniture except the examination table. The room is cold and well lit, but Marcia (we'll start with her) can't tell where the light is coming from, except for the one bright light shining down on her as she lies on the table. There are strange instruments around the room, and a probe of sorts hangs over the table.

The beings who examine Marcia are short, about four feet tall, and have pasty-gray skin and expressionless faces with slits for mouths. Their heads are large and round (and hairless) on top, tapering down to pointy chins, with noses and ears barely protruding. They wear skin-tight, one-piece pullovers. They are neither kind nor cruel, but totally dispassionate and business-like in their behavior.

Marcia's examination is pretty thorough, if somewhat superficial by earthly medical standards. It involves a lot of touching of the whole body: face, arms, back, legs, and feet. Marcia's clothing is removed wholly or in part to facilitate this process. Although Marcia is embarrassed and frightened, she doesn't think the aliens are deliberately trying to hurt her. Indeed, she may be receiving telepathic reassurance from one of the other "grays." These other grays are taller than the examiners; they are slender and

155

The examining alien.

elegant and seem to be in command. The relationship between the tall grays and the short grays appears to be like that between the officers and crew on a naval ship.

In Britain and Scandinavia, the visitors tend to be tall, blond, blue-eyed Nordic types. Why this should be I cannot tell.

Close Encounter

The following are among the more interesting variations of aliens reported:

➤ A "praying mantis" type
➤ A five-foot tall humanoid with slanted eyes and a slit-like mouth wearing a silver uniform and a pilot's helmet
➤ A creature with wrinkled gray skin and lobster claws for hands
➤ A ten-foot tall creature with green hair, pointed ears, and three eyes
➤ A short furry creature with a round head and hands with retractable claws

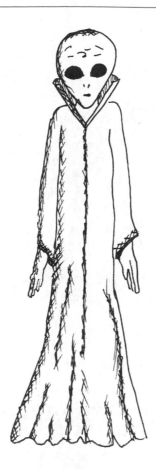

The tall gray alien: an artist's depiction.

Marcia may be artificially inseminated during the examination. Apparently, the aliens are trying to grow a race of alien-earthling hybrids. Or, if Marcia is a repeat abductee, a fetus may be removed from her to continue growing outside the earthly womb. The examiners may take little bits of skin tissue, leaving scars on the side of the knee or elsewhere.

John, who you will remember is being examined separately, may be induced to give a semen sample, possibly by electrical stimulation. He will probably not have sex with a beautiful alien woman, as some early abductees reported. The aliens seem to have given up that practice.

Post Exam

After the examination, John and Marcia are taken past several other rooms and allowed to look in. They see a bridge from which the ship appears to be controlled, a meeting room where the crew congregates, and a nursery where babies are being cared for. They also see some other members of the crew, including a third type of alien that resembles a reptile.

The reptile-looking alien.

"You Will Forget...Forget...Forget"

The next thing John and Marcia know, they are back in their car with no clear memory of what happened or how much time has passed. They forget the entire experience very quickly. The aliens seem to have a very powerful, but defective, method of mind control. John and Marcia are troubled by bad dreams and have a feeling that something is wrong with their lives, their marriage, or something. They feel restless and ill at ease; they suffer several of the symptoms outlined in the "ten signs" at the beginning of this chapter.

The intense anger that I spoke of earlier will be unfocused, because they do not consciously remember the cause of it. Their anger often turns into severe depression.

Hypnotic Regression

Then either John or Marcia (or both) seek professional help. The professional—psychiatrist, psychologist, therapist, or lay hypnotist (possibly an interested, self-taught UFOlogist)—uses hypnotic regression to lead them through the events, now suppressed, that caused their psychic trauma. With understanding some people find relief, others suffer from the discovery that their abduction was part of an ongoing pattern, that they have already been abducted perhaps a dozen times, and that they quite naturally fear they are going to be abducted again.

Betty Hill Speaks

If this composite story sounds a lot like the tale of Betty and Barney Hill from the preceding chapter, Betty Hill agrees with you. She thinks that deep, medical hypnosis probably produces valid results, and she is sure that the events *she* discovered under hypnosis actually happened. This is due, in part, because she and her husband had medical hypnosis, the kind used in surgery, and partly because Dr. Simon, their therapist, wasn't looking for the results he got.

Report from the Field

"In the more than three and a half years I have been working with abductees I have seen more than a hundred individuals referred for evaluation of abductions or other "anomalous" experiences. Of these, seventy-six (ranging in age from two to fifty-seven; forty-seven females and twenty-nine males, including three boys eight and under) fulfill my quite strict criteria for an abduction case: conscious recall or recall with the help of hypnosis, of being taken by alien beings into a strange craft, reported with emotion appropriate to the experience being described and no apparent mental condition that could account for the story."

—John E. Mack, M.D., *Abduction*

"The first stage of hypnosis is one of suggestibility," Betty Hill told the *Fortean Times*. "It's supposed to be useful to have a person lose weight, or help them cut down on smoking or something like that. But if you say to a person, 'You murdered someone!' in the first stage of hypnosis, they're going to spend the rest of their lives looking for the body." People who believe they are being completely honest can be remembering events that never happened but that were implanted by the hypnotic process.

Possible, Probable, True, False

If it sounds as though I'm skeptical about the abduction phenomenon, you're right. My skepticism, however, is aimed at what Betty Hill calls the "me too people." Too many reports are too similar and contain elements that transcend the laws of science for me to accept them as true without some sort of physical proof. I believe some things that are difficult to explain may have happened to some people but that nothing of note happened to most of those who have been hypnotized into believing they were abductees. Nothing, that is, beyond the experience of hypnotic regression itself. These are my standards; they don't have to be yours. Wherever in the continuum of response your convictions put you—from total acceptance to total disbelief—is okay with me.

I don't think the problem is with the abductees. Many, if not most, are sincere, honest people. Unbridled hypnotism and hypnotic regression practiced by people with their own agenda, however, have been the culprit in many a recent miscarriage of justice, with innocent people being accused of, and sometimes convicted of, child molesting, Satanism, and murder on the testimony of someone who has a "recovered memory" aided by hypnotic regression.

Report from the Field

Stephanie Kelley, a graduate student at the University of Kansas, is doing a study on alien abductions—or, as she puts it, "a rhetorical analysis using abduction narratives as my texts." If you are, or think you are, an abductee, Ms. Kelley would like you to fill out a questionnaire. All the information will be kept confidential, and any identifying data will be removed from the questionnaires before anyone else sees them. The information could prove to be useful in understanding the abduction phenomenon. For more information, including how to contact Ms. Kelley, see Appendix C.

I am not saying there is no such thing as hypnotic regression, or that memories can't be recovered with the aid of hypnotism. I am saying that, like any other tool, hypnotism properly used can be of great benefit. Used improperly it can be immensely destructive. Indeed, hypnotism can be helpful in recovering memory. The police in several countries have used it to help victims or witnesses to a crime recall faces or license plates or other details that might help apprehend the criminal.

But what are we to think when one therapist finds that most of her patients under hypnosis reveal they had been molested by their father as children, while another therapist finds that most of her patients have been dragged onto flying saucers and examined by unfriendly eyes? Could the fault, dear reader, lie not with the patient, but with the therapist?

Am I saying, or even hinting, that nobody has ever been abducted by a flying saucer? I am not. In numerous murder cases, particularly notorious ones, many people confess to the the crime. Because 50 innocent people confess to a crime, however, doesn't mean that no murder has been committed. To study the abduction phenomenon properly, a method must be developed to separate the few possibly genuine cases from the "true believers" who have become abductees at the will of their hypnotist-therapists.

The Least You Need to Know

➤ Contact is not abduction.

➤ There are said to be ten signs by which an abductee, whose memories are suppressed, can tell whether he or she might have been abducted.

➤ The number of people who may have had an abduction experience is in the tens of thousands.

➤ Many abductees have had similar experiences.

➤ The abduction experience is retrieved from the unconscious mind of the abductees through hypnosis.

➤ A subject under hypnosis is in a very suggestible state and often creates complex stories to please the hypnotist.

➤ Although most abduction stories (I believe) are induced by the hypnotist, images of aliens have become so ubiquitous that they must have originated somewhere.

Chapter 16

Another Time, Another Place: Alternate Explanations

In This Chapter

➤ UFOs might not be extraterrestrial craft

➤ The hollow earth theory

➤ Various occult explanations

➤ Men in Black

➤ Parallel universes

➤ Paraphysical possibilities

➤ Archetypes

The idea that the UFOs are extraterrestrial visitors has superseded and supplanted all the other possible explanations for the phenomenon in the popular mind. Even those who don't believe in the existence of UFOs know that what they're *not* believing in is aliens from outer space.

This was not always the case, however. In medieval times, apparitions in the sky were thought to be angels or possibly devils. In the late 19th century, when it seemed the sky was full of dirigibles that hadn't been invented yet, the occupants of the craft were said to be the inventors, who were test-flying their devices before delivering them to Washington, or flying off to fight the Spanish, or starting on a round-the-world voyage. The World War II foo-fighters were thought to be a secret enemy weapon. The fact that both sides were plagued by them wasn't known until after the war.

With the modern wave of UFO sightings, starting with Kenneth Arnold's "skipping saucers" in 1947, some consideration was given to the possibility that the Soviets were testing new secret weapons in the sky over the state of Washington, but as there was no rational explanation as to why they should do that, the notion lost favor. The idea that the crafts were from another planet soon became the most common explanation. Then the wave of flying saucer movies of the 1950s brought both the flying saucers and their alien crews into the public consciousness.

The claims of the contactees—and later the abductees—set forth in book after book and dramatized in movie after movie, solidified the concept. When you say "UFO" to a random stranger, he will have a good image in his head what you're talking about. (Actually, if you say UFO to a random stranger, he'll probably smile politely and move as far away from you as he can get.)

Of course UFO sightings have been explained away by the doubters and debunkers as many different things, if not dismissed as merely outright hoaxes. (For the hoaxes, see Chapter 17.) In his book *Flying Saucers,* premier debunker Professor Donald H. Menzel explained the sightings as the planet Venus, the planet Jupiter, sun dogs (refractions of the sun showing up elsewhere in the sky, related to rainbows), mirages, lenticular clouds, fireballs, and other atmospheric phenomena. He backed up his explanations with pages of mathematical formulae. What he succeeded in proving is that anything, true or false, can be explained away if you try hard enough.

There are other possibilities, however, about just what "aliens" are and where they and their saucer-shaped crafts are from.

Close Encounter

In July 1977, UFO buffs assembled in Roswell, New Mexico to celebrate the events described in Chapter 12. Two clerics offered differing views of the meaning of the UFO phenomenon. According to Michael Lindemann, editor of *CNI News,* an online newsletter of UFO happenings, the pastor of Roswell's non-denominational Calvary Chapel announced that the weekend visitors were attracted by the devil's "alien minions." "People are looking to UFOs as a replacement for God," Pastor Jim Suttle said. "This is Satan distracting people from the Lord."

Chuck Missler, a Christian minister from Idaho, doesn't see the aliens as being from another planet, but rather as "fallen angels" from another earthly dimension. Christ will return shortly, according to Missler, to battle with the alien hordes.

The Hollow Earth Theory

In the 1950s, Raymond Palmer, editor of *Fate* magazine, several flying saucer magazines, as well as various science-fiction magazines over the years, promoted the idea of one of his writers, Richard Shaver, that the earth was hollow. The theory first appeared in a science-fiction story, but Palmer and Shaver quickly promoted it to fact.

Inside the hollow earth, according to Shaver, is the country of Lemuria, populated by a race of evil dwarves called the *Abandondero* (or just *dero*), who pilot flying saucers and delight in wreaking havoc on the surface of the earth.

The hollow earth theory was not new with Shaver. Baron Holberg's *Journey to the World Under-Ground* (1742) takes its hero Nicholas Klimius into the earth where he finds a sun surrounded by planets.

A Hole at the Pole

In 1818, Captain John Cleves Symmes, of Ohio, published his theory that the earth is hollow, with good-sized entrances to the interior at the North and South Poles. In 1825, he suggested to Congress that the United States mount an expedition to the North Pole to test his theory. A bill to that effect was introduced. It didn't pass but did get 25 votes. In 1826, Symmes and a collaborator wrote *Symmes Theory of Concentric Spheres*, outlining his elaborate theory that within the earth are five hollow spheres, one inside the other, each inhabited on both sides. His son, Americus Symmes, took this one step further and declared that the lost tribes of Israel were now located on one of these spheres inside the earth.

Agharta

In his book *The Hollow Earth* (1964), Raymond Bernard, Ph.D., starts with the ideas set forth in a book he found in a Brazilian bookstore called *From the Subterranean World to the Sky: Flying Saucers*, by Huguenin, who in turn based his ideas on a theory of Professor Henruique Jose de Souza, president of the Brazilian Theosophical Society. It seems that flying saucers come from the "great Subterranean World with innumerable cities in which live millions of inhabitants." This land, called "Agharta" (Buddhist for "Subterranean World," according to Huguenin), is located "in a hollow inside the earth large enough to contain cities and fields where live human beings and animals, whose physical structure resembles those on the surface."

Sighting

If you are wondering how the citizens of Agharta got where they are—and who wouldn't be?—Bernard says that they came from the prehistoric continents of Lemuria, which sank into the Pacific Ocean 2,500 years ago; and Atlantis, which sank into the Atlantic Ocean long before that. The final sinking event occurred 11,500 years ago, "according to Plato's account, derived from ancient Egyptian records." (Or so Bernard would have you believe; as far as I know, Plato didn't say that, and there are no such records.)

Parallel Evolution

Actually, Bernard makes one very good point. If flying saucers come from planets circling other stars, then the evolution of the beings piloting them would be entirely unrelated to our own, and the odds of them looking anything like us would be very slight. Remember, if a giant meteor hadn't crashed into the earth 65 million years ago, the dominant intelligent species on the planet might well be some sort of dinosaur. And yet in most accounts of contact with saucer people, they look no more alien than do the Klingons or Vulcans—clearly not the product of separate paths of evolution. Bernard's notion of the saucers originating within the earth at least allows for a common ancestor with the rest of us.

Unfortunately, this doesn't improve the case for there being a gigantic hollow inside the earth. Now that satellites have photographed the entire surface of the earth, and no hole to the interior has been found—these were supposed to be good sized holes, remember—we can probably let the hollow earth theory lie fallow.

Saucers and the Occult

No sooner did flying saucers come into the common vocabulary than the concept was adopted by the occultists and made over into a variety of spiritual, supernatural, and psychic manifestations.

Some of the occult accounts of extraterrestrial beings predate the flying saucers. Toward the end of the 19th century, Madame Helena Petrovna Blavatsky developed the occult religion she called Theosophy. In her six-volume *The Secret Doctrine*, she speaks of "the Ascended Masters," some of whom live on various planets around the solar system.

Sananda

In the early 1950s, a Chicago woman named Dorothy Martin began receiving messages from an extraterrestrial named Sananda, who warned her that a major catastrophe was going to take place on earth on December 21, 1954. Sananda communicated by automatic writing, a process in which the receiver (Ms. Martin) allows the sender (Sananda) to guide her hand telepathically as she moves a pencil over a piece of paper. Ms. Martin spread the word, and soon a band of faithful followers waited to see what else Sananda would tell them.

Sananda, who told Ms. Martin he had been Jesus in a previous incarnation, promised to save her and her followers from the coming cataclysm by sending a flying saucer for them. Some of her followers quit their jobs and sold their homes and belongings to prepare for the coming destruction of the earth and await the final saucer. (I do not know what they planned to do with the money they got for the sale of their property.)

At Sananda's suggestion, Ms. Martin notified the press of the coming end of the world. When December 21, 1954 came and went with no destruction of the world and no flying saucer, the group was disillusioned. Ms. Martin changed her name to Sister Thedra and moved to Mount Shasta, California, where she continued to pass on the advice of higher beings to a waiting world.

The One World Family

In 1947, Allen Michael Noonan was working at his job at an outdoor billboard when he was suddenly transported to a great room where a group of elders sat around a glowing throne. A booming voice told him that his job was to save the world. He would have the telepathic help of Ashtar, a Venusian from the 12th dimension in producing his massive twelve-volume *Everlasting Gospel*, and in founding the One World Family. Extraterrestrials in UFOs outside the orbit of earth would also telepathically give him the help and advice he needed. Apparently, Ashtar also was a hollow earth fan, as Noonan related in an interview:

> The space command flies in and out of the earth. The earth is hollow and the Higher command—the Galactic Command—already has bases inside the earth. There are great openings at each pole of the earth, and what we call the Northern Lights is only the Great Central Sun shining out of these openings. Many people coming from the Polar regions have reported seeing flying saucers there which disappeared into the ocean.

In the 1970s, Noonan and his One World Family were running a vegetarian restaurant in Berkeley, California. Since then, I don't know—maybe the UFO went back into the earth.

Close Encounter

In their 1975 book *Encounters with UFO's*, John Welden and Zola Levitt carefully study the UFO phenomenon and come up with an answer: UFOs are run by demons as part of a great plan to prepare the way for the Antichrist by making the world "ready to think in terms of the new and the strange." They will do this by either 1) solving all the world's problems, 2) helping to set up the scientific study of the occult, or 3) causing us "to combine forces against a common enemy—in this case, hostile invaders from other worlds."

Men in Black

One recurring tale that should be mentioned in our discussion of UFO-related phenomena is of the Men In Black (MIB). They have been reported as appearing after a UFO sighting, especially when there has been some physical evidence of the event. Wearing black suits, black ties, black hats, and very serious expressions, they typically gather the evidence, threaten everyone who saw the event into silence, and leave. It is variously hypothesized that they are aliens who live among us and have the job of cleaning up after alien accidents, or that they are secret government agents, part of a conspiracy to keep the truth about extraterrestrials from the public.

The Men in Black stories have been taken up by the professional storytellers and so far have resulted in a movie by that name, a children's animated television show, and a computer game.

Parallel Universes

A respectable scientific theory, which exists in several variants, says there is not merely one universe but a number—possibly an infinite number—of universes stacked parallel to each other. If there were some sort of multi-universal force, like gravity but working through several side-by-side universes, then there might be a sun in the universe right alongside our own in a similar position as our sun, and it might have a family of planets much like our solar system.

If this theory were so, then the flying saucers might be from a planet like earth in the universe one over from this one. Perhaps the saucer people are several thousand years ahead of us in development and have discovered a way to travel among the universes. That would explain how their ships can appear and disappear the way they have been reported to do, and how they can suddenly vanish from radar screens. They merely flip back into their own universe. It's easy when you know how.

The Paraphysical Explanation

Another possibility, offered by Arthur C. Clarke (among others), is that the flying saucers are not material objects at all but manifestations from the realm of paraphysics. Since "paraphysics" means either "beyond the physical," or "beyond the laws of physics as we know them," this certainly opens a number of possibilities. In a sense, because "paraphysics" is such a non-specific term, meaning whatever we want it to (and the further out the better), we're practicing a form of name magic here.

When a scientist calls something "para"—parapsychology, paraphysics, parabiology, and so forth—this is sometimes a polite way of saying not merely, "I don't know how this works," but also, "I'm not sure there's really anything there."

Leaving out the claims by contactees whose stories taken as a whole make them less than believable, let us consider some of the aspects of flying saucers, as described by multiple separate observers, that possibly put them outside the realm of regular physics.

➤ Flying saucers move with no visible means of propulsion; they rise and hover in place completely silently.

This suggests a propulsion system other than any known on earth. Electromagnet repulsion—traveling on the planet's magnetic lines of force—has been suggested, as has some sort of gravity- or anti-gravity–based device.

➤ Flying saucers, or the beings in them, seem to be able to selectively stop car engines and silence radios.

Nothing on earth is known that could do this to the engine of a car. Electromagnetic forces powerful enough to immobilize a working combustion engine would probably twist the metal frame of the car into a free-form sculpture of a vortex, if it didn't melt it into a steel puddle.

➤ Flying saucers have been seen to make sharp turns at high speeds, something no earthly craft can do, and something that creates accelerations that would probably squash any human pilot.

In the 1930s, E.E. Smith, Ph.D. proposed an "inertialess drive" for the spaceships in his science-fiction stories. The spaceships would be capable of high accelerations without harming the people inside. Alternatively, the pilots of the UFOs could be related to cockroaches, which are said to be able to withstand very high accelerations.

➤ Flying saucers occasionally completely vanish, disappearing from view and from radar screens at the same instant.

Perhaps they use a Romulan cloaking device, à la Star Trek. Or perhaps the aliens are from a parallel universe, as discussed previously, and are able to switch instantly from one planet to the next.

➤ Our extraterrestrial brothers have been known to communicate with both contactees and abductees by a form of telepathy.

Telepathy, the ability to "read" someone else's mind, is one of the most widely accepted parapsychological abilities in science fiction and various occult and metaphysical disciplines. Scientific experiments conducted by such people as Dr. Rhine of Duke University have even found some basis for a slight amount of telepathic ability in some subjects. But it is very slight and uncontrollable. One argument against the existence of telepathy is that if such an ability actually existed, surely evolution would have selected it as an incredibly useful "sixth sense," and we could all do it by now. On the other hand, if there is no such

Report from the Field

"For if the materiality of UFOs is paraphysical (and consequently normally invisible), UFOs could more plausibly be creations of an invisible world coincident with the space of our physical earth planet than creations in the paraphysical realms of any other physical planet in the solar system. Given that UFOs are paraphysical, capable of reflecting lifelike ghosts; and given also that (according to many observers) they remain visible as they change position at ultra-high speeds from one point to another, it follows that those that remain visible in transition do not materialize for that swift back transition, and therefore, their mass must be of a diaphanous (very diffuse) nature, and their substance relatively etheric...The observed validity of this supports the paraphysical assertion and makes the likelihood of UFOs being earth-created greater than the likelihood of their creation on another planet."

—R.A.F. Air Marshal Sir Victor Goddard, K.C.B.

thing as telepathy, why is it that as soon as I start thinking about going for a walk, my dog Archie jumps up and waits impatiently by the door?

➤ On occasion, our extraterrestrial brothers are able to enter a room through a closed window, or walk through a wall.

This violates all the laws of physics as we understand them. We could pass it off as some sort of projection device, except some abductees claim they were removed from the house through the same wall the aliens came in. Your guess is as good as mine on this one; if you have a good guess, let me know.

Archetypes

Dr. Carl Jung, a highly respected psychiatrist and analyst of the psychic and psychological problems of the human race, wrote that flying saucers were a modern myth, an archetype taking the place of earlier manifestations of angels and other visions. In his 1959 book, *Flying Saucers: A Modern Myth of Things Seen in the Skies*, Jung suggests the sightings can be attributed to the fact that "the whole world is suffering under the strain of Russian policies and their still unpredictable consequences." He says that when the conscious mind sees no way out of a situation, a psychic dissociation can occur "giving rise to unexpected and apparently inexplicable opinions, beliefs, illusions, visions, and so forth."

Jung wrote that the round shape of the flying saucers could be considered a God-image, quoting the old saying that "God is a circle whose center is everywhere and circumference nowhere." As for cigar-shaped craft, well, even Jung admits that sometimes a cigar is just a cigar.

The Least You Need to Know

➤ The majority opinion today is that UFOs are extraterrestrial craft, but there are other possibilities.

➤ The two-century–old theory that the earth is hollow and that another civilization lies within it was brought up to date by Richard Shaver and others, who claimed that the UFOs emerge from the hollow land within the earth. But satellite photographs, which have mapped the entire globe, have failed to find a suitable hole.

➤ Occultists claimed to communicate with beings from flying saucers, superior beings who had a lot to teach us earthlings, by automatic writing, telepathy, or other psychic means, and received instructions about saving the earth or selected portions thereof.

➤ A recurring UFO tale involves the Men In Black (MIB) who show up after an encounter to clean up and remove the evidence. There is a lack of agreement as to who is sending them.

➤ UFOs might be coming from a universe parallel to this one, but how this could be done is not known.

➤ The various UFO manifestations that defy known physical laws require an explanation that matches the explanation of where the UFOs originate from.

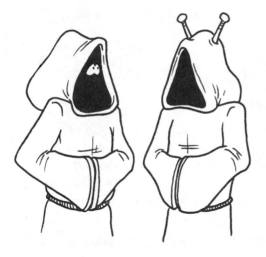

Chapter 17

Hoaxes, Frauds, and Cults: Approach with Care

> **In This Chapter**
>
> ➤ Hoaxes, frauds, and cults defined
>
> ➤ Some sample hoaxes
>
> ➤ George Adamski
>
> ➤ The Aetherius Society
>
> ➤ The Unarius Academy of Science
>
> ➤ Heaven's Gate

I am lumping hoaxes, frauds, and cults together because they all promote false ideas and they succeed and thrive by preying on the human need to believe. It's very hard to convince someone of something that isn't so unless that person is prepared to believe and willing to believe. By "prepared" I mean that his or her view of the way the universe works includes the possibility of the hoax being true. By "willing" I mean that the story claimed by the hoax fills a felt spiritual, social, political, or economic need. The victim may not have known of the need before the hoaxer got busy, but afterward felt that it might become anything from a minor interest to an overriding passion that must be met.

Close Encounter

The way I'm using these words, a *hoax* is a lie told or a trick played for fun or even with malice, but without any attempt to gain personally or financially from the event. A *fraud* is a lie told or an event staged to enhance the prestige, the status, or the finances of the stager. Sometimes a hoax slides imperceptibly over to become a fraud. A *cult* is a group of people following a charismatic leader in untraditional beliefs that require obedience on the part of the cult members.

The easiest example of creating needs is the American advertising industry. We now need things daily that didn't exist a hundred years ago, things our grandparents did very well without. We use germ-killing mouthwash and deodorants for the underarm, the rug, and the room. We buy separate cleansers for the bathtub, the sink, the tile, the toilet, the clothes washing machine, the dish washing machine, and hand washing dishes and clothes.

Cults combine the need to believe with the need to belong. They tend to attract the most vulnerable people in our society, those with nothing to believe in and nothing to belong to. Often the members are young people who are on their own without a familial support system or a network of friends. Many of them have what they fancy are good reasons to disbelieve the life lessons they were taught at home. They are open to new ideas and lack the critical screening necessary to sort the good from the bad, the wise from the foolish.

Cult leaders tend to be charismatic almost by definition, since charismatic means having the ability to impress and influence others. Some of them have been accused of using brainwashing techniques to control the members of their organization. This is not unknown, but in many cases it is unnecessary; the people who join the cult react to good treatment (compared to what they have known) and love (spiritual and otherwise) and the sense of purpose imparted by the beliefs of the cult, and manage to brainwash themselves.

Many would-be cult leaders espouse causes and beliefs already common in the community they are aiming at. If you teach a combination of astrology, spiritualism, and the coming doom for the whole world, you will find many believers in the occult community. If you add to this mix the possibility of salvation and redemption through doing good works, forswearing sex, and awaiting the arrival of Our Space Brothers in their flying saucers, you can probably build a membership list.

Flying Saucers Hoaxers

When the stories of flying saucers entered the American consciousness, they must have filled several different psychic needs; they were rapidly accepted as true by a large minority of the public. The hoaxers and frauds quickly moved in, capitalizing on the public interest.

This, incidentally, is not a comment on the validity of the UFO phenomenon as a whole. Hoaxers and frauds have always appeared in the midst of truth. As the laws and properties of electricity were being discovered and electrical devices were being developed, the con men went to work devising fraudulent electrical motors, electrical generators, and medical instruments that could cure all diseases by their electrical powers. The FDA is still trying to get several "electrical" cure-all devices off the market.

A Minor Sort of Hoax

On 30 July 1953, the *Atlanta Journal-Constitution* reported that the body of a space alien had been found. That day three young men flagged down a police car and told the officers that they had just accidentally run down and killed a small, humanoid-looking spaceman. The alien had come from a small red UFO that had been parked in the middle of the highway. Several other aliens had been walking around outside the UFO, but they had retreated into their craft and departed when the accident happened, leaving their defunct comrade behind.

The officers found the body of a small recently deceased humanoid lying on the highway, and several charred circles in the road where the boys claimed the spacecraft had been.

When the story broke, the police got several calls from people who said they had seen the UFO as it flew by. The story was a sensation for a couple of days until a professor of anatomy found that the little alien body was actually that of a monkey. Eventually the boys admitted that they had bought a monkey from a pet store, killed it, removed its tail and fur, and brought it to the highway. The scorch marks on the road had been made with a blowtorch. Even after the revelation of the hoax, some people wrote into the paper insisting that it was a cover-up, and that a real alien had been run over that night on the highway outside of Atlanta.

George Adamski and the Venusians

George Adamski saw his first flying saucer on 9 October 1946 and spent the next few years photographing dozens of them as they flew over his house on the southern slope of Mount Palomar, California. By the time he met with the saucer man in 1952, by his account, he had seen hundreds. Strangely, the astronomers at the Hale Observatory atop Mount Palomar did not photograph, and presumably did not see, them. Surely the astronomers would have mentioned sighting any such celestial objects.

In 1949, Adamski began lecturing about flying saucers. He also wrote (actually, his secretary Lucy McGinnis wrote and he took credit for) a science-fiction novel called *Pioneers of Space: A Trip to the Moon, Mars and Venus*. This novel had many elements in it that were to show up later in his allegedly true accounts of his experiences with the space people.

They Have Landed

In 1953, Adamski collaborated with Desmond Leslie to write *Flying Saucers Have Landed*, which became the first *contactee* best seller. Leslie contributed a history of saucers and sightings, in which he declared, with admirable precision, that, "Venus is the 'Home of the Gods'. From Venus in the year B.C. 18,617,841 came the first vehicle out of space to alight on our planet." Adamski added five chapters that detailed his meeting of a Venusian in the California desert on 20 November 1952.

On that date, Adamski and six compatriots drove to a point "10.2 miles from Desert Center toward Parker, Arizona." There they saw "a giant cigar-shaped silvery ship, without wings or appendages of any kind." Shortly thereafter Adamski had his friends drop him off, because he somehow realized that the ship had come to contact him.

While the friends waited a distance away, Adamski went forward to meet, as he put it, "a man from space—A HUMAN BEING FROM ANOTHER WORLD!"

Sign Language

This alien looked to be completely human, although his trousers looked different and his hair was long. "The beauty of his form surpassed anything I had ever seen. And the pleasantness of his face freed me of all thought of my personal self." They spoke of many things—well, Adamski spoke; the alien used sign language. The alien used gestures to tell Adamski that nuclear testing was a bad thing, and that too many explosions ("Boom! Boom!" the alien explained, gesturing with his hands) would destroy the earth. He also succeeded in getting across to Adamski that there was a mothership in orbit above, and that the saucers worked by "the law of attraction and repulsion."

Over the next few years, Adamski met Orthon from Venus, Firkon from Mars, and Ramu from Saturn. They took him for long voyages among the planets, and he came back and wrote (or had written for him) more books. The knowledge that Adamski's space brothers show of the physics and geology of the planets of our solar system is amazingly slight and inaccurate, considering that they lived there.

To counter the belief that Adamski, who died in 1965, was a fraud, living off the credulity of his readers and listeners (he lectured a lot), some conspiracy theorists espouse a theory that Adamski himself was duped by the saucer people into telling ridiculous stories to undermine belief in his claims, thus in him, and by a stretch, in the UFOs themselves.

The Destruction of Chester

The January 1978 issue of *Official UFO* published an incredible story, scooping all the mainstream press. On Saturday, 2 July 1977, the town of Chester, Illinois, population 5310, had been attacked by flying saucers and totally destroyed. Reporters from the daily papers went to Chester, found it standing, and wrote a few humorous pieces after interviewing a few Chestertons. Myron Fass, the editor of *Official UFO*, didn't give up his story, insisting that the aliens had returned, rebuilt the town, and given the townspeople selective amnesia.

The Aetherius Society

George King, a London taxicab driver, first heard from the Cosmic Masters when he was 35 years old. At first it was a disembodied voice telling him to prepare himself. And then, a week later, a man in white robes walked through the door to his room and lectured him on what was wrong with the world and how he, George King, had been selected to put things right.

Master Aetherius

Shortly thereafter, King had a spiritual visit from Master Aetherius, a superior being from the planet Venus, one of the planets in the highly advanced Interplanetary Parliament, which met on the planet Saturn. King was to represent the Interplanetary Parliament here on earth as their "primary terrestrial channel." It would be his job to gather about him those spiritually and intellectually able to grasp this cosmic truth.

One night shortly after these revelations, King rented Caxton Hall, a favorite place in London for those with mystical messages to seek an audience.

Report from the Field

"On a cold Saturday morning in March 1954, Mr. George King was washing up the dishes in his bed-sitter in Maida Vale when a voice boomed out from nowhere: "Prepare yourself, You are to become the voice of Interplanetary Parliament." Struck by the unexpectedness of the message, George King dropped a plate."

—Dr. Christopher Evans, *Cults of Unreason*

King faced the audience and Master Aetherius took over his body and spoke through him. It was a great success.

Jesus Christ

Since then, the Aetherius Society has had other speakers from the cosmos, speaking through the bodies of their earthly vessels. "Mars, Sector 6" is a common visitor as, on special occasions, is Jesus Christ. The Society has spread out from its humble beginnings in Caxton Hall, with organizations now in Australia, New Zealand, and a big one in the United States, headquartered in Los Angeles. And, with speakers like that, it's no wonder.

The Unarius Academy of Science

"In 2001, Earth will be visited by the Muons of Planet Myton from the Pleiades on a mission of peace." So says the Unarius Academy, and it is preparing for the event. Unarius stands for UNiversal ARticulate Interdimensional Understanding of Science, and the Academy is made up of "countless thousands of advanced spiritual beings," most of whom look a lot like you and me, and live in southern California.

Report from the Field

"Higher beings, living on higher physical worlds, have been building the 33 spacecraft that will form a gigantic city when attached one atop the other! The Star Center, a gigantic college or city, will descend and remain on Earth! These Starships will land on large acreage, purchased for this purpose in Southern California, and will serve as a gigantic university, where people can come from all over the world to visit and study!"

—Archangel Uriel of the Unarius Academy

Archangel Uriel

Unarius was founded in 1954 by Ernest L. Norman, "the Moderator of the Universe," and his wife Ruth E. Norman, "Archangel Uriel." Ernest died, from our earthly point of view, in 1971. Ruth, as Uriel (Universal Radiant Infinite Eternal Light), continued and expanded on her husband's teachings, possibly with his continued advice and support. After his earthly death, he assumed his true identity as Archangel Raphiel and moved to Mars.

The First Stave

The Unarius Academy is headquartered in El Cajon, California, near San Diego. Its teachings, now in over 100 books published by the Academy, are a mixture of Theosophy, Christianity, Buddhism, and science fiction, with heavy emphasis on flying saucers and past lives. The members are now planning for the landing of starships on earth, which will be, "the first stave in the alignment of 33 planets, of which planet Earth is to be the thirty-third and final linking member, forming an Interplanetary Confederation for the Spiritual Renaissance of Humankind on Earth!"

Ruth Norman passed beyond in 1994, possibly joining her husband on Mars. Since her death, Charles Spiegel, a retired psychology professor at San Diego State University, has headed the Academy. "The West Coast of the United States used to be the East Coast of the sunken continent Lemuria," Spiegel explains. "That's why so many people move out here— they're lured here in their pre-history."

When the Muons arrive in 2001, they are going to bring an extra spaceship with them so that we earth people can visit the other planets. I wonder how they feel about carry-on baggage?

Heaven's Gate

In 1995, the members of a cult calling itself Heaven's Gate moved to San Diego and went into the Internet Web site-creating business. Their company was called Higher Source, and it created the graphics and hypertext for commercial Web sites. The business did well, and a year later the cult members moved into a house at 18241 Colina Norte in Rancho Sante Fe, an upscale San Diego neighborhood.

The Two

Heaven's Gate was the creation of a couple called "the Two," or "Bo" and "Peep." Bo was Marshall Herff Applewhite, a onetime choral director at the University of Alabama, professor of music at the University of St. Thomas, and patient at a psychiatric hospital in Houston. Peep was Bonnie Lu Nettles, who had first met Applewhite in 1972 when she was a nurse in the Houston hospital where he was a patient. Nettles was deeply into astrology and channeling, and professed to have a "spirit guide" named Brother Francis, a monk who died in 1818.

The connection between Heaven's Gate and the mythos of UFOs went back to 1973, when Bo and Peep experienced an enlightenment and came to believe that passages in the Book of Revelation referred to them. They founded a spiritual group called Human Individual Metamorphosis (abbreviated HIM) and decided that they were really extra-terrestrials or angels (same thing, they thought) who were on earth to raise mortals to the next level. HIM taught a mix of Christian belief, astrology, spiritualism, science fiction, and salvation by UFO.

The Two told Hayden Hewes, who was the director of the International UFO Bureau in Oklahoma City, that they were there, "to show and tell how man may make the ascension into the next evolutionary level." They predicted that they were going to be assassinated, but that three days later, they would publicly return to life.

A Cloud of Light

By 1975, Bo and Peep were beginning to gather disciples, and UFOs were figuring more strongly in their teachings. The story now was that three and a half days after their assassination, the Two would ascend to heaven on a cloud of light. After which, flying saucers would come to take away their disciples. As time went by and none of this happened, disciples would get disheartened or bored and leave the group, but new members would replace them. Membership stayed at around 150.

Close Encounter

A recruiting poster the Two used in San Francisco in 1975 read like this:

UFO's
IN SAN FRANCISCO AREA
Why they are here
Who they have come for
When they will land

Two individuals say they were sent from the level above human, and will return to that level in a space ship (UFO) within the next few months. This man and woman will discuss how the transition from the human level to the next level is accomplished, and when this may be done.

This is not a religious or philosophical organization recruiting membership. However, the information has already prompted a number of individuals to devote their total energy to the transitional process. If you have ever entertained the idea that there might be a real PHYSICAL level in space beyond the Earth's confines, you will want to attend this meeting.

Applewhite was not into sex, and the group actively discouraged any sort of sexuality among its members. Some of the men went so far as to have themselves castrated, as Applewhite himself had been, to lessen their sexual urges. Somewhere along the way, Bo and Peep became Ti and Do, as in the musical scale. In 1985, Bonnie Lu Nettles (Do) died of cancer. "Shedding her container," and returning, as one believer put it, to the next level to resume her position there.

The Spaceship Following Hale-Bopp

Applewhite believed that the appearance of the Hale-Bopp comet in 1997 was the sign he had been waiting for. He declared that a dark body that was believed to be following the comet (this later turned out not to be so) was a spacecraft that had been sent for him and his followers. He also believed that to board this spacecraft, he and his followers had to leave their bodies, their "earthly vehicles" behind.

On Wednesday, 26 March 1997, the San Diego County Sheriff's Office found the bodies of 21 women and 18 men in the Heaven's Gate communal home. They were dressed in their usual black shirts and pants and wearing new Nike sneakers. They had committed suicide in three shifts, each of them eating up to 50 Phenobarbital pills mashed up in pudding or applesauce and washed down with vodka. The second shift layed out the bodies of the first on their cots and covering them with purple shrouds and, in some cases, putting plastic bags over their heads to make sure of death. Then the second shift did the same, leaving two members to arrange them properly.

All the members had one bag packed with personal belongings, a passport, and $5.75. Because they were leaving their earthly vehicles behind, it is hard to see the point of that. It is, however, a minor point to quibble about with 39 people who have committed suicide en masse.

Several members of the cult who did not happen to be at the house for the mass suicide killed themselves shortly thereafter, one of them leaving a note that read: "I'm going on the spaceship with Hale-Bopp to be with those who have gone before me."

Riding the Comet

We can see no sense in what happened to the Heaven's Gate cultists, draw no easy moral from their mass demise. They were not brainwashed in any usual sense of the word, no ex-members have come forth to tell tales of deprivation or forced compliance with the group's ethos. They were all adults who knew as much about death and its finality as any of us. Perhaps they lacked a basic grounding in general science, or didn't stop to think that a spaceship would have no reason to hide behind a comet, or that there are easier ways to board an interstellar craft than swallowing 50 barbiturates.

There is a story that when the philosopher Voltaire lay dying, a priest came to him and told him that it was time that he gave up his foolish notions about this and that.

"Why are you here?" Voltaire asked.

"God sent me," the priest replied.

"Ah!" said Voltaire. "And may I see your credentials?"

Perhaps we should adopt the same standard when someone tells us that extraterrestrials are here to save us, and all we have to do is swallow a bottle of pills, or gather in the desert to greet the ship, or take a very expensive course in reaching some "higher plane," or stand on one foot, or otherwise put our free will in someone else's keeping.

Visits from Another Galaxy

And it continues. Malachi York is the leader of the United Nuwaubian Nation of Moors, a commune living on 476 acres of farmland near Eatonton, Georgia. He is also a musician, a writer, an entrepreneur, and a visitor from another galaxy. The commune—which has constructed large replicas of the pyramids and the Sphinx—is waiting for the intergalactic spaceships to arrive in 2003 to take 144,000 chosen people back with them whence they came. While they are waiting, the commune is thinking about building a theme park.

The Least You Need to Know

➤ My definitions: A *hoax* is a joke or trick, a *fraud* is done for monetary gain, and a *cult* is a group gathered around a charismatic leader for a common purpose.

➤ Hoaxes are common in the UFO community, but not all UFO reports are hoaxes.

➤ George Adamski had either friends from Venus or an active imagination, take your pick.

➤ George King spoke to Master Aetherius, also from Venus, and was enlightened.

➤ The Unarius Academy of Science is awaiting the landing, in 2001, of the Muons from the planet Myton.

➤ The members of the Heaven's Gate cult decided that they couldn't wait, so they committed mass suicide to rid themselves of their earthly bodies and join a spaceship coming in behind the Hale-Bopp comet.

Chapter 18

What Does It All Mean?

In This Chapter

➤ UFO ignorance

➤ Today's magic as tomorrow's science

➤ Impossible or highly illogical UFO behavior

➤ UFO stories as obvious frauds

➤ Contactee stories: hoaxes or frauds

➤ Abductee stories: hard to judge

Many years ago, John W. Campbell Jr., then the editor of *Astounding Science Fiction* magazine, pointed out that the technology of any sufficiently advanced society will seem like magic to a more primitive culture. And the technology of the future would seem like magic to those in the past. If, for example, I were somehow able to go back to the 1950s and hand my pocket calculator or my digital wrist-watch to Campbell, or to any of the leading scientists of the day, they would understand what it did (tell time, solve equations), but they would have no idea how it worked and would not have the means to figure it out. To them it would be the functional equivalent of magic. And that is only half a century ago.

Any civilization able to visit us from some distant star system is certainly hundreds, if not thousands, of years ahead of us in technology. The fact that their ships can travel at tremendous speeds, make sharp turns, dive into the water and continue on, and hover above the earth with no visible means of propulsion—the fact that they can stop car engines, lift people into the air with invisible beams, and abduct people without their remembering it—the fact, in other words, that what they can do seems like magic to us does not mean that it is impossible, or that it is not happening.

Close Encounter

Flying discs, called *vimanas,* are mentioned in two ancient Hindu religious poems, the *Mahabharata* and the *Ramayana,* which are both around 2,000 years old. The description of how to build one sounds suspiciously modern and other-worldly.

"Strong and durable must the body be made like a great flying bird of light material. Inside it one must place the mercury engine with its iron heating apparatus beneath. By means of the power latent in the mercury which sets the driving whirlwind in motion, a man sitting inside may travel in a great distance in the sky in a most marvelous manner."

And the description from the *Mahabharata* of a vimana's attack of the city of Varanasi could be out of a science-fiction movie.

"Varanasi burned, with all its princes and their followers, its inhabitants, horses, elephants, treasures and granaries, houses, palaces, and markets. The whole of a city that was inaccessible to the gods was thus wrapped in flames by the vimana and was totally destroyed."

On the other hand, the fact that they have not yet contacted our government and made their presumably non-negotiable demands, the fact that they have not left any artifacts anywhere where our wise men can examine them, and the fact that some of the stories of contact with them have more natural explanations and others have turned out to be hoaxes means that the evidence of their existence should be carefully weighed and considered.

One of the arguments made in favor of the truthfulness of many UFO reports is that the people making the report are good, sober, honest people with respectable backgrounds and good jobs, and have nothing to gain by lying. Unfortunately the human psyche is very complex and there are countless incidents on record of good sober respectable people lying when they had no discernible reason to do so. This doesn't make all UFO reports hoaxes, it just makes the job of separating the true from the false that much more difficult.

So it's a good idea at this point to pause and consider what questions we should ask while considering this phenomenon, and what sort of answers we should expect.

A List of Whys

From the point of view of us poor humans, the behavior of the flying saucers, as recorded by those who claim to have seen them, is at best bizarre and at worst totally incomprehensible. I am not discussing their science or their technology, the possibilities of which are adequately (I think) gone over in other chapters, but their psychology. Why do they do what they do? For example:

Report from the Field

"It's not a spaceship unless you can read the Mars registration plate."

—Sir Arthur C. Clarke

➤ Why do they play tag with earth aircraft? Are they testing our reflexes? Are they just having fun?

➤ What can they hope to learn from us? Surely these beings from another place are here for a reason. Surely they have something better to do.

➤ Why are there so many different designs of alien spaceships—saucers, triangles, eggs, cigars, octagons, balls of fire? Are they having a convention?

➤ If they want to avoid contact with humans, why do they allow themselves to be seen at all?

➤ If they're contacting us on purpose, why not just land on the White House lawn?

➤ Some contactees claim that they have been given messages by the aliens. And the messages are always some version of "play nice, don't fight." What about some practical advice on how to accomplish that? What about a cure for cancer? What about a solution to global warming? What about a really good barbeque sauce? What about a couple of tips on the market?

➤ Other contactees claim to have been poked, prodded, and otherwise violated by the aliens, and to have had strange objects inserted into various parts of their bodies. What do our extraterrestrial visitors hope to learn from this?

Report from the Field

"I think the evidence for the reality of Unidentified Flying Objects is beyond a reasonable doubt, and that the phenomena is deserving of scientific attention in spite of the existence of organizations on the lunatic fringe that have tended to discredit such attention."

—Dr. James A. Harder, Associate Professor in the College of Engineering, U.C. Berkeley

Nothing but the Truth

I'm not claiming that the lack of an adequate answer to any of these questions means that the people who claim that particular experience are speaking less than the absolute truth. Many of them certainly are, but others are not. Even those who are speaking the truth as they see it, however, may not have seen what they thought they saw. As I said earlier, it is not easy to separate truth from fiction in the study of UFOs.

You have probably noticed a certain ambivalence on my part, in one paragraph discussing UFOs as though they are certainly here and the aliens are among us, and in another talking about how many hoaxers there are and that even those who think they're telling the truth may be mistaken.

I have found that to be unavoidable in taking the middle road that I've striven for in this book. Many flying saucer advocates, especially among the contactees, are certainly hoaxers or worse, and you should know that. But as for the others, I will leave you the fun of deciding on your own.

Sighting

Although there are increasingly interesting reports that there well may be life on Mars (see Chapter 21), it almost seriously hasn't progressed beyond the stage of bacteria.

You must make your own judgements as to who is prevaricating or exaggerating and enhancing, who may be telling the truth, and who is certainly telling the truth, as they know it.

The facts about astronomy can be of some help in the elimination process, however. Given the advances in planetary astronomy, and what we now know about our nearest neighbors in space, anyone who claims to have spoken to visitors from Mars or Venus (and I name no names, Mr. Adamski) is either prevaricating or has himself been hoaxed. Venus is too hot for anything we might think of as life, and Mars is too dry to have anything but the most primitive forms of life, if any.

All Things to Some People

"When I use a word," Humpty Dumpty told Alice in Lewis Carroll's *Through the Looking Glass*, "it means just what I choose it to mean—neither more nor less. …The Question is which is to be master—that's all."

Many practitioners of the art of the UFO follow Humpty Dumpty's practice, and use words and concepts and scientific facts to mean just what they choose them to mean, which makes it difficult for the rest of us to follow in anything like a rigorous, intelligent manner. And so we tend to take a deep breath and plunge in to the story being told, and follow along behind the narrator the best we can. If we're trying to separate the probably possible from the probably impossible and the possible but probably phoney—how's that for careful qualifications?—we have to develop an ear for truth and an eye for detail.

This Is Only a Test

Here's a test to see how well your ear and eye are developed at spotting the false. This problem is stolen by me from an early intelligence test:

If the following story were told to you as true, could you believe it, and, if not, why not?

A man falls asleep in church during the sermon. He dreams that he is a French aristocrat back in the days of the French Revolution. He gives a ringing speech in his dream in defense of the aristocracy, but the Committee drag him off to be guillotined anyway. Just as, in his dream, he is placed in the stocks and he hears the *snick* of the blade being released, the woman in the pew behind him drops her prayer book and it lands on the back of his neck. The poor man dies instantly of a heart attack.

Possibly true? Definitely false? Why? Think about it for a minute. And then read on.

Possible, Probable

My problem with the story the first time I heard it was the man's poor choice of epochs. If he had chosen any time during the 300 years before the Revolution to be a French aristocrat, it could have been a very pleasant dream indeed. But no. Luckily the story is definitely false.

That's what you said, right? And you knew why. You analyzed the story for its internal logic. Every part of the story could be true, you realized, but the story *as a story* didn't hang together. If it were true, you wouldn't know about it. You *couldn't* know about it. Why?

If he died instantly of a heart attack, you wrote in the margin of this very page, how could anyone know what he was dreaming?

Very astute of you. Now, keeping your hard-won logical abilities where you can get at them, let's look at UFOs.

Timeline

Here is a list of the more important UFO encounters, many of them discussed elsewhere in this book. Note how the experiences grow and change.

➤ **August 12, 1883:** While conducting solar studies from his observatory in Zacatacas, Mexican astronomer José A. Y. Bonilla sees more than 100 objects crossing the disc of the sun. He photographs this phenomenon, and the picture reveals that the objects are cigar- or spindle-shaped.

➤ **November 22, 1896:** A "winged cigar" appears in the sky over the streets of Oakland, California.

➤ **1942–1945:** Some British and American military pilots report seeing mysterious bright lights following, and sometimes preceding, their planes. On occasion, the lights are resolved into 8- to 12-inch flying discs. These objects are nicknamed "foo fighters" and at first are believed to be an enemy secret weapon. After the war, it is discovered that German and Japanese pilots saw similar apparitions and thought they might be Allied secret weapons.

➤ **June 24, 1947:** While flying a search mission for a downed plane, Kenneth Arnold reports seeing a formation of nine objects flying south near Mount Rainier, Washington. He described them as boomerang-shaped, but said they flew "like saucers skipping across the surface of a lake." The term "flying saucers" was born.

➤ **July 7, 1947:** In Tacoma, Washington, Gene Gamachi and I.W. Martenson claim to have seen a UFO land on a neighbor's roof and "little men" get out. The craft and the men had vanished by the time reporters arrived.

➤ **July 8, 1947:** An alien spacecraft is reported to have crashed in the desert northwest of Roswell, New Mexico.

➤ **January 7, 1948:** While chasing a UFO near Godman Air Force Base in Kentucky, Captain Thomas F. Mantell was killed when his plane crashed.

➤ **October 1, 1948:** Captain George Gorman of the North Dakota Air National Guard has a dogfight with a UFO near the Fargo, North Dakota airport.

➤ **December 16, 1948:** Air Force Project Sign has its code name changed to Project Grudge. The final report of Project Sign [Technical Report TR-2274-IA of the Technical Intelligence Division, Air Materiel Command, Wright-Patterson AFB] is issued on February 11, 1949. The report, originally classified "Secret," was declassified in 1961.

➤ **January 1950:** *True* magazine publishes Major Donald Kehoe's article on flying saucers, which claimed that, "For the past 175 years the planet Earth has been under systematic close-range examination by living, intelligent observers from another planet." The article, which offered little proof of its assertions, caused a sensation.

➤ **1953:** George Adamski and Desmond Leslie publish *Flying Saucers Have Landed*, in which Adamski claims to have talked to beings from the planet Venus.

➤ **March 1954:** In London, George King is in telepathic contact with "Master Aetherius" telling him that he is to be the voice of the "Interplanetary Parliament." He founds the Aetherius Society.

➤ **1954:** In California, the Unarius Academy of Science is founded by the Normans, Ernest and Ruth, to spread the teaching of, among others, the Muons of Planet Myton, who are arriving here in 2001 on a mission of peace.

➤ **September 19, 1961:** Betty and Barney Hill have a close encounter with a UFO in the White Mountains of New Hampshire. Their experience will bring them, in December of 1963, to the offices of psychiatrist Dr. Benjamin Simon. Their complete and frightening suppressed memories will be brought out over a period of seven months. The best-selling book, *The Interrupted Journey*, by John G. Fuller is an account of their experiences.

➤ **January 1969:** *Scientific Study of Unidentified Flying Objects*, written under the direction of Dr. Edward U. Condon, is published. Universally known as The Condon Report, the study was commissioned by the U.S. Air Force on October 7, 1966, and is the compilation of two years research by many people. A fair, balanced, objective, and very thick book, it quickly becomes the touchstone for all future UFO research by both believers and skeptics.

➤ **1972:** Crop circles begin appearing in fields in England.

➤ **1987:** Bestseller fiction author Whitley Strieber publishes *Communion*, his supposedly nonfiction personal account of abduction by aliens.

➤ **March 26, 1997:** Thirty-nine members of the Heaven's Gate cult commit suicide at their home in San Diego, to spiritually join the spaceship that is following the Hale-Bopp comet.

The problem for someone trying to make some definitive statements about flying saucers is that all the previously discussed events are flying saucer phenomena. But are we to believe that the same beings who played tag with Captain Mantell or had a dogfight with Captain Gorman landed on the California desert and told George Adamski they were from Venus? Or that they were in telepathic communication with the Aetheriuns or the Unarians? Or that they abducted Betty and Barney Hill? Or passed through a wall into Whitley Strieber's bedroom to abduct him? Or that they were in a spaceship following the Hale-Bopp comet?

Okay, we agree, we should throw out some of these stories before even considering the rest. But which ones? Will your list be the same as mine?

You see the problem.

Contact!

We cannot argue with the people who *claim* to have seen lights, or solid objects, in the sky looking like nothing made on earth and dashing about in a manner our man-made craft are incapable of. We can attempt to find objects that we know of in the sky that might be what they were seeing, like that old favorite the planet Venus, or mirages, or wayward weather balloons. But if they insist that whatever they saw had portholes and blinking red and blue lights, and that it made an abrupt right turn, and sped off faster than anything earthly had a right to travel, or suddenly dived under water, or just disappeared—Poof! Like that!—we will probably decide how much faith to put in the observation, depending on how much faith we put in the observer.

But the contactees have provided us with enough data to analyze their claims. George Adamski met an alien from Venus who could read his mind but who had to communicate to him with crude gestures. He went for long voyages to other planets with Orthon from Venus, Firkon from Mars, and Ramu from Saturn. Sure he did. Venus is too hot, Mars is empty of higher life forms, and Saturn is a gas giant with no breathable atmosphere and a surface gravity that would crush soda bottles.

George King has communicated with the reincarnated spirit of Jesus Christ on another planet. Ruth Norman talked telepathically to the Muons from the planet Myton, just one of the 33 planets that make up the Interplanetary Federation. Bo and Peep were going to show "how man may make the ascension to the next evolutionary level." Their chosen method turned out to be mass suicide.

Looking at these claims from either a scientific or a religious viewpoint, they have too many inconsistencies and fallacies to be taken seriously. Unfortunately many people do take them seriously. If joining one of these societies or cults merely is to add color and excitement to your otherwise drab existence, how can anyone gainsay it? If it is too costly of your time, your material wealth, or your life, however, you may have made a bad bargain. Then there is the point that truth is of intrinsic value, and anything that leads away from the truth in one field may make you more susceptible to lies in other fields.

Report from the Field

"All in all, the alleged evidence [for flying saucers] seemed thin—most often devolving into gullibility, hoax, hallucination, misunderstanding of the natural world, hopes and fears disguised as evidence, and a craving for attention, fame, and fortune. Too bad, I remember thinking."

—Carl Sagan,
The Demon-Haunted World

There seems to be what I will call the "genre principle" in storytelling. Patterns recur from story to story in the same genre; a western these days is nothing like the old west, but it's a lot like other westerns. Private detective novels are nothing like what real private detectives do, but they're a lot like other private detective stories. Sometimes it's possible to find the progenitor, the story from which all the other stories flowed. A great group of modern fantasy novels are thinly disguised Tolkein, modern vampire stories have descended and evolved from Bram Stoker's *Dracula*, and most of the abduction stories owe their existence to Betty and Barney Hill.

Their story was original when they told it, not drawing on anybody else's recollections, not patterned on any pre-existing model of what an abduction story was supposed to be.

Abduction stories are harder to parse than stories of contact. The people tend to be more believable, but the facts tend to be as strange or stranger. The aliens are not from Venus. They are not reincarnations of Jesus. They do not come with messages from the Grand Parliament of the Stars. They do, however, walk through walls and have the ability to induce amnesia. Their amnesia-inducing powers are imperfect, however; otherwise we wouldn't know any of these stories. In addition, the aliens seem overly interested in the bodies and sex organs of the abductees.

The tales of the UFO are ongoing. The latest ones are triangular and gigantic and have a deep throbbing sound; most of the others have been silent. Look at Appendix C for a list of UFO organizations if you want to keep up with what's happening. Several of them have email newsletters and Web sites. It will be interesting in two or three decades to look back on this and see whether it turned out to be a complex hoax or series of unrelated hoaxes, or our introduction to the universe, or still an abiding mystery. As you make your own decision, remember what J. Allen Hynek said: "Absence of evidence does not constitute evidence of absence."

The Least You Need to Know

➤ Many questions about the actions and intent of the UFOs need answers.

➤ The technology of any sufficiently advanced society will seem like magic to a more primitive culture.

➤ Most of the stories of the contactees read like neither magic nor science, but like hoaxes and frauds.

➤ As to the rest, sightings and abductions, they are a mix of the possible and the impossible; it's hard to sort them out.

➤ I am trying to give you enough information to make informed decisions, when added to your own store of knowledge.

➤ As new UFO-related stories come along, do not accept them uncritically. Instead, remember Hynek's dictum: "Absence of evidence does not constitute evidence of absence."

Part 4
It's Out There—Isn't It?—
The Scientific Search for
Extraterrestrials

If intelligent extraterrestrial life forms have not arrived on earth—or if they have remained shy and refused to show themselves—then we will have to seek them out where they live. For a real scientist to discuss the possibility of extraterrestrial life was, until recently, a good way to get drummed out of the corps, but of late, it has become respectable.

The possibility of finding life on the other planets of our solar system or their satellites is not great, and the probability of finding other intelligent life is just about nil. There may be bacteria in the soil of Mars, however, and who knows what we'll find in the oceans of Europa or Ganymede. We now know that there are planets out there, probably millions of them, circling millions of other stars. Furthermore, it is beginning to seem as though life is a natural condition of the universe and will form wherever it has a chance.

Discovering intelligent life elsewhere in the universe would be one of the greatest happenings since humans learned to speak. Even if we had to communicate with extraterrestrials by radio—which at the speed of light would take a while, since even the nearest star is more than four light years away—an interstellar dialog would give us a better idea of how we got here and just what we're supposed to be doing here.

Chapter 19

The Meaning of Life

In This Chapter

➤ Life elsewhere—not like life on earth

➤ It all started with a Big Bang

➤ Second-generation stars

➤ Life on earth began early

Until a being from a UFO walks up to a noted scientist and says, "Hi! I'm from a small planet circling the star you call Betelgeuse. Where are you from?" the scientific community as a whole is going to doubt the existence of "flying saucers." But this doesn't mean that most scientists doubt the possibility of finding extraterrestrial life. These days scientists are more than willing to entertain the idea that earth does not hold the exclusive franchise for life. There is a fair amount of consideration being given to the possibility that there is life on other planets, possibly planets circling other stars, and there is much scientific discussion as to just what that life might be like.

In the Beginning...

We'll take up the development of life on earth in the next chapter, to give us a starting point for considering the possibilities of life elsewhere. And in Chapter 21, we'll consider the planets themselves and see if we can determine just which ones might

Report from the Field

"The number of advanced civilizations in the Milky Way Galaxy today depends on many factors, ranging from the number of planets per star to the likelihood of the origin of life. But once life has started in a relatively benign environment and billions of years of evolutionary time are available, the expectation of many of us is that intelligent beings would develop."

—Carl Sagan, *The Dragons of Eden* (1977)

become covered with that surface disturbance we call life. For now let's look at where the earth itself came from and how it ended up the way it is.

I'll start with a history of the universe itself, from the first blip to last Thursday, complete in three pages. And I'll do my best along the way to explain how we figured it out. We'll look deeper into some of these ideas in later chapters. Hold on to your hat!

All the Colors of the Rainbow

It all began in 1665, when Sir Isaac Newton put a prism in the way of a beam of sunlight coming through his window. The prism bent the light passing through it and cast a rainbow of colors onto a nearby wall. Newton found out that the white light of the sun is made up of—literally—all the colors of the rainbow, and that each color is refracted—bent—a slightly different amount when passed through a prism. This creates a "spectrum." The rainbow is the sun's white light, made up of all the colors, bent into a spectrum by raindrops.

Close Encounter

Light is caused by an object, usually a very hot object, emitting a beam of particles, called *photons*, which sometimes behave like waves. A good explanation of that takes up a fat chapter in a high school physics text, but because we don't need it here, I refer you to the nearest physics textbook if you're interested. Colors are the way we perceive the different wavelengths of light. The basic rainbow of colors are usually listed as red, orange, yellow, green, blue, indigo, and violet. These make up the visible spectrum. All the hundreds of other colors we have names for can be placed somewhere on this line from the deepest red to the thinnest violet.

In 1863, William Huggins, an English astronomer, used a gadget called the spectroscope—basically a prism or a *diffraction grating* and a screen to show the pattern of refracted light—to divide the light of distant stars into its basic colors. This enabled him to determine the chemical composition of the stars. Different elements, when heated into their gaseous form as they are inside of stars, emit or absorb light at different frequencies, thus making bright lines of emission or dark absorption lines on the spectroscope screen. Each element has its own unique "signature" of emission and absorption lines. By looking at the pattern of bright and dark lines produced, astronomers could tell what the star was made up of.

The Stuff the Stars Are Made of

Each star has a slightly different composition, but all stars are mostly hydrogen, with a touch of helium, and all the other elements together make up less than one percent of a star's volume.

Contact

The **diffraction grating** made up of closely spaced thin wires or fine lines scratched on a glass plate, was invented by Joseph von Fraunhofer in 1820. Light passed through one bends as though it had gone through a prism.

Here is a percentage breakdown of the most common elements that make up the stars in our universe:

Hydrogen	87.609
Helium	12.262
Oxygen	0.059
Carbon	0.026
Neon	0.024
Nitrogen	0.008
Everything else	0.002

Notice that many of the elements we think of as common here on earth, and which are very important to our lives and to our industry—iron, sulfur, tin, copper, even silicon (the major ingredient of sand)—are part of that two-thousandths of a percent of "everything else." How that "everything else" came into being is discussed later.

The Red Shift

In 1923, an astronomer named Edwin Powell Hubble studied what was then called the Andromeda *nebula* with the new 100-inch telescope on Mount Wilson in California, which could see much clearer and much farther into the universe than any other instrument up until then. He found that Andromeda was actually a galaxy composed of billions of stars, much like our own Milky Way, but so far away that it looks like a tiny patch of bright fuzz in the sky. By studying certain stars called *Cepheid variables* that he located in the Andromeda Galaxy, as it was now renamed, he was able to

Contact

Nebula, from the word *nebulous* (which means cloudy or indistinct), was the name given to small, indistinct cloudy patches in the night sky. As telescopes improved, many of them turned out to be distant galaxies, while others were expanding clouds of interstellar gas, possibly from exploding stars.

Cepheid variables (so called because the first one discovered was in the constellation Cepheus) are stars that periodically vary in brightness. The American astronomer Henrietta Swan Leavitt discovered in 1912 that Cepheids with the same period have the same brightness. This enabled astronomers to figure out the distance from earth to the Cepheids—because if you know how bright something actually is, you can measure how far away it is by how bright it appears.

estimate just how far away it was. (His estimate was 750,000 light years, but modern measurements have almost tripled that.)

Over the next few years, Hubble found many more galaxies scattered about the sky, and, by 1929, was ready to announce an astounding fact about them. They were all—*all*—going away from us.

Hubble found that the spectrographic lines of the elements in these new galaxies he had discovered were shifted more to the red than they should be, and, curiously enough, the farther away they were, the more the shift. Since there's no reason to assume that a heated element emits a different frequency when it's far away, Hubble decided that the red shift was a Doppler effect. This is what makes train whistles seem shriller when the train is heading toward you and deeper when it's going away. Light waves also show a Doppler effect. If a light source is coming toward you, its spectrum is shifted toward the blue; if its headed away from you, the shift is toward the red.

Since there was no known reason that we were particularly unpopular with the rest of the universe, the most logical explanation for this red shift was that the universe itself was expanding in all directions. Picture the surface of a balloon as it's being blown up. Each point on the balloon is getting farther away from every other point. Well, the universe is like that in three—maybe four or more—dimensions.

So it seemed that we live in an expanding universe. There were several possible explanations:

➤ The universe was actually infinite in all directions, a so-called "steady state universe." But new matter or energy was constantly popping into existence from wherever, so everything else had to move over to make room for it, making it look as though the universe was expanding. There was no idea of where this new stuff might be coming from, but everything had to come from somewhere sometime. This theory, developed by British astronomer Fred Hoyle and some others, held that it was doing it all the time rather than all at once.

➤ The universe had a built-in wave form, making it expand and contract continually over some tremendously long period. We just happened to be around while it was expanding.

➤ Since the universe was getting bigger, at some time in the past it had to be much smaller.

The Biggest Bang of All

It seems to be the *Big Bang* theory that best explains the universe we see all around us. It holds that about 15 billion years ago, give or take 5 billion years, the entire universe was the size of a pin head and unimaginably hot—so hot that matter as we know it couldn't exist. All at once, with an incredible explosion, it began expanding. As it expanded, it cooled down, and the basic particles—quarks of different colors and flavors and the like (if you don't know what that means, just accept that they are very elementary particles)—were formed.

Sighting

Curiously enough back in 1917, it was pointed out by a Dutch astronomer named Willem de Sitter that, if Einstein's theory of general relativity was right, the universe was expanding. This went against the prevailing wisdom, and de Sitter was ignored.

Close Encounter

The term "Big Bang" was coined by Fred Hoyle, who thought he was making fun of the idea when he named it. He didn't like the theory at all, preferring his own "steady state" theory (see the preceding section). Hoyle's greatest objection was that if the universe expanded from a tiny point at some time in the past, it would be impossible to know what had happened before that point, or how it came into existence. This was, in Hoyle's opinion, an inelegant way to create a universe.

In the first little while after the Bang—it's hard to say how long, because time didn't have much meaning right then—some of these particles linked to form protons and electrons, which then joined to become hydrogen atoms, the simplest atom of them all (1 proton + 1 electron = 1 hydrogen atom). Gravity pulled these hydrogen atoms together into gaseous clumps. The clumps came together to form bigger clumps, and their increased gravity pulled in more hydrogen. When the globs of hydrogen were big enough, they heated up because of internal pressure (gravity again) until they were so hot that atomic fusion began, and they lighted up and became stars. As the hydrogen is burned, the fusion process creates helium.

Smaller Bangs

Sometime around a billion years after the Big Bang, much of the gas had condensed into stars, and the stars had formed great clumps of galaxies. Some of the stars thus formed were much larger than the average stars around today, possibly because they formed where the gas was a little thicker, and therefore the gravity stronger. These massive stars burned up their stellar fuel quickly, and collapsed in on themselves. For a brief time, these super-stars became unbelievably dense, their interiors unbelievably hot, and then they became what we call "supernovas," blowing up in explosions that dwarfed anything except the Big Bang itself.

In the incredible heat and density of the super-stars right before the explosion, and during the explosion itself, the nuclear fusion would produce elements much denser than helium, including everything on the list a couple of pages back—from oxygen to the .002 percent of "everything else." This matter, ejected from the star when it exploded, was then available to join in the creation of new stars and planets.

A New Generation

Our sun and its family of planets came into being about four and a half billion years ago, about ten billion years after the Big Bang. The sun is a second-generation star, formed from the debris left after the explosion of one or more supernovas. This is why it has planets with iron cores and oceans, and life. Life on earth needs those second-generation elements to exist. The area in space around the sun and other second-generation stars is actually richer in the elements other than hydrogen and helium than the average; they account for about three percent of the mass of the solar system.

If our sun and solar system can form after the universe has been around for ten billion years, then it's clear that all the stars were not formed at once way at the beginning, shortly after the Big Bang. It seems that star formation is a continuous process, new stars coming into existence out of the dust and ashes of the exploding old stars.

We can date the age of the earth, and thus the solar system, thanks to radioactivity. It was chemist Bertram Borden Boltwood back in 1907 who realized that, since the element uranium was radioactive, slowly decaying into lead with a *half-life* of 446 billion years, one could determine the age of a uranium-bearing rock by analyzing just how much of it had already turned to lead.

The three percent of elements other than hydrogen and helium that make up the universe might not seem like much, hardly enough to make the planet earth, but it suffices. The total mass of the solar system (and I steal these figures freely from Isaac Asimov, who knew everything worth knowing) is 343,600 times that of the earth. Three percent of that is enough to make 10,000 earths and have some left over.

When the mass of dust and gas coalesced to form the sun and our solar system, the metals, being denser, tended to gather at the center of the proto-planets. If you want to see the process at work, fill a glass most of the way to the top with salt and then drop some pennies

Contact

The **half-life** of a radioactive element is the amount of time it takes for half of it to decay (change) into another element. If half of it decays in, say, 100 years, then half of the remainder will decay in the next 100 years, so in 200 years three-quarters of the original mass will have changed into something else. And so on.

in it. Put your hand over the top and shake the glass for a long time; the pennies will end up at the bottom. That's because the copper in the pennies is more dense than the salt.

If the planet is too small or too close to the sun, all the atmospheric gasses will eventually drift off because there isn't enough gravity to hold them, or they'll be boiled off by the heat of the sun. If the planet is too far away from the sun, everything will be frozen solid. But if it is in just the right orbit—which we call the *ecosphere* (the zone around a star in which a planet can sustain life)—it will have an atmosphere, and the water will be mostly liquid rather than ice or steam, and life can form.

For the first half-billion years after it was formed, the earth was being bombarded by the leftover bits of rock that hadn't originally clustered to form the planets. We can see the results of such continuous bombardment on the surface of the moon, but the winds and rains and tides of earth have eroded away most of the craters that once pockmarked the earth. That's the advantage of having an atmosphere, that and the fact that it makes life possible.

Eventually, the inner solar system was swept clean—well, pretty clean. We do occasionally still get hit by a pretty big chunk of rock flying in from somewhere in the outer reaches of the solar system. And, pretty much as soon as conditions would allow it, life came into existence on the earth and started its climb toward creatures intelligent and curious enough to wonder where we came from, and where we're headed, and who's on first base.

And we are almost certainly not alone in the universe. As we'll see in the next few chapters, scientists who study such things now believe that where life can form, it probably will.

The Least You Need to Know

➤ If there is life on other planets, it probably looks nothing like us.

➤ The chemical composition of the stars can be told by their spectrum.

➤ The universe came into being with a Big Bang some 15 billion years ago.

➤ Over 99 percent of the matter in the universe is hydrogen and helium.

➤ The heavier elements are created by the explosions of supernovas—the death throes of giant stars.

➤ Our sun and the solar system were formed about four and a half billion years ago.

➤ Life began on earth about as soon as conditions would allow it to.

This Island Earth

The hunt for intelligent life elsewhere in the universe presents several interesting problems for the hunter. Both "life" and "intelligence" are terms that defy easy explanation. There is still no general agreement as to whether viruses are alive, for example; and as for intelligence, I have seen some computer programs that can do a great job of simulating it. Computers now play chess as well as the best human grand master, but they are neither alive nor intelligent.

There are many ways for life to have evolved, and we have experience with only the one chain of evolution that has produced all life on this planet. If there is life elsewhere in the universe, it will almost certainly look and behave quite differently from what we think of as life here on earth.

And I don't mean that they will have blue skin or bulging foreheads or funny ears or be significantly taller or shorter than the average human—I mean *different*! And we have no way to predict what those differences might be.

We know for sure of only one way for life to evolve: the way that produced bacteria and plants and dinosaurs and turtles and us. If we go back far enough—billions of years—we will find the primitive one-celled organisms from which all the rest of earthly life has sprung. In a very real sense, you are related, not just to apes and other mammals, but to every living thing on the planet. That oak tree outside your window is a very distant cousin.

Sighting

In a short story called "Firewater," noted science-fiction writer William Tenn hypothesized a race of aliens who looked kind of like blue lights in soda bottles, and flitted about on their own business, and we couldn't communicate with them or even figure out what they were doing or what they wanted. And anyone who tried to went crazy in the attempt.

Vive la Difference

But if life started with a different set of instructions, even slightly different, somewhere else, what might a billion years of evolution have produced?

Before we take a serious look at the odds of finding extraterrestrial life, and more particularly extraterrestrial intelligent life, and the way we go about the search, we have to agree on just what it is we're looking for. The "extraterrestrial" part is easy: life that did not originate on the planet earth. But the "life" part is not as obvious as it seems. We must agree on what we mean by "life," and how we'll recognize it if and when we run across it somewhere in outer space.

The Living and the Not-So-Living

It sounds silly, doesn't it? Of course you know what life is, or at least you know it when you see it. Living things are distinct from non-living things because they can grow and move (even plants move, not from place to place, but flowers open and close and some plants can turn to face the sun) and reproduce. Oh yeah? Well consider the following:

➤ A potato
➤ An egg
➤ Roast beef
➤ Hair
➤ Your fingernails
➤ A sponge

➤ Salt
➤ A virus
➤ The computer HAL from the movie *2001: A Space Odyssey*
➤ A computer virus

The Potato, the Egg, and the Roast Beef

A potato and an egg are both food for life, energy sources supplied by the potato plant and the chicken for the benefit of the next generation of plant or bird. An unfertilized egg or an unbudded potato does not move or grow or aid in reproduction—yet they are the products of life, and are intimately involved in the life process of their species.

A roast beef was once undoubtedly alive, as part of the body of a steer (usually). And in it's present state, it will soon provide nourishment to another living creature. But it can no longer move or grow or reproduce. Should the designation of life be given to an object that is no longer living?

Hair, Fingernails, and Sponges

Your hair, fingernails, and toenails, although continuously grown by your body, cannot be said to be alive, which is a lucky thing or haircuts and manicures would probably hurt like hell. The shells of clams and oysters likewise, along with cows's and rhinoceros's horns—a rhino's horn is actually a kind of hair—are the products of life, although not alive themselves.

Salt

As many of you will remember from your high school chemistry class, you can grow salt. In an aqueous saline (watery, salty) solution in the right temperature range, it forms a crystal that will continue to grow as long as conditions are favorable. But we can agree that it isn't alive.

HAL

Was the HAL computer featured in Stanley Kubrick's movie *2001: A Space Odyssey* alive? Are intelligent computers alive? The question, of course, is supposing that computers are capable of intelligence, and that is still undecided, with learned books being written on both sides of the issue. But let's assume that sometime—the day after tomorrow or in the far future—we create a computer that passes every test of intelligence we can dream up for it. Is it alive? Will I be committing murder if I unplug it?

These are truly philosophical questions, by which I mean I don't know the answer. A good case could be made either way. Some people say that the computer isn't alive because it wouldn't care whether you turn it off (unless you add self-preservation software to the programming—which might not be a good idea).

But human beings sometimes don't care whether they live or they die. Some people commit suicide. This is not considered a sign of good mental health, but does it mean that they were not truly alive? I don't think so.

Viruses

Viruses, both biological and computer, are a sort of half-life. They are incapable of reproducing on their own, but depend on taking over another organism—a living cell or a computer program—and inducing it to become a little virus factory, churning out copies of the virus and neglecting its own duties. For both biological entities and computer programs, this can mean disaster. But the biological organism may die; the computer program merely needs to be expunged of the virus and rebooted (although it may be very costly in terms of data lost).

205

So are biological viruses alive? Is the glass half full or half empty? It depends on just how narrowly you define life. Are computer viruses alive? No.

What Is Life?

The dictionary defines "life" as the condition of animals or plants that distinguishes them from rocks or dead organisms. Not a big help. The characteristics by which life can be recognized include metabolism, growth, response to stimulus, and reproduction.

Contact

Metabolism is defined as, "those processes necessary to maintain life," which pretty much takes us around in a circle. It includes the processes of growing, such as tissue and muscle building, as well as the processes of breaking down, such as the burning of body sugars to make energy.

Scientists discovered a long time ago that the first thing they must do when they sit down to discuss anything from atoms to black holes is define what they're talking about. It's a good idea for the rest of us, too, and it's *essential* when talking science. If we're discussing bats, and you're thinking baseball while I'm picturing flying mammals, we have the start of a good comedy routine, but we probably won't come to any meaningful conclusions. This is why scientists have a specific, often Latin, name for almost everything. You may call them tomatoes while I insist they're love apples; but if we both agree we're talking about *Lycopersicum esculenium*, we can communicate.

So when we speculate in a serious, scientific manner about the possibility of life elsewhere in the universe, we're presented with the interesting problem of defining just what we're talking about. What is life? How will we know it when we see it? How did it get started on earth, and how might it get started elsewhere?

It Just Grew

It wasn't so long ago that people, even highly intelligent and greatly learned people, believed that life could be created from non-life, a process called *spontaneous generation*, and that it was happening all the time. If there was a God and he created life, the reasoning went, presumably he could do it again and again whenever he felt like it. It was generally believed that a horsehair kept in a bottle of water could turn into a worm. Maggots were thought to be spontaneously generated in rotting meat, and then mysteriously turned into flies.

While spontaneous generation was believed to be the way life was created, there was no reason to think that life couldn't exist anywhere. The need for air and water was recognized, but if there was air and water on earth, why wouldn't there be air and water everywhere else as well?

It wasn't until 1864 that Louis Pasteur put the theory of spontaneous generation to rest by showing that if a meat broth is heated to kill any microbes in it, and sealed off in some way so that no new microbes can get to it, it will stay free of life. Even microbes need other microbes to bring them into existence.

Close Encounter

Pasteur's experiments with meat broth led to pasteurization, the process of making milk safe and microbe-free without destroying the flavor by heating it to 145 degrees Fahrenheit for 20 minutes. In addition to this boon for babies, Pasteur also improved the lives of their parents by discovering how the fermentation of beer happened, giving brewers some control over their product for the first time. He also developed the first effective treatment for rabies, a disease that is invariably fatal unless treated.

But if life can only spring from other life, how did it begin? Which came first, the chicken or the egg? And where did *it* come from?

Your Father's an Ape

In 1859, Charles Darwin revealed his theory of evolution in a book called *On the Origin of Species by Means of Natural Selection*. It created quite a stir. But the theory provided an answer for part of the question of where chickens—and humans—come from. To greatly simplify a complex theory, Darwin showed that simple forms of life could, if given enough time, evolve into more complex ones, and one species could over time diverge into two or more distinct species.

The process is actually well understood. We do it all the time with cattle, horses, and dogs. There are, at last count, 143 breeds of dog recognized by the American Kennel Club, and they are all descended from one ancestor. But that is done by deliberate selection; you only allow Lady Byrenne Von Dusselpecker Pickwick, your prize Peke, to roll in the hay with another grand master Pekinese, keeping the bloodline pure. What Darwin showed is that there is a natural process of selection that encourages species to evolve over time—a long time, but there has been plenty of time available since the world began.

At the Beginning

So we know, at least in general principle, how primitive one-celled life grows in complexity to become trees, frogs, and us. But where, and how, did it all begin?

Contact

The word **organic** in this sense means formed from the same complex carbon compounds that are produced by the processes of life. Some of them, such as various amino acids (the basis for the proteins that are the building blocks of life), have been shown to be produced by natural processes.

Well, frankly, nobody knows. Until quite recently, it was thought that after the earth was formed, it was a sterile world for several billion years. It was believed that for a long while natural processes did this-and-that, creating various *organic* substances from the materials at hand, but not quite succeeding in bringing forth life. Then finally, by some cosmic accident, or by the hand of God (or, if you prefer, by the hands of the gods or the tentacle of Cthulhu), the first biological organism appeared.

What this would mean, or at least strongly imply, is that the appearance of life on a planet was not inevitable. If earth could have gone lifeless for half of its existence, then other planets, even if placed in their equivalent to earth's favorable orbit around their home star, might continue for much longer, or indefinitely, without producing living organisms.

It's in the Chert

The story has recently been rewritten to have a happier ending, if you're a fan of life. In the 1950s, *paleontologists* Elso Barghoorn and Stanley Taylor decided to look for

Contact

Paleontologists are people who study fossils, which are the remains, in whatever form, of long dead things that were once alive.

fossils in beds of chert, which is a rock made of silicon dioxide. Nobody had looked there before because most chert is formed by volcanic action, and the heat would burn up any living thing unfortunate enough to land on it. But some chert is formed in the ocean and, Barghoorn and Taylor realized, would be perfect for preserving tiny fossils.

It was. Fossil bacteria has now been found in rocks dating back more than 3 1/2 billion years. This is within half a billion years of the time the earth itself was formed and started cooling down. In geologic terms, a mere moment.

Just Add Water, Zap, and Stir

This suggested strongly to scientists like Carl Sagan, Isaac Asimov, and others that, given the least opportunity—a planet the right distance from the sun, sufficient water, carbon, and other chemicals—life would occur. It might never get past the one-celled critter stage, since it seems to have taken quite a while to do that here on earth, but quite a variety of single-celled organisms would probably evolve.

Way back in 1951, Melvin Calvin, a chemist at the University of California at Berkeley, and some of his colleagues filled a flask with a mixture of carbon dioxide, hydrogen, and water and sealed it. Then they shot a burst of homemade cosmic rays through the flask (using the university's 60-inch *cyclotron*).

When they unsealed the flask and analyzed the contents, they found that a variety of organic molecules, namely formic acid, glycolic acid, and formaldehyde, had been created. It was proof that organic compounds could be created from inorganic substances and the right kind of energy.

A year later, chemists Harold Urey and Stanley Lloyd Miller at the University of Chicago added sterilized water to their apparatus, and topped it off with an "atmosphere" of hydrogen, ammonia, and methane. This was a sort of primitive earth in micro-miniature, duplicating the conditions on earth as they might have been 4 or 5 billion years ago, before life appeared. They circulated the mixture past an electric spark for a week, to simulate the effects of lightning, and then uncorked it to see what had happened. They found a variety of organic molecules, including many different amino acids, which are the basic constituents of proteins— and proteins are what all life that we know of is made up of.

Nobody has yet (as far as I know) achieved the next step—actually creating life in the laboratory— except in science-fiction movies. But experiments have suggested various ways in which it could have happened, in tidal flats or clay sediment or volcanic vents on the ocean's bottom. We can't be sure just which environment created the first life on earth. Life is probably not being created today because the nutrient soup from which it would spring would be immediately eaten by already-living microbes.

Panspermia

In his book, *A World in the Making* (1908), a Swedish chemist named Svante August Arrhenius suggested that life is universal. But not by separate creations on a myriad of life-supporting planets, but with one origin, and then spread through the universe by bacterial spores floating through space for millions of years until they land on a suitable

Contact

The **cyclotron** was developed by physicist Ernest Lawrence in 1930. It accelerates atomic particles (usually protons) around a circular course, guiding them with powerful magnets, until they achieve high speed and energy, and then it smashes them into a target. It is sometimes called an "atom smasher."

Sighting

In 1650, Bishop James Ussher determined, based on analysis of the "begats" in the Bible, that the universe was created in the year 4004 B.C. (Four years later, theologian John Lightfoot refined that further to 9:15 in the morning of 26 October 4004 B.C.—a Wednesday). If you choose to believe the bishop, I can only suggest that God must have planted many false clues such as the fossil record and the radioactive decay of uranium and the movement of the continents in an attempt to convince us otherwise. Perhaps it would be an act of politeness and religious faith to pretend to believe what God obviously wants us to believe.

planet. Then the process of evolution can start on the colonized planet, leading finally to intelligent beings. This would make every living thing in the entire universe a distant relative.

The theory, called *panspermia*, has some appeal, and has been modified and improved on over the years. But it has a few fatal flaws: The universe is so huge, and the distances are so vast, that untold billions of these spores would have to begin traveling through space every year at reasonably high speeds to accomplish their mission. And they would all be killed by cosmic radiation before they had traveled too many million miles. And no mechanism for starting these spores on their way has been suggested.

And in any case, it begs the question. Life would still have to have started somewhere.

We Have Met the Garbage and It Is Us

Biologists Francis Crick and Leslie Orgel have suggested that the spreading might have been done purposefully. The life-spores might have been placed in robot spacecraft programmed to hunt for suitable planets and plant the seeds of life. They call this "directed panspermia."

Close Encounter

In 1953, Francis Crick and his associate James Watson developed the idea that DNA—deoxyribonucleic acid, the material that makes up our chromosomes—is arranged in a double helix—like two spiral staircases twined around each other—and that it is the splitting apart of this double helix, with each half making a duplicate copy of the other half, that allows the passing of genetic information on to new cells (and to the next generation). For this insight, Crick and Watson and Maurice Wilkins, a New Zealand physicist who aided them, shared a Nobel Prize in 1962.

Other people, such as Cornell astronomer Thomas Gold, have suggested that an alien spaceship might have landed on earth before life developed, perhaps to refuel, or to camp surrounded by the unspoiled beauty of a pristine planet before it is despoiled by life. And perhaps they left their garbage behind, and we are descended from the bacteria in that garbage.

The preceding argument holds for these theories as well. Life had to originate somewhere, and the question of how that happened is not answered merely by moving the point of origin of life to somewhere else.

As We Know It

As I've said before, the one thing almost all scientists agree on is this: Whatever alien life exists on whatever distant planets, it won't look like us. If that giant asteroid hadn't hit the earth 35 million years ago, and the dinosaurs had opted to go for intelligence instead of mere bulk, then a large lizard might be typing these words and pondering these problems. And he/she/it might have done it 34 million years earlier.

There are a couple of other possibilities for intelligent life here on earth besides humans and our close cousins the chimpanzees and gorillas. One theory of why the beings on the UFOs have not communicated with us yet is that they're actually here to talk to the porpoises and dolphins and orcas.

And, if we weren't around, elephants might develop a civilization of their own in a few hundred thousand years—the wheel of evolution turns very slowly except when it's shaken up by something like a great asteroid hitting the planet.

Carbon Chauvinists

Then there is the possibility that, not only won't an intelligent alien look at all like us, it might not even be made of the same stuff. We are made of (among other things) proteins built up from amino acids, made up of carbon, nitrogen, oxygen, hydrogen, and sulfur. Biologists tend to think of life as carbon-based, since almost all of the life processes—respiration, energy production, growth, and replication—intimately utilize a chemical reaction involving a carbon compound.

And yet, given a sufficiently different starting point, couldn't another entire biological chemistry have come into being—using, perhaps, sulfur or silicon?

When we manage to get out into the universe and meet the beings already there, perhaps far advanced compared to our civilization, they may be so alien from us that we can't even breath the same air. Water might be a deadly poison, and they might freeze to death at temperatures lower than the melting point of lead.

Perhaps some gas cloud in interstellar space, awash in radiation from a nearby star cluster, has developed a wispy sort of life. Perhaps this life has over the aeons developed an awareness and intelligence. And perhaps it communicates by radio waves the way we communicate by sound waves. What will it think of our radio broadcasts when it hears them? What sort of reply will we get? And have we enough in common beyond the bare fact of intelligence to be able to communicate and share information?

The discovery of extraterrestrial life could answer some of mankind's oldest questions, and show us how we relate to the universe and how meaningful our existence is. It will also certainly pose many questions that we cannot foresee and change our future in ways we cannot imagine.

The Least You Need to Know

➤ The difference between life and non-life is not always obvious.

➤ Louis Pasteur proved that life could not begin spontaneously.

➤ Charles Darwin showed how higher forms of life evolved from the lower forms.

➤ As several chemists have shown, given the right conditions, and a few million years to work, a simple life form might emerge from the primal soup.

➤ The evolution of life on other worlds will almost certainly follow a completely different path from life on earth.

Life Around the Sun

The first time that we here on earth reached out to touch another world was on Monday, 10 January 1946. Two weeks later, the feat was made public; the headline in the *New York Herald Tribune* announced that "Radar Pushes Into New Frontier of Interplanetary Space."

The United States Army Signal Corps aimed a radar pulse at the moon from a laboratory in Belmar, New Jersey. The pulse bounced off the surface of the moon and was received back in New Jersey, completing a round trip of 480,000 miles in two and a half seconds.

Twenty-three years later, on 16 July 1969, much sooner than anyone would have guessed even a decade before, the first humans landed on the moon. By then we were pretty sure no moon men would greet them. The rest of the solar system, however, was still filled with possibility.

As the decades pass and our unmanned probes explore the solar system, the possibility becomes more and more remote. Of the planets we first looked to for life, Venus and Mars, one is too hot for anything we can imagine to live on it, the other is too dry and cold and airless for anything but the most primitive microbes. To find even primitive microbes, however, would be the most exciting discovery since Columbus failed to discover a quick route to Asia.

But now, curiously, worlds that we had thought to be frozen, barren, and lifeless turn out, on closer inspection, to have possibilities.

The Moon

The moon was, of course, the first place the fabulists of the past thought of placing extraterrestrial life in their stories. It was large, it was close, and it seemed comparatively easy to get to. The Greek satirist Lucian (ca. 120–200 A.D.), in his *True History*,

Sighting

Facts about the moon:
Mean distance from the earth:
238,855 miles (384,400 km)
Diameter at the equator: 2,160 miles
(3,476 km)
Rotation period around the earth:
27.3 days

had his hero ride to the moon on a whirlwind. Another hero flew there on wings made from bird feathers. (Several writers had their heroes get to the moon in a dream, but that's cheating and we won't count them.) Cyrano de Bergerac had his hero collect bottles of dew; when the dew rose in the morning, so did the character, and thus he was drawn up to the moon. Another fictional journey to the moon had Cyrano's hero in a basket pulled by swans. In yet another he used a rocket.

Life on the moon wasn't envisioned as being particularly different from that on earth. In "The Elephant in the Moon," a satirical poem, Samuel Butler (1612–1680)— not the Samuel Butler who wrote *The Way of All Flesh*; he came 200 years later—described living on the moon as follows:

Th' inhabitants of the Moon
Who, when the Sun shines hot at Noon,
Do live in Cellars underground
Of eight miles deep and eighty round,
(In which at once they fortify
Against the Sun and th'Enemy)
Which they count Towns and Cities there,
Because their People's civiler
Than those rude Peasants, that are found
To live upon the upper Ground,
Call'd Privolvans, with whom they are
Perpetually in open war.

Heavy stuff, huh?

Today, we know that there is no life on the moon. I suppose I should hedge that a little, so I will. To date, scientists examining the rocks brought back from the moon and the close-up studies done by various unmanned and manned spacecraft orbiting the moon have found no signs of life. It is possible that millions of years ago, before the moon lost what atmosphere it had, some sort of life developed. There probably wasn't enough time, however, and besides, if any life developed, it is long deceased.

Let me demonstrate why it's necessary to not state more than you know when discussing planetary science and the possibility of life: Until last week I would have written that the moon has no atmosphere and no water, both being necessary for life to exist, or at least to prosper. All the text books will tell you so.

Well, all the text books will have major changes in the chapter on the moon in their next editions. As of last week (the first week in September, 1998), we now know that the moon does have water. Not a lot by earth standards, but big enough to fill a couple of pretty good-sized lakes. The estimate is that there is enough water at each pole to fill a lake ten miles on a side to a depth of about 50 feet. This water is frozen and hidden under the surface in various spots around the moon. It was detected by an instrument called a *neutron spectrometer* aboard the Lunar Prospector, an unmanned spacecraft now in orbit around the moon. The best guess is that it is a result of comets, which are mostly water, hitting the moon, digging in, and then getting covered over as the surface dirt falls back down.

Contact

A **neutron spectrometer** detects and measures neutron emission, in this case from the hydrogen atoms in the moon water.

This is good news for future visitors to our companion in space; now we know that they won't have to bring their own water, air, or fuel to power the trip back to earth. Water can be decomposed to hydrogen and oxygen. The oxygen can be breathed, and the hydrogen can be burned (with the oxygen) in a rocket motor. And, best of all, the waste product of the burning is water, which will fall back onto the moon to be used again.

The Sun

The sun, as we all know, is not a planet and cannot be the home to any sort of life we know of. The heat would blast apart any organic compounds and most compounds of *any* sort. But the light and heat of the sun, at a suitable distance, are what make life on this planet possible. If we find microbial life on Mars, it, too, will have the sun to thank.

Sighting

Facts about the sun:
Mean distance from earth: 93,000,000 miles (149,600,000 km)(Also known as 1 astronomical unit [au])
Radius: 432,474 miles (696,000 km)

Mercury

The closest planet to the sun, Mercury would have long ago lost any atmosphere it started with due to its constant baking in the sun's heat. This was verified in 1974/75 when the Mariner 10 spacecraft got a close-up look on three different passes. For a long time, scientists thought that Mercury always presented the same face to the sun as the moon does to earth. This would have meant that there might be some atmosphere, or even water, frozen on the perpetually dark side away from the sun. We now know, however, that Mercury does rotate, although very slowly. Its day is 58.6 earth days long, which makes a Mercurial year about one and a half Mercurial days long.

Sighting

Facts about Mercury:
Mean distance from the sun:
36,000,000 miles (58,000,000 km)
(0.4 au)
Diameter at the equator: 3,030 miles
(4,876 km)
Length of year: 88 earth days
Length of day: 59 earth days

Venus

For most of this century, the planet Venus was thought to be a prime possibility for being another home for life in our solar system. Mercury is about the same size as the earth. It's closer to the sun, but not too close, and the heavy cloud cover detected by our telescopes seemed to be a good sign that it had water—probably a lot of water. With all those clouds, it seemed that much of the planet must have a hot and steamy atmosphere. But what the planet actually looked liked under the perpetual bank of clouds—whether it was one vast ocean or there were continents and islands poking up through all that water—was a mystery. Many science-fiction stories were written about the jungles of Venus or the great underwater civilization in the Venusian world-ocean.

But in 1956, a team of radio astronomers succeeded in isolating radio waves from Venus. Every celestial body with internal heat radiates electromagnetic energy. The frequency of this energy is somewhere between the infrared and x-rays, depending on the internal temperature of the body. The radio waves picked up from Venus showed that the surface of the planet was much hotter than anyone thought. On 14 December 1962, the American unmanned spacecraft Mariner 2 passed close enough by Venus to get a good reading of its temperature. To be sure, the Soviet Venus probes Venura 4 (12 June 1967), Venura 5 (16 May 1969) and Venura 6 (17 May 1969), which dropped through the Venusian atmosphere and took temperature readings on the way down, confirmed the earlier findings.

Sighting

Facts about Venus:
Mean distance from the sun:
67,000,000 miles (108,000,000 km)
(0.72 au)
Diameter at the equator: 7,520 miles
(12,102 km)
Length of year: 225 earth days
Length of day: 244 earth days

The atmosphere of Venus is about 95 times as dense as the earth's, and it's mostly (95 percent) carbon dioxide. This creates the ultimate greenhouse effect, trapping all the sun's energy that makes it through the cloud bank. The surface temperature of Venus is about 480° C (900° F), which is hot enough to melt lead. And those clouds that first caused astronomers to think Venus must be a water planet seem to be made up largely of sulfuric acid.

It might be possible to turn Venus into a livable planet when we get technically advanced enough to think about such things. We would probably begin by introducing some single-celled plants into Venus's atmosphere. Plants thrive on carbon dioxide, and their waste product is oxygen. If we do it right, after a few hundred years the atmosphere of Venus will be much lower in carbon dioxide, which will reduce the greenhouse effect and lower the surface temperature. And the atmosphere will have enough oxygen in it for animals to breathe. Figuring out what to do next and in what order would be a good extra-credit project for your science class.

The computer game SimLife lets you play these sorts of games, and is good practice for anyone who sees exobiology as a possible career path.

Earth

We are reasonably sure that there is intelligent life on earth. How it originated, however, is still one of the great unanswered questions. Many possibilities are being investigated (to the extent that anyone can investigate something that happened four and a half billion years ago). One interesting consideration is that amino acids, the most basic building blocks of life, have been found in meteorites that have fallen to earth from outer space. This could mean that life, or the ability to form life, is ubiquitous, occurring everywhere it has a chance. Or it could mean that all life began somewhere else in the vastness of space, and that the rest of the universe has been seeded from this original creation.

Sighting

Facts about Earth:
Mean distance from the sun: 93,000,000 miles (150,000,000 km)(1.0 au)
Diameter at the equator: 7,926 miles (12,756 km)
Length of year: 365.256 days
Length of day: 24 hours

Mars

Mars has been our great hope for finding life off earth in the solar system. The finding of canals on Mars (see Chapter 3) was so exciting to those who read about it, which was just about everyone who could read, because the canals seemed to have been built by intelligent beings. That was both hopeful and scary. Hopeful because Mars was believed to be much older than the earth—until recently, the best theories of the

Sighting

Facts about Mars:
Mean distance from the sun:
141,540,000 miles (227,786,000 km) (1.52 au)
Diameter at the equator: 4,222 miles (6,794 km)
Length of year: 687 earth days
Length of day: 24 hours, 37 minutes

creation of the solar system had the planets being formed from the outside in—and therefore the Martian were an ancient race and could teach us a lot, such as how to live in peace and harmony. Scary because they might not be peaceful and harmonious; if Mars was an old, dying planet, the Martians might be jealous of our oceans and atmosphere. They might want to either conquer us or just kill us off.

Mars, however, does not have canals. They seem to have been an artifact of the refracting telescopes that 19th-century observers used to stare at the planet, or maybe just an effect of staring too long at a distant, fuzzy point of reddish light. Mars does have ice caps at the poles, and dust storms, and surface creases that could be ancient river beds that dried up millennia ago.

There is, as yet, no definite answer whether there is, or ever was, life on Mars. The various missions to Mars have landed on the surface, taken wonderful pictures, and searched for life. None has yet been found, but some of the results were less than clear, so the possibility has not been ruled out.

In March 1998, NASA scientists announced they thought they had found signs of ancient life on a couple of meteorites discovered in Antarctica and believed to have originated on Mars. It is possible that a comet, for example, hitting Mars might throw up debris hard and high enough for it to escape Mars gravity and eventually end up on earth as a meteor. And these rocks seem to have the right chemical composition to be from Mars. The question is: Are the tiny patterns found in the rock really signs of microscopic life? Some noted scientists say yes, others say no. The argument continues.

Several of the Viking orbiter photographs taken in 1975 showed what seemed to be a giant stone face on Mars. If it is a face, it is staring straight out at the universe. Recently, the area has been re-photographed. The new pictures have convinced most people that the "face" is a result of chance weathering of the rock, even as it convinced other people that it is definitely a sculptured face.

It seems odd to me that anyone would construct a stone face to stare straight up at the sky, a position from which few on the ground could even tell what it is. Maybe it was to welcome visiting spacecraft.

Jupiter

We do not understand the processes of life well enough to state positively that there is no life on Jupiter, but there is certainly no life of the sort we find on earth. Jupiter is a gas giant, one of four in the solar system, and by far the largest. (The others are Saturn, Uranus, and Neptune.) The gas that makes up the giant is mostly hydrogen, with a touch of helium and trace amounts of methane, ammonia, and a few other chemicals in its outer atmosphere. Astrophysicists, the people that study how stars work, say that if Jupiter were 100 times larger, the pressure and temperature at its center would be high enough to start nuclear fusion, and our solar system would have two suns.

Jupiter's Children

Jupiter has an extensive collection of moons: 16 at last count and still growing. Of these, the four largest are known as the "Galilean satellites," because they were first discovered by Galileo when he peered at Jupiter through his telescope in 1610. They are large enough to be planets on their own if they were circling the sun directly. The largest, Ganymede, is larger than the planet Mercury, and the other three, Callisto, Europa, and Io, are not much smaller. There is an outside chance—not enough to bet the farm, but maybe enough to wager a couple of haystacks—that one or more of the Galilean satellites is home to life of its own.

Sighting

Facts about Jupiter:
Mean distance from the sun: 483,000,000 miles (777,300,000 km) (5.19 au)
Diameter at the equator: 88,640 miles (142,652 km)
Length of year: 11.9 earth years
Length of day: 9 hours, 50 minutes

Callisto

The Galileo spacecraft that flew by Callisto in 1997 found signs in the magnetic signature of the fourth largest of Jupiter's moons that somewhere under its rocky surface, Callisto has an ocean of liquid saltwater. The possibility for life on Jupiter's moons looks promising. Scientists are not sure why the water would be liquid at Callisto's distance from the sun, but there are two main possibilities: Callisto may have a hot core like the earth, or the tidal effects from Jupiter and the other Galilean moons may generate heat.

Europa

The Galileo spacecraft flew within a couple of hundred of miles of Europa in 1997 and took close-up pictures of its surface. Geologists studying the pictures think that maybe they have found signs of a great ocean under Europa's rocky surface. The surface itself seems to be mostly ice, and the occasional crater holes are mostly filled in and smooth, which seems to indicate that an upwelling of liquid water from under the ice filled in the crater.

NASA is now thinking of designing a Europa-lander to burrow through the surface layer of ice to where the liquid water is and test it for life. The lander will be able to take pictures and send them back, probably by way of an orbiting unmanned spaceship, so that we can see for ourselves what it looks like down in the ice-locked seas of Europa. Perhaps the first thing we'll see is a Europan sea monster staring back.

Saturn

Saturn, with its system of rings belting the equator, is probably the most beautiful sight in the solar system. It is a gas giant, much like Jupiter but not quite as gigantic.

Sighting

Facts about Saturn:

Mean distance from the sun: 886,000,000 miles (1,426,000,000 km) (9.53 au)

Diameter at the equator: 74,500 miles (124,724 km)

Length of year: 29.5 earth years

Length of day: 10 hours, 39 minutes

Titan is Saturn's largest moon, the second largest in the solar system (Jupiter's Ganymede beats it), and one of the most interesting. With a diameter of 3,200 miles (5,150 km), Titan is larger than the planet Mercury and, unlike Mercury, has an atmosphere.

Titan's atmosphere is mostly nitrogen (as is earth's, coincidentally), with a smattering of methane and other hydrocarbons. A thick haze, which extends about 200 miles from the surface, covers Titan and makes it hard to see what's underneath. The surface must be too cold for liquid water, but there may be oceans of liquid methane.

The building blocks of life exist on Titan, but as far as we know Titan is too cold for the life processes to have started. We might be wrong, however. There may be pathways to the creation of life available to the natural processes on the surface of Titan. If we ever go to explore, we just might find something alive waiting for us.

The Outer Planets

The gas giants Uranus and Neptune are out past Saturn and the small, rocky planet Pluto. Pluto is usually the ninth planet out from the sun, but its orbit is so erratic that at times—and this is one of them—it's actually closer to the sun than Neptune. At the moment, it is the eighth planet. It will be the ninth planet again for a couple of hundred years beginning in 1999.

There is no reason to believe that the search for life will find anything rewarding at or around any of these outer planets, but their very distance means we don't know that much about them yet.

The Nemesis Theory

There is a theory that the sun has a dark companion star—a massive star-like object whose atomic fires have burned out or for some reason never ignited—on a great elliptical orbit that takes it out into the vastness of space for 26 million years, and then swings it back close to the sun. This star, called "Nemesis" after the Greek goddess of retribution, would upset the Oort cloud, a thick cloud of comets possibly orbiting at a great distance beyond the planets, as it came close. This would cause a hailstorm of comets to head toward the sun.

If one of these massive comets hits the earth, it would cause great tidal waves that could inundate continents, and raise a cloud of dust that would circle the earth and cut off sunlight for decades. In the resulting cold nothing could grow, and many animals, including complete species, would die of starvation.

The idea that comets stirred up by Nemesis periodically hit the earth is being offered as a possible explanation for the mass extinctions of entire species that have occurred in the past. They do seem to happen regularly every 26 million years or so. Some are, so to speak, more "mass" than others, and we seem to have been missed by comets big enough to cause major disruption on a couple of the cycles.

The major extinctions, which wiped out much of the life on earth and caused major species to go extinct, occurred at the end of the Cambrian Period, about 500 million years ago; at the end of the Devonian Period, about 340 million years ago; and at the end of the Permian period, about 225 million years ago. The last such extinction, which occurred at the end of the Cretaceous Period, about 65 million years ago, wiped out the dinosaurs.

The Least You Need to Know

➤ Enough water has recently been discovered on the moon to make it much easier for us to establish a base there—or an amusement park.

➤ The cloud cover over Venus was long thought to indicate a watery world, but it turns out the atmosphere is straight carbon dioxide, the clouds are sulfuric acid, and the surface temperature is hot enough to melt lead.

➤ Mars has no canals, and there is great doubt whether there is or ever was any life there. A Martian rock discovered here on earth, however, may show signs of bacterial life.

➤ There is a great stone face on Mars. Is it real or simply the result of man's tendency to see faces in everything?

➤ There may well be oceans, and possibly life in the oceans, under the surface ice of Europa and Callisto, two of Jupiter's satellites.

➤ Titan, Saturn's large moon, has a nitrogen atmosphere through which we cannot see.

➤ Uranus, Neptune, and Pluto are so far from the sun that there is little possibility of life as we know it.

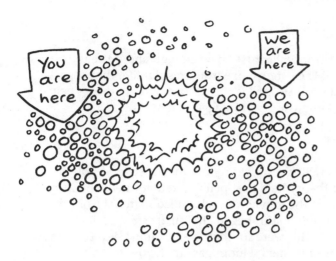

Chapter 22

Life Far Away

In This Chapter

➤ Planets circling distant stars

➤ Detecting a wobble that means there's a planet

➤ The ecosphere

➤ The life equation

The universe is gigantic, which is a good thing. Since that's all there is, it's lucky that there's so much of it.

Don't ask what happens when you reach the end of the universe, because it doesn't work that way. According to Einstein, and he's been right so far, the universe is curved in four dimensions the way the surface of the earth is curved in three. Although the earth appears to be flat when you're standing on it, if you draw a perfectly straight line anywhere on the earth's surface you'll eventually (after about 24,902 miles) come back to where you started. Likewise, if you go in a perfectly straight line out into the universe, you'll eventually end up back where you started. It's the length of that hypothetical line that determines the size of the universe. As the universe expands (see Chapter 19), the line will take longer to meet itself.

But in all that vastness of space, among the billions of galaxies each with its billions of stars, are there any other planets that are home to intelligent life?

Quite probably. But we earthlings haven't always thought so.

Rarer Than Diamonds

From the late 19th century, when astronomers first knew enough about the universe to begin to seriously consider the possible existence of extraterrestrial life, they were very pessimistic about there being any. Life, it seemed, depends on so many things being just right that the odds of finding it elsewhere were staggeringly small.

Planets Needed

First of all, there has to be a planet circling a star, and nobody understood how stars came to have planets. One popular theory held that planets were formed when two stars passed so close to each other that the gravity of each pulled material from the other and, as they separated again, the star stuff began circling its star, gradually cooling and coalescing into planets. If this were so, then planets must be a truly rare occurrence throughout the universe since stars seldom pass that close to each other.

Water Must Be a Liquid

Then one of the star's planets had to be in an orbit that approximated earth's orbit around the sun as far as the amount of energy it received: too much closer and the planet would fry; too much farther out and it would freeze. The critical temperatures were the boiling and freezing points of water, since as far as we know all life needs liquid water to exist. Water is a liquid from a temperature of 0 degrees Celsius (32 degrees Fahrenheit) to 100 degrees Celsius (212 degrees Fahrenheit). If the surface temperature over most of a planet does not fall between these two numbers for a substantial part of its year, all the water will either freeze solid or remain gaseous. And with the number of possible orbits, from nearer to the sun than Mercury to farther away than Pluto, being at just the right distance seemed very unlikely.

Contact

The range of orbits around a star that are suitable for a life-bearing planet is known as that star's **ecosphere**.

There were also great questions associated with the idea of creating life. Since no one had any idea of how life came into being, it was assumed to be very difficult. After all, as far as we know, it isn't happening any more on earth. Life may be evolving, but no new forms of life are being created from scratch. (Refresh your memory of life on earth in Chapter 20.)

Every Star a Mother

As we discovered more about stellar processes this view changed. Today most scientists believe that planets are created along with the star they circle, and as part of the same process. Thus it seems probable that most stars have planets. We now have evidence that several nearby stars have planets. This evidence is indirect, but powerful.

The description of any star as being "nearby" is a relative one. All stars but our own sun can be considered distant. The nearest star to our solar system, *Alpha Centauri*, is 4.3 light years away. (Light, traveling at 186,282 miles *per second*, takes eight minutes and 20 seconds to travel the 93 million miles from our sun to earth, but it takes four years and four months to travel the more than 25 trillion miles from Alpha Centauri to here.) Planets circling any star but our own cannot be seen directly, as they do not shine on their own but merely reflect the light of their sun. And, being (relatively) so close to their sun and so far away from us, its light drowns out their reflected light.

Close Encounter

Alpha Centauri, the brightest star in the constellation *Centaurus*, the Centaur, (hence the "Alpha"), is the third-brightest star in the sky, but it can be seen only from the southern hemisphere. Thomas Henderson, a British astronomer, was the first to measure its distance from earth from his observatory in Cape Town, South Africa in the 1830s. It turns out that Alpha Centauri is actually a three-star system, with two stars orbiting each other fairly closely and a third, smaller star orbiting the other two at some distance. This third star, called *Proxima Centauri* is the one that approaches us most closely; during part of its orbit, it is as close as 4.2 light years.

Hand Me That Spectroscope

These distant planets were discovered by a clever use of the spectroscopic analysis of the light from certain stars. It involved considerations of the effect of the pull of gravity a planet would exert on its star, and of the Doppler effect of the light shining from that star. (Refer to Chapter 19 for a discussion of spectroscopy and the Doppler effect.)

The Dance of the Planets

Astronomers who were examining a star to see if it might have planets would keep a record of the spectrum of that star to see if it changed over a period of time. By looking at one of the characteristic absorption lines—say that of iron—to see how it was shifted by the Doppler effect, they could tell what direction the star was going. If it was shifted toward the red, the star was headed away from us. If it was moved toward the blue, then the star was approaching.

But if it alternated, into the red for some weeks or months and then toward the blue for the same length of time, and then red, and blue, back and forth as if the star were dancing in place, then something had to be causing that dance.

The most logical cause was the pull of gravity of one or more planets circling the star. As a planet swings around a star, the star wobbles just a bit toward the planet. It was that tell-tale wobble that made the apparent spectrum swing from red to blue. Next time you jump out of an airplane reflect that, just as the earth is pulling you toward it, you are likewise pulling the earth. You are moving a lot farther and faster toward the earth than it is toward you, but the attraction is mutual.

Even Smaller Wobbles

At the moment, the smallest planet that the wobble technique can detect is somewhat larger than Jupiter, which is over 300 times the mass of the earth. Finding more Jupiters is fascinating, but what astronomers interested in the question of extraterrestrial life really want to know is whether there are more earths. We don't know whether life can exist on Jupiter, but we think not. But we have very good evidence that life can exist on earth.

A new instrument has been developed by astronomers at the United States Naval Observatory that should make it possible to detect even earth-size planets circling distant stars. Called the Multi-Channel Fourier Transform Spectrometer (mFTS), it uses a process called interferometry to detect even smaller wobbles in a star, as would be produced by planets as tiny as the earth.

And, as part of a project called The Exploration of Neighboring Planetary systems (ExNPS) Study, NASA plans to launch the Terrestrial Planet Finder (TPF), which would be stationed out beyond the orbit of Jupiter in the darkest part of the solar system, and search for the faintest wobbles in stars that could establish the existence of earth-type planets.

Out of the Dust

In addition to investigating the wobble of the stars, new and more sensitive telescopes and imaging techniques now make it possible to detect the presence of a dust cloud—actually more like a dust disc—around a nearby star. A disc of cold dust circling a star is believed to be a sign that the star might have planets, the dust being left over from the formation of those planets.

Such discs have been found around the stars *Vega* and *Fomalhaut*, and a star named *Epsilon Eridani*, which is about the same size as our sun and only 10.2 light years away. Even more interesting is the discovery that these discs are donut-shaped, with an area clear of dust about the size of our solar system between the inner edge of the disc and the star.

Astronomers hypothesize that the reason for this is that the star does have a family of planets, and these planets are sweeping up the dust as they orbit around the star.

There are more than 40 stars that we now are pretty sure have planets. And since astronomers haven't had a chance to check out many more than that yet, it seems that having a retinue of planets is a fairly common condition for a star. Most of the ones that have been found are the size of Jupiter, or larger, but that's because really large planets are much easier to detect.

Size Does Matter

So it seems as though planets are ubiquitous, but astronomers still have to determine what percent of them might have the necessary conditions for creating and sustaining life.

For life to come into existence on a planet, the star it circles can't be too big or too small. If the star is too big, then its lifetime will be too short—really big stars burn themselves out in a billion years or so, hardly enough time for life to get beyond the stage of primitive bacteria. If the star is too small, the ecosphere, the range of orbits where water on the planet would be liquid, would be so small as to make it unlikely for a planet to be in it.

Sighting

Remember, we're talking about life *as we know it*—based on carbon compounds. See Chapter 19 for other possibilities.

The Right Stuff

Now that we have found a star with the right lifetime, and a planet at the right distance, we have to make sure that the ingredients for life are present. And for that we need a second- or third-generation star. First-generation stars, born shortly after the great expansion of the universe we call the Big Bang are almost entirely made of hydrogen and helium (as is explained in Chapter 19). That's all that was around then. Most of the other elements are created when a star ends its life by blowing itself up, becoming what we call a nova. That creates enough heat and pressure to cause the light elements to fuse into the heavier elements, like carbon, oxygen and iron, that we need for life.

This process is still going on; stars are reaching the end of their lives and blowing up on a regular basis, adding to the supply of heavier elements.

Sighting

Remember that, even after the novae have done their work, 99 percent of the universe is still hydrogen and helium (see Chapter 19). Even our sun, a second-generation star, is 97 percent hydrogen and helium. So we carbon-based life forms shouldn't get the idea that we're in any way important in the greater scheme of things—whatever that may turn out to be.

The second- or third-generation stars, formed in areas where some part of the cosmic dust is made up of these heavier elements needed for life (as we know it), are clearly the best bets for planets on which life might form.

Let There Be Life!

There is no way of knowing just—or even approximately—how many stars have second-generation planets with metal cores and rocky mantles circling them, but the number must be large. After all, the amount of mass in the universe is so great that even the one percent of it that isn't hydrogen or helium is enough to make billions of planets. Our local Milky Way galaxy alone is home to more than 100 billion stars. And it is beginning to look as though having planets is the normal condition for a star.

The next question is what about life? How many of these planets can we expect to support life, and more particularly intelligent life—and how can we tell?

Well we don't have enough information to tell, but perhaps we can decide what questions we have to ask to get that information.

Sighting

Dr. Frank Drake, professor of astronomy and astrophysics at the University of California, Santa Cruz, was interested in the possible existence of extraterrestrial intelligence for many years. He served as president of the SETI institute (see Chapter 23) and co-authored *Is Anyone Out There?—The Scientific Search for Extraterrestrial Intelligence* with science writer Dava Sobel.

Doctor Drake's Equation

Back in 1961, a group of people interested in the problem gathered together in Green Bank, West Virginia, for the Green Bank Conference on Extraterrestrial Intelligent Life. During this conference, astronomer Dr. Frank Drake thought over the problem of how many intelligent civilizations there might be out there for us to try to find (or that might try to find us). He listed all the factors that had to be considered to resolve the problem of extraterrestrial intelligent life, and put it together in the form of an equation.

Don't be nervous. This equation is easy to understand, and is a really wonderful way for examining all the factors involved and seeing how they interrelate. It is usually expressed as:

$$N = Rf_p n_e f_l f_i f_c L$$

Where

➤ N is the number of intelligent races we might find if we were to look at any given time.

➤ R is the number of stars coming into being in an average year.

➤ f_p is the percent of these stars that form planets.

➤ n_e is the number of these planets that are in the star's ecosphere.

➤ f_l is the number of those planets where life happens.

➤ f_i is the percentage of this life that evolves into intelligent beings.

➤ f_c is the percentage of these intelligent beings that try to communicate with the rest of the universe.

All this multiplied by L, the lifespan in years that a technologically advanced civilization can be expected to continue to exist.

Sound complicated? Follow along and you'll see that it's actually quite simple.

The Equality of Life

Let's plug in some reasonable approximations and see what we get. Before I start picking out numbers, I must point out that one person's reasonable approximation is another's wild-eyed fantasy. I'll do the best I can.

We'll confine our estimates to our local galaxy, the Milky Way, since it's quite big enough all by itself, and anything farther away is too far to worry about.

Sighting

Just to keep perspective, the Milky Way is one of millions of galaxies, each containing billions of stars.

➤ What we're trying to determine is N: How many extraterrestrial intelligent species have developed a technologically advanced civilization, and might be interested in communicating with us if we start looking for them.

➤ We need to find out first how many stars are possible homes for these races (actually the planets circling these stars, but we'll get to that next). We assume that biological life comes into being at a certain point in a star's lifetime, and intelligent life develops within a certain time after that. Therefore knowing how many stars are created on average in a given year, R should tell us how many are around at the right age. We can get this figure by dividing the number of stars estimated to make up the Milky Way with the estimated age of the Milky Way. Notice all those "estimated" hedges.

The estimated age of the Milky Way, last I heard, was 10 billion years, give or take a couple of billion. The estimated number of stars is somewhere around 100 billion. This gives us 100/10 or about 10 stars being created in any given year.

➤ Now for f_p—the number of these stars, as a percent, that form with planets. It seems from recent evidence (see "Every Star a Mother," earlier in this chapter) that the number is almost unity—that is, that almost every star comes equipped with planets. But let's not go all the way (where have I heard that before?). Let's just say that 8 out of 10 stars have solar systems. So f_p = 80 percent.

➤ n_e, the number of planets in an average star's ecosphere, is a tough one to estimate. Some of the planets that have been discovered so far seem to be gas giants, like Jupiter, that are orbiting their star at distances closer than the earth is to the sun. That would leave little room for earth-type planets in the ecosphere. So, purely arbitrarily because we really don't have enough information yet, let's say that one out of every two stars with planets has one in the right place. Which would make n_e equal to one-half or 0.5.

➤ To balance that, judging by what happened here on earth, and the experiments in creating amino acids that are described in chapter 20, it would seem a good bet that every planet in the right orbit that can produce life, will do so. This would put f_l equal to 1.

➤ But f_i is a problem. How many of these supposed extraterrestrial species would develop intelligence? If that giant meteor hadn't hit the earth 35 million years ago and wiped out the dinosaurs, would they have developed brains larger than prunes? Or would size, bulk, speed, and big teeth have been enough for Tyrannosaurus Rex to have stayed in charge through the centuries, and prevented mammals from developing any species larger or smarter than tree-shrews?

Let's give the utility of intelligence the benefit of a doubt, and say that the leading species on any planet will get there through superior brainpower, which will eventually lead to beings as smart as we like to think we are. This puts f_i also equal to 1.

➤ We have no basis to make a decision about f_c, and must wildly speculate. Is curiosity a natural requirement of intelligence? And will that curiosity inevitably focus itself toward the stars? Perhaps the intelligent species on one planet lives under water, would they even see the stars? Perhaps the dominant sense is smell, or something like that, rather than vision—would they care about the stars? Perhaps the intelligent species has seen too many movies about invaders from distant planets—wouldn't they choose not to try to communicate if only to make sure we don't know where they are?

Sighting

There is a theory that a gas giant in a solar system—located, like Jupiter, at a comfortably great distance from the host star—would be a great aid to the future of life on the inner planets. It would serve as a mighty broom, sweeping the solar system clear of many of the meteors that would otherwise continue to bombard the life-bearing planet. Too many hits like the one believed to have wiped out the dinosaurs would make life a chancy occupation.

But let's be generous and assume that any species that develops intelligence is going to be curious about who else is out there, and what they might have to say. Let's assign a value of .1 to f_c.

Now, putting an attempt to get a value for the last term in the equation, the length of time an advanced civilization can expect to stay around, L, aside for a moment, let's plug in values for what we have:

$$N = Rf_p n_e f_l f_i f_c L$$

$$= 10 \times .8 \times .5 \times 1 \times 1 \times 1 \times L$$

$$= 4L$$

Which means that, if our figures are right, at any given time (like right now) there are four times as many advanced civilizations out in the galaxy willing to contact us as the average length of time in years that such a civilization will last without destroying itself or dying of old age.

The *L* You Say

In galactic terms, the beginning of technological civilization is the advent of radio, since that is the earliest technology that makes it possible to communicate with other planets. By this definition, we have been a technologically advanced civilization for less than a century, and already we're showing signs of blowing ourselves up or poisoning the earth until it can no longer sustain life. To judge by us humans, and we have nothing else to judge by, once a civilization becomes technologically adept, it quickly develops the skills necessary to destroy itself, and all other life on the planet.

But let's be very hopeful and assume that most advanced civilizations manage to get by the first critical couple of centuries and learn to live in peace, and not use up or destroy the resources of their planet before they learn to leave it. In which case, L could be a million years or longer. Let's stop at a million.

If L is equal to a million, then N equals four million. By our very cobbled together estimate, that would make four million advanced civilizations out there in the Milky Way just waiting for us to communicate with them.

If these four million are parceled out at random, that means that there should be one of them within 250 light years of us. And our early radio shows have been spreading out from earth with the speed of light since the 1920s. Sometime in the next 200 years,

Report from the Field

"Once life has started in a relatively benign environment and billions of years of evolutionary time are available, the expectation of many of us is that intelligent beings would develop. ...The entire evolutionary record of our planet...illustrates a progressive tendency toward intelligence. There is nothing mysterious about this: smart organisms by and large survive better and leave more offspring than stupid ones. ...Once intelligent beings achieve technology and the capacity for self-destruction of their species, the selective advantage of intelligence becomes more uncertain."

—Carl Sagan, *The Dragons of Eden*

some being who looks as much like us as we look like horseshoe crabs, but who could play a pretty mean game of chess if we teach it the rules, is going to be listening to the *Jack Benny Show*.

The Truth Is Out There

I think it might be a good idea to admit that many of those plugged-in numbers are ballpark estimates, and it's a very big ballpark. So I'll allow for one order of magnitude in the figures each way (that's adding or removing a zero).

Therefore let me state with absolute (un)certainty that there's good chance that N equals somewhere between 400,000 and 40,000,000 intellectually aware, technologically advanced civilizations out there, trying to get in touch with us. In the next chapter, we'll look at what we're doing to locate them.

The Least You Need to Know

➤ The planets circling distant stars can be detected by a wobble in the star's motion.

➤ Planets are a much more frequent occurrence than was previously thought.

➤ A planet must be in a star's ecosphere to develop life.

➤ Filling in the numbers in the Drake equation can give us an approximation of how many civilizations are out there. The number I come up with is between 400,000 and 40,000,000, but I could be wrong.

Chapter 23

The Search for Extraterrestrial Intelligence

In view of the odds I quoted in the preceding chapter on the probability of intelligent life elsewhere in our own galaxy, you're probably wondering why we aren't being visited right now by some curious citizens of the Milky Way.

It's a good question. It was first (as far as I know) asked in 1943 by Nobel Prize-winning physicist Enrico Fermi, and has become known as the *Fermi Paradox*. It could be stated as follows:

> The Milky Way Galaxy hosts tens of billions of stars. It and most of the stars in it are more than 10 billion years old. That gives billions of chances for an intelligent life form to develop, and billions of years for it to travel about the Milky Way, colonizing millions of planets and investigating any planets developing their own life. So how come they're not here among us negotiating intergalactic treaties, curing diseases, teaching us not to kill each other, visiting Disney World, buying souvenir statuettes of the Eiffel Tower and Empire State Building and tee

Sighting

Science-fiction writer, poet, and philosopher Randall Garrett once suggested that the most important benefit of joining the Galactic Federation might well be the right not to be considered food by any other member.

shirts that say "My grandsire visited Earth, and all I got was this lousy tee shirt with only two arm holes."

Over the past half century, a variety of reasons have been put forward as to why there is no confirmed presence of extraterrestrials on earth at the moment or in the recent past. Let me suggest a few.

We're It

It could be, despite our carefully figuring of the odds that make it seem almost certain that there is life out there (see Chapter 22), that the Universe has rolled the dice of life and they've come up blank except for our tiny ball of rock circling an unimportant star. If so, it seems like an awful waste of real estate.

They Were Here and Left

As far as the human race is concerned, recorded history goes back for—and let's be generous—about 5,000 years. The latest figures date our planet as being close to 5 billion years old. If members of an advanced space-traveling civilization had come to visit Earth anytime during 99.999 percent of its lifetime, they would not have found anybody around worth talking to. If they left anything behind them, it's probably been buried hundreds if not thousands of feet beneath the surface as the continents drifted and the sheets of ice moved forward and back.

Report from the Field

"Innumerable suns exist; innumerable earths revolve around these suns in a manner similar to the way the seven planets revolve around our sun. Living beings inhabit these worlds."

—Giordano Bruno (1548–1600)

We've Been Taken Off the List

We were due to be visited and the advance party of the aliens has been studying our radio and television signals, which after 80 years of broadcasting now reach 80 light years in all directions. By some cosmic joke, they have not been able to receive *Masterpiece Theatre*, *Sesame Street*, or even *60 Minutes*, but only *Gilligan's Island*, *Barney and Friends*, and *My Mother the Car*. They have decided not to bother coming.

Our Timing Is Bad

It could be that my figure for "L" in the preceding chapter is way off, and the lifespan of an intelligent species is comparatively brief. Perhaps only a few manage to make it past 10,000 years of civilization without committing racial suicide through warfare or so polluting their planet that it becomes unlivable. If this is so, then although there might have been tens of thousands of races possessing intelligence throughout the galaxy, only a few of them would coexist at any given time. Most of them will have gone extinct before being able to get out of their own solar system—a trick we still haven't figured out how to accomplish in anything like a reasonable manner (see Chapter 24 for the possibilities). And we may well be extinct before anyone gets around to visiting us.

The Yokel Effect

The Milky Way Galaxy is shaped sort of like a fried egg, with a bulging center surrounded by a thinner disc. It has a diameter of about 100,000 light years. Our sun is in the thin disc part, about three-fifths of the way out from the center. This area is not particularly rich in stars. As you head toward the galactic center, the number of stars increases and they get much closer together. If you were the captain of a spaceship exploring the galaxy, charged with going where no Xnapfingak has gone before and finding new worlds and new life, which way would you order the ship to go: toward a galactic center probably teeming with life, or out to the sticks where they don't know the latest dances and they dress funny?

Report from the Field

"Physicists have stumbled on signs that the cosmos is custom-made for life and consciousness. It turns out that if the constants of nature—unchanging numbers like the strength of gravity, the charge of an electron and the mass of a proton—were the tiniest bit different, then atoms would not hold together, stars would not burn and life would not have made an appearance."

—*Newsweek*, 20 July 1998

We're Being Watched

The Galactic Federation of Planets has sent observers to watch our development from a safe distance, and as soon as we rise above the level of savagery and show ourselves capable of not blowing ourselves or other members up, the observers will show themselves and invite us to join.

We Don't Know It When We See It

Someone once pointed out to me that a modern jet flies at an altitude and speed that would put it out of reach of the best fighters of World War II. The whole air war in Europe could be being fought as a Boeing 747 flies overhead, and nothing the combatants could do would touch it. Well, it could be that the aliens are here, but their technology is so far advanced that we can't even detect them—although there's no apparent reason why they would be here, if not to communicate with us. Perhaps we are wrong in our conceit that we are the intelligent species on earth. Perhaps the aliens are deep in discussions with the whales, or the elephants, or the ants.

Einstein Was Right

In Einstein's view of the universe, the speed of light (186,282 miles a second) is the absolute limiting speed anything can travel, and even that takes more energy than the entire universe can provide. Perhaps there really is no way around the Einstein equations, and all we can hope to do is carry on a conversation with some other intelligence by radio or laser, and we will have to wait hundreds of years for each question to be answered.

UFOs

As you realize from Parts 2 and 3 of this book, UFOlogists believe that we *are* being visited. That may well be so. But if so, the visitors are being very subtle about it, and scientists are trained to seek tangible proof of any assertion before they accept it. Although many, perhaps most, scientists today are willing to accept the possibility of extraterrestrial visitors, nobody has yet shown them an extraterrestrial, living or dead, or even a piece of a UFO.

Several of the reasons already stated for the lack of contact could also explain the UFOs. They don't want us to know they're here, or they're scouting us until we're ready, or they're already in touch with the only intelligent species on earth (the octopi, for example). If this is so, they, whoever they are, could be a little bit more subtle about it and not go around getting people so excited about the sightings and abductions. But then aliens are by definition alien, and they certainly don't think like us.

Report from the Field

"The problem is colossal. There are millions of stars to aim at, and we have no idea at what frequency someone might be sending us signals. Imagine driving your car in another state and trying to tune in to a radio station you like, and then multiply this by a factor of a billion or more and you'll have an idea of what we're up against."

—Michael Papagiannis, *Boston* magazine, January 1983

The Answer Is out There

Just because extraterrestrial intelligent life forms have not visited us (openly?) yet, or at least have not chosen to land on the White House lawn and appear on national television to explain themselves, does not mean that we can't be looking for them. And so we are.

By These Signs Shall Ye Know Them

We don't have to wait for our alien brothers to announce their presence here for us to prove they exist. As a hunter searches for the footprints of his prey, so we can look for the signs that an extraterrestrial civilization would be sending out—radio waves, for example. To repeat myself (and who better?), we have been broadcasting radio into the universe for about 80 years now, and television and radar and microwave signals have been heading out for the past 50 years. This means that other intelligences, in an ever-widening circle that is now almost 160 light years wide, might be listening to our earliest radio shows, and will shortly be able to watch Uncle Miltie.

We cannot expect another civilization to be beaming signals directly at us, because unless they're doing a really good job of listening for us, they don't know we exist. But any radio signals they send out for their own use will keep spreading until they reach us. So, if we do a really good job of listening for them, we might just hear them.

An advanced civilization might make other signs besides radio signals. Perhaps they communicate between the planets in their solar system by laser beam. In which case, if the laser were pointed in just the right direction, we might catch a glimpse of it.

The Dyson Sphere

Way back in 1960, physicist Freeman Dyson published a paper in *Science* magazine in which he suggested that the more advanced a civilization becomes, the greater its need for energy will be. Because most energy comes from the sun, Dyson suggested that a really advanced civilization might cage their sun in a sphere constructed at an appropriate distance, perhaps the distance earth's orbit is from our sun. We don't know how to even begin such a project here on earth, but then we are not a really advanced civilization.

Such a "Dyson's Sphere" would probably emit waste energy in the infrared, which should be detectable at great distances if the energy trace has had time to reach here.

Sighting

If a star that we had been watching for some time were to suddenly—over the course of a couple of centuries, say, which is pretty sudden when we're considering things in an astronomical time frame—stop shining in visible light and shift its spectrum to infrared, we could be pretty sure that we were watching an advanced civilization building their own Dyson Sphere.

Project Ozma

The first serious attempt to search for communications from beings elsewhere in the universe was Project Ozma, initiated by astronomer Frank Drake (see Chapter 22) in 1960. Drake named his project after the storybook Princess of Oz, which, as he explained "is a place very far away, difficult to reach, and populated by exotic beings."

There was not much time or money available for the project, and the people involved wanted to keep it fairly quiet, because looking for signs of extraterrestrial intelligence was not a good way to further one's scientific career back then. They decided to concentrate on stars like the sun, because we know that the sun is capable of producing a planet capable of supporting life, and on stars that are close to us in space, because any signal would be stronger.

Our Stellar Neighbors

There are just seven sun-like stars (not counting the sun itself) within 25 light years of earth:

Star	Distance in Light Years
Epsilon Eridani	10.8
Tau Ceti	12.2
Sigma Draconis	18.2
Delta Pavonis	19.2
82 Eridani	20.9
Beta Hydri	21.3
Zeta Tucanae	23.3

Three of these, Delta Pavonis in the constellation Pavo (the Peacock), Beta Hydri in the constellation Hydrus (the Water Snake), and Zeta Tucanae in the constellation Tucana (the Toucan) are located in the southern sky, and therefore are invisible to an observer north of the equator. 82 Eridani, in the constellation Eridanus (the River), is visible in the North. Because it is pretty far south, however, it never rises high in the sky.

Of the three remaining stars, Epsilon Eridani (also in Eridanus, but higher in the sky), Tau Ceti (in the constellation Cetus (the Whale), and Sigma Draconis in Draco (the Dragon), they picked the two closest to earth (possibly for that reason).

Drake and his comrades used the radio telescope at the National Radio Astronomy Observatory at Green Bank, West Virginia. They pointed the 29.5 meter (85-foot)

A radio telescope aims at the night sky.

telescope at Tau Ceti and Epsilon Eridani for more than 150 hours spanning the months of April through July, 1960.

A radio telescope is designed to "see" radio-frequency waves emitted by the natural action of stars and other celestial objects. Most of them look a lot like a television satellite receiver disc, but much bigger. The quoted size of the telescope, 29.5 meters in this case, refers to the width of the parabolic mirror that reflects the radio waves to a receiver mounted above, just as a visible-light reflector telescope reflects light waves.

Radio telescopes have discovered several interesting classes of stellar objects such as *quasars* and *pulsars* that don't show up in visible-light telescopes.

The Natural Frequency of Hydrogen

Following the suggestions of physicists Philip Morrison and Giuseppe Cocconi, the Ozma group tuned their radio telescope to listen at a frequency of 1420 megahertz (21.1 centimeters wavelength). This is the natural frequency of the hydrogen atom, and it seemed like a natural idea for an intelligent race to use that frequency to communicate. The notion was that hydrogen gas is the most common material in the universe, and any race with an interest in astronomy would, sooner or later, tune radio telescopes to that frequency to work out the distribution of matter throughout the universe. And any race not interested in astronomy wouldn't have radio telescopes and wouldn't be listening at any frequency.

Bandwidth

So, to increase the chances of someone out there hearing you, it makes sense to send your signal on a frequency that other races will probably be listening to. Because most natural signals have a wide bandwidth, a narrowband signal will attract the attention of whoever happens to run across it.

Assuming that our hypothetical alien race would reason the same way, and besides you have to start somewhere, the Ozma team listened to the faint

Contact

Quasars, quasi-stellar radio source, are distant objects that emit tremendous amounts of energy, in some cases more than an entire galaxy, but seem to be not much larger than stars. They remain one of the great mysteries of the universe.

Pulsars are stars that emit very regular bursts of radio waves, so regular that at first, radio astronomers thought they might have found intelligent communications. But regular as they are, the bursts contain no information. It is now thought that pulsars are rapidly spinning neutron stars—very dense stars perhaps left over from a supernova explosion—that are emitting a beam of energy.

Contact

The **bandwidth** of a radio signal is the span from the number of hertz (cycles per second) at the low end of the signal to the number of hertz at the high end. An FM station that's listed as broadcasting at 88.5MHz (megahertz: million cycles per second) can probably be heard from 88.3–88.7MHz or more. So its bandwidth is at least 0.4MHz.

buzz of background hydrogen, hoping to hear the clicks and whines of intelligent communication. They didn't hear anything worth reporting, although there was one exciting moment where a signal was received, but it turned out to be radio noise from a passing plane. But at least they began the process of listening.

SETI

Project Ozma was the first attempt in what has become a continuing search for intelligent life beyond earth. Since then there have been more than 30 projects of varying durations and complexities, searching on various radio bands. For a while, an ambitious SETI (Search for Extraterrestrial Intelligence) effort was carried on by NASA, financed by our glorious leaders, but in 1993 Congress cut off funding for the project. In response to this piece of short-sighted policymaking, several organizations have sprung up to take over the task of searching for our interstellar companions.

Close Encounter

We may already have eavesdropped on an interstellar conversation. It was at 11:16 p.m. (eastern standard time) on 15 August 1977, that the "Big Ear" radio telescope at Ohio State University recorded a narrowband signal at the hydrogen frequency coming from the direction of the constellation Sagittarius. It lasted for 37 seconds and, unfortunately, was never repeated. The astronomer who first noticed it wrote "Wow!" along the side of the printout, and ever since this has been known as the "Wow!" event. Continued analysis of the signal over the past decades has ruled out most of the other possibilities, leading the scientists involved to conclude that they indeed *may* have recorded an ETI (Extraterrestrial Intelligence) event.

Project Phoenix

When Congress canceled NASA's SETI program in 1993, the privately funded Project Phoenix took its place. In February 1995, Phoenix began using the largest radio telescope south of the equator: the Parkes 210-foot radio telescope in New South Wales, Australia. It is now also using the 140-foot radio telescope in Green Bank, West Virginia. Phoenix plans to look at (or listen to) about 1,000 stars that are within 200 light years of our solar system. Phoenix is looking for signals between 1,000 and 3,000MHz. It has surveyed about half of its list by now, and has not yet picked up the local weather report from outer space. Considering the limited number of stars and the limited frequency span it is examining, however, there's still a long way to go before getting disheartened.

The SETI League

Another result of the unfunding of NASA's SETI project was the founding of the SETI League, a gathering place for amateur radio and amateur radio astronomy fans and hobbyists, who are going to do their best to search for and find that elusive ETI signal with small backyard radio telescope dishes and a couple of thousand dollars (or less) worth of radio and computer equipment. Even though their equipment is nowhere near as sensitive as that of the big boys, they think that with so much sky to cover and so many frequencies to listen to, they have as good a chance of making that once-in-a-millennium discovery as anyone else. Their search is called Project Argus, and their goal is to have 5,000 amateur radio astronomers pointing their dish antennas at the sky by the year 2001. (For information on these two groups see Appendix D.)

SERENDIP

The University of California at Berkeley has an ongoing SETI Program called SERENDIP (Search for Extraterrestrial Radio Emissions from Nearby Developed Intelligent Populations). The project operates as a "piggyback" SETI system on the 1,000-foot dish at Arecibo Observatory in Puerto Rico. Without interrupting whatever radio astronomy observations are going on, SERENDIP takes a feed of the telescope's output and passes it through the SERENDIP spectrum analyzer and looks at millions of narrowband chunks to see whether any of the signals overheard show signs of intelligence. Because we have no way of telling from what direction an ETI signal may come, listening in the whatever direction is being used for other science experiments is just as good as listening in any other direction, and this piggybacking enables the SERENDIP group to do almost continuous eavesdropping on the universe. The U.C. Berkeley SERENDIP group is shortly going to add its piggyback receivers to several other radio telescopes around the world.

Close Encounter

In 1989, the International Academy of Astronautics agreed to a set of procedures for what to do when an extraterrestrial signal is discovered. As set forth in the "Declaration of Principles Concerning Activities Following the Detection of Extraterrestrial Intelligence," anyone finding an ETI signal would, 1) eliminate all other possibilities; 2) notify the Central Bureau for Astronomical Telegrams of the International Astronomical Union; 3) notify the secretary-general of the UN; 4) make all the data regarding the signal available to scientists worldwide. The SETI establishment would then 5) clear any competing earth–originating signals from around the ETI frequency; and 6) consult on when and how (and whether) to reply. To which I may add, 7) accept the Nobel Prize.

SETI@home

If you have a home computer and would like to be a part of the hunt for signals from extraterrestrial civilizations, talk to the people at SETI@home. They are working with SERENDIP to get computer analysis of the billions of bits of data being recorded by SERENDIP's receivers. And the computer they want to use is yours.

The idea is that SETI@home would supply you with a screen saver that would go to work while you are not using your computer, and analyze a small chunk of the SERENDIP data. Then in the middle of the night, or whatever time you pick, your computer would call SERENDIP up and turn in the analyzed data for a new chunk. This is called distributed computation, and allows 50,000 small PC computers to do the work of one or two giant computers, and do it faster. Also, because SERENDIP works on donated money, it enables the financing to go much further.

As currently planned, the experiment will run for two years starting in either late 1998 or early 1999.

The Least You Need to Know

➤ Nobel Prize winner Enrico Fermi wondered why we haven't been contacted by extraterrestrial visitors.

➤ There are many possible reasons for this lack of communication.

➤ Perhaps, as some people believe, we have already been visited or are being visited right now.

➤ If extraterrestrials are out there, we should be able to find them by radio.

➤ Project Ozma was the first attempt at communicating with alien beings. It didn't find anything, but it taught us how to look.

➤ There are many ongoing SETI (Search for Extraterrestrial Intelligence) projects.

➤ SETI@home enables you to get involved yourself if you have a home computer.

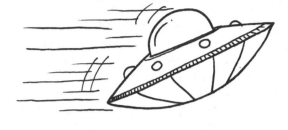

Chapter 24

Faster Than a Speeding Bullet: The Science of Space Travel

In This Chapter

➤ The universe is larger than we imagined

➤ The speed of light

➤ Sending an unmanned ship to the stars

➤ The generations ship

➤ Suspended animation

➤ Ways around the light-speed barrier

As our understanding of the universe increases, our view of our place in it diminishes. Primitive humans thought that the earth was flat and that their place on this flat earth, wherever that might be, was the center of everything. They also believed that the earth and everything on it had been placed there for their special benefit. This view is still with us today, not the flat earth part (although there is a Flat Earth Society that professes to believe that the globes of the earth are a sham), but the rest. It is only slowly and with great protest that many people are being brought around to the view that plants and animals have a right to exist, and that indeed our own existence may be tied up with theirs.

It is now clear that to understand the universe and our place in it, we are going to develop a perspective larger than that afforded from this tiny planet. We have already begun with our probes to the planets, but sometime in the near future, I believe, human curiosity being what it is, we will do our best to travel to the stars. Let us look at how our knowledge of the possibilities of interstellar travel grew, and what we now know about how such flights may become more than science fiction.

Sighting

Around 280 B.C., the Greek astronomer Aristarchus figured out, on the basis of clever observation and sound mathematical reasoning, that the earth must go around the sun instead of the reverse. Nobody who was anybody believed him.

It's Greek to Me

The ancient Greeks and others realized that the earth was round (way before Columbus), but still maintained that the earth was the center of the universe, and that the sun and the stars revolved around it. It wasn't until the 16th century that Copernicus began the scientific revolution by realizing that the problems with determining the orbits of the planets would disappear (mostly) if he assumed that the earth and the other planets were all in orbit around the sun. He wrote *De Revolutionibus Orbium Coelestium* (Concerning the Revolution of Heavenly Bodies), which was promptly banned by the Church. (The ban was finally lifted in 1835.)

Kant and the Island Universe

In 1755, German philosopher Immanuel Kant suggested that the Milky Way was an "island universe," along with the Andromeda nebula and other such bodies. When this was finally accepted as so, it moved the whole solar system to far out along one arm of one galaxy in a vast sea of galaxies. Our place in the universe was getting smaller, but with this reduction in our perceived importance came the possibility that there were other races out there that might be worth looking for.

It's Getting Bigger

The creator of the universe, whoever that might be, seems determined to increase our isolation. It seems that the universe itself is expanding. That means that everything in it is moving away from everything else. Picture a balloon being blown up with all the stars and galaxies and whatnot on the surface as it expands. The stars also have a random motion, and local gravity has an effect inside galaxies, so some stars are approaching each other. But on the average, everything is getting farther away from everything else.

And stars are pretty far apart to start with. Alpha Centauri, the closest star to the sun, is about four and a half light years off. If we hope to do more than listen in to the conversations of extraterrestrials, if we ever hope to meet them face to face—or face to beak or whatever—we are going to have to be pretty clever to figure a way to get there.

If aliens are indeed visiting earth right now, they have solved a scientific problem that seems to be much more difficult than building a craft that can stop or hover or dive into the sea, or even more difficult than hypnotizing their human subjects so that they almost forget what happened. They have traveled between the stars. I would very much like to meet one, just to ask him how he managed it.

Einstein Said It First

The problem is that, according to Einstein's special theory of relativity, which he proposed back in 1905, the speed of light, 186,282 miles a second, is the absolute fastest speed of anything having mass. Nothing with mass can go faster, and if you've got much mass you would find it almost impossible to even approach that speed. And at that speed, which we can't get anywhere close to, the nearest star would take considerably more than four and a half years to get to.

Acceleration and Deceleration

Why, you may ask, would it take more than four and a half years to get to the nearest star at the speed of light if the nearest star is only four and a half light years away? Ignoring the other problems, which we will get to in a minute, first you have to get your craft up to the speed of light, or as close as you can manage, and then you have to slow it down again at the other end. At a rate of acceleration comfortable for humans, say 32 feet per second, which would make your space ship feel as though it had the same gravity as earth, it would take about a year to accelerate to light speed. During that year you would have gone about half a light year. And then the same thing in reverse to slow down to zero. This works out to taking a bit over five and a half years to travel four and a half light years at the speed of light with comfortable acceleration and deceleration at each end. And you will want to spend some time exploring whatever you find before you go back. Let's say about a year would be right.

So a round-trip to Alpha Centauri, with acceleration and deceleration and exploring time, would take about 12 years. And that's travelling most of the way at the speed of light, which we can't. This proposition also ignores such problems as carrying enough fuel to manage the trip, and the risk of hitting something on the way. Hitting even a grain of sand when you're travelling near the speed of light and the sand is stationary would probably blow your ship apart.

The Faster You Go the Bigger You Get

Einstein's limit seems to go against common sense; why can't a spaceship just keep accelerating until it's going way past the speed of light, if it has the fuel? Well Einstein's limit has been scientifically tested many times by now, and it's proved to be right each time. The reason also goes against common sense: Increasing the acceleration of a body also increases its mass. As you go faster, you get heavier. Trust me on this (or read a good physics text).

We know this is so from accelerating subatomic particles (neutrons and protons and the like) up to very high speeds in cyclotrons. Scientists do this to smash them into other particles, and see what comes out of the collision. But they've managed to get the particles going fast enough so that Einstein's equations are demonstrated, and the particles really do gain appreciable mass as they increase speed.

Slower Than Light

If we can't travel faster than light, and we can't get any object with mass even up to the speed of light, can we still get to the stars? It depends on how badly we want to go. A practical limit on the speed we can hope to attain is about ten percent of the speed of light. Various ways are proposed for doing this, all very much in the design stage at the present time.

Project Orion

In the early 1960s, a study called Project Orion was done by the Unites States government on the feasibility of using atomic power as the propulsion system for an interplanetary ship. The notion was to build a ship, probably in orbit, with a great curved plate at its rear end. Every couple of seconds a small atomic bomb would be dropped out the back and detonated. The resulting atomic explosion would push the ship forward. The study had to be dropped when the United States signed the Limited Nuclear Test Ban Treaty in 1963.

Project Daedalus

In 1973, the British Interplanetary Society began a six-year study called Project Daedalus, in which a team of scientists and engineers worked out one possible method of accomplishing interstellar exploration. Their design called for an unmanned spaceship with a pulsed-fusion rocket engine to head for Barnard's star, a red dwarf star about 5.9 light years from the sun. the ship's engine would burn deuterium, a comparatively rare isotope of hydrogen, and helium 3, a really rare isotope of helium.

Sighting

Einstein's equations indicate that as a body approaches the speed of light its mass approaches infinity. That seems to mean in practice that nothing with mass can actually reach the speed of light. Particles with no mass, photons and the like, travel at the speed of light the instant they are produced. But zero (no mass) times anything, including infinity, is still zero, so they can get away with it.

Sighting

Project Orion was also the name of a 1976 NASA-sponsored study to determine the best way for finding planets circling distant stars. We are now starting to find such planets (see Chapter 22).

The ship would be assembled in earth orbit, and then head for Jupiter, where the Jovian atmosphere would have been skimmed for helium 3, in a sort of floating mine operation. Filling up its tanks with helium 3, the ship would then take off for Barnard's star. The scientists figured that the pulsed-fusion engine could probably get the ship to about .12 c, their way of saying about 12 percent of the speed of light.

The engines would run for about four years, perhaps in two stages, with the first stage of engines and fuel tanks being jettisoned after two years much as a multistage rocket works today. After that the ship would coast at about .12 c for the rest of the trip, about another 50 years.

Because there would be no way to slow the ship down, its information-gathering time around Barnard's star would be brief. To get around this, the unmanned ship would carry 18 robot scout ships, which would be sent to specific points of interest as soon as the main ship got close enough to determine by telescopic observation what those points were.

The ship's computers would have to be very clever and capable of making independent decisions, because the control center back on earth would have no way to issue commands in a timely fashion. Of course there would be a constant exchange of information and data, but as the ship approached Barnard's star, the radio messages would take more than five years each way.

As the mothership passed through the Barnard's star system, it would gather the information radioed to it by the scouts and transmit this and the data it collected itself back to earth. And about five years and eleven months later, if everything went right, we would know an awful lot about Barnard's star and its planets.

The spaceship, unable to stop or even slow down, would continue on past Barnard's star for the next billion years and more, unless it ran into something or someone decided to collect it.

Close Encounter

Some of you special theory of relativity buffs are probably wondering why I'm not discussing the time dilation effects of approaching the speed of light. Okay, here: Einstein predicted that as you near the speed of light, time would slow down in your vehicle as compared to the place you left from. If you were to go at 90 percent of the speed of light to a nearby star and return, four or five years might have passed inside your spaceship, but to the people on earth, 200 or 300 years went by. From what we can tell by observation—having astronauts take an atomic clock on board their orbiting craft, and then comparing it to one back on earth when they return—Einstein was right about that, too. But the effect only becomes important at speeds near the speed of light. At the 10 to 15 percent of the speed of light, we can hope to travel if we're very clever; the difference is so slight it doesn't matter.

Several inventions need to be made, and several technological advances need to be accomplished, before the Project Daedalus ship can be sent on its way:

➤ The "pulsed-fusion rocket engine" doesn't exist yet.

➤ We have no practical way to mine the atmosphere of Jupiter yet.

➤ Computers aren't smart enough yet.

But we're working and learning, and the British Interplanetary Society didn't figure we would be ready to send the ship off until the end of the 21st century, so we have almost a hundred years to work out the kinks.

Manned and Womanned Expeditions

The use of unmanned robots is all well and good, but a strong case can be made that we should send people. If we do, I know some people I would like to send. (Oops, ignore that, just a joke.)

Report from the Field

"Earth is the cradle of man's civilization, but one cannot live forever in a cradle."

—Rocket pioneer Robert Goddard

The people sent on such a trip would be explorers in a sense of that word that we haven't seen for a couple of hundred years. They would be devoting not just a couple of months for an expedition, but a lifetime for a journey. It would be the greatest adventure, with the most promise for advancing the knowledge and potentiality of the human race since our ancestors left the trees and strode upright into the savannahs.

The Generations Ship

If we can't conveniently go faster than about 10–15 percent of the speed of light, and it will take 50 years to get to one of the nearest stars, how are we to travel into the vastness of the universe? One possible answer, one that has been popular with science-fiction writers for many years, is the generations ship.

Close Encounter

In 1960, physicist Robert Bussard proposed a super ramjet for use in interstellar travel. The ship using this propulsion system would generate a magnetic field for about 2,000 miles around, which would attract and gather in the occasional protons found in not-quite-empty space. (Bussard first proposed a physical scoop, but building one of the necessary size would be exceptionally difficult, and it would soon be ripped apart if the ship passed through any sort of dust cloud, no matter how fine the dust.) The protons would then be a fuel source for a nuclear jet engine. The advantage is that the ship wouldn't have to carry all its own fuel. The disadvantage is that nobody knows how to do it. If it could be done, the method might be able to accelerate a starship up to almost half the speed of light.

The ship, which would be assembled in earth orbit, would in effect be an ark, entirely self-sustaining, carrying perhaps 25 to 100 families and all their belongings in a voyage that can go on as long as necessary. The children of the original crew would take over as their parents retired and died, and then their children, and so on. Hypothetically such a ship could go on forever, stopping at solar systems it discovered to stock up on supplies. It would be fully equipped with machine shops and furnaces and the like, quite capable of turning raw materials into whatever was required.

It would have plants and animals and trees, divided into possibly two or three different earth habitats. There would be a large lake with many sorts of fish, or probably several lakes in case one got diseased or something. Any plants that might be useful that were not being grown on the ship would be carried as seeds. Any animals that were not carried live would be carried as DNA or as frozen embryos. It would start out the size of several huge aircraft carriers all clobbered together, but could grow in any direction as space was needed. Possibly the whole ship, or some part of it, would rotate to provide artificial gravity.

The ship couldn't land on any planet that it ran across, so it would have to have some kind of shuttlecraft for exploring the surface. If it found a desirable planet that wasn't already occupied by an intelligent race, it could leave off settlers and supplies and start a colony. Of course if we already knew of a desirable planet, a generations ship could be sent to it directly to start a colony.

Suspended Animation

If we learn how to put people into suspended animation and bring them out again, the way they did in the movie *2001: A Space Odyssey*, we could make our trips to the stars with much smaller spacecraft. People in suspended animation don't eat or drink, and they don't take up much room.

The only method of accomplishing this that I know of would be cryogenic suspension—freezing the person to as close to absolute zero as you can manage, and then trying not to drop him until he's defrosted. At the moment we can do the first half, freezing the body. But we're not even close to knowing how to bring the person back to life when he's defrosted. Some people are being cryogenically suspended now when they die, under the assumption that someday we will know how to bring them back to life and how to cure whatever it was they died of. The odds of that don't seem particularly high, but as a friend of mine who wants it done to him says, "What have you got to lose?"

Sneaking Around the Light-Speed Barrier

If we can't go faster than the speed of light and going slower means that it will take much too long to get anywhere, how are we to go scooting around the galaxy and saving the rebel forces from the evil empire? It would, I think, be cruel of the universe to exist and not to have provided some way for us to travel about in it, if only we're smart enough to figure out how.

Wormholes

A black hole is created when a collapsed star or other incredibly dense object is so compacted that its gravity field bends any light that hits it so strongly that the light cannot escape again. Its effect on matter is just as drastic. Any object entering its gravity field is trapped, squeezed to a paste of atoms, and pulled into the hole. However...

If the black hole is rotating, which it probably would be, there's a chance, according to the complicated theories of how black holes work, that an object falling in at one place would be ejected back into regular space somewhere else. And that somewhere else might be clear across the galaxy. And the trip would be instantaneous.

So, if we could chart the entrances and exits to these "wormholes" and we could figure out some way not to get smeared into an atomic paste when we entered, we would have a way to hop about from place to place in the universe provided both of the places are near the entrances to wormholes.

Isaac Asimov suggested that a possible reason the earth isn't being visited by one of the many extraterrestrial civilizations that he was sure existed (Isaac didn't believe in flying saucers) was that we weren't located anywhere near a convenient wormhole.

Hyperspace

The favorite gimmick of science-fiction writers for having their characters speeding around the galaxy was "hyperspace." A starship would merely leave regular space and enter hyperspace, which lay right outside and congruent to normal space. The physical laws are different in hyperspace, and distances are not what they seem. A couple of days in hyperspace and you can travel from one side of the galaxy to the other, a couple of weeks and you can traverse the universe.

Well, it could be. Several of the mathematical models of the universe allow for multiple dimensions, I believe 11 is one of the favorite numbers, and we are aware of only three—four if you count time. If we could devise a way to twist around into one of the other sets of dimensions, the physical rules would be different and we might be able to travel vast distances with only a few steps.

An Alternate Possibility

Recent theories of how the universe came to be offer the fascinating possibility that our universe is but one of a possibly infinite number of universes. And as each universe was created, in its own Big Bang presumably, the underlying structure might have emerged slightly different so that different physical constants—the laws of nature—might have emerged. Gravity might work differently; the speed of light might be much faster or much slower; different sorts of atoms might have been created with vastly differently properties than those we're familiar with. There might be complete chaos, from our point of view, or overly oppressive order.

And some of those universes might coexist with our universe, and we might be able to find a way to step (or jump, or fall, or twist) from our universe to one next door. But the neighbor universe might map differently. That is, the point on the other universe that is touching Chicago might be right next to a point that is touching a spot on the third planet circling a star in a distant galaxy.

We might someday be able to figure out a way to cross over from our universe to some of the others, if others there be. And then we could take a few steps one way or another and see where we come out. But we had better be very careful to mark well the spot where we entered if we ever want to get back home.

The Least You Need to Know

➤ It took a long time for us to realize how big the universe is, and that it's still growing.

➤ Einstein's special theory of relativity shows that the speed of light is the fastest anything can go.

➤ Project Orion suggested propelling a spaceship by setting off atomic bombs behind it.

➤ Project Daedalus designed a fusion-powered unmanned spacecraft for a trip to Barnard's star. A few of the devices needed hadn't been invented yet, however.

➤ The generations ship would take families to the stars at about one-tenth of the speed of light; their descendants would actually be the ones arriving.

➤ There are various possibilities for going faster than light, or somehow around the light-speed barrier, but so far they are all merely possibilities.

Part 5

Take Me to Your Agent: Extra-terrestrials in Popular Culture

Science expands our knowledge in small, steady steps and takes us into the future. Science fiction expands our imagination in great leaps and prepares us for a future. (Okay, so sometimes science manages a leap or two, and sometimes it heads us into fields that science fiction didn't predict at all, such as the personal computer or genetically altered potatoes. But I like the metaphor, so we'll just ignore the contradictions.)

The science fictional view of extraterrestrials has usually not been a kind one. From the "bug-eyed monsters" of the early science fiction magazines to the alien horror in the movie Alien, *our myth makers seem to have been doing their best to warn us against otherworldly creatures.*

Running counter to the scare stories are the feel-good tales of warm-hearted aliens who wish only to serve and help humanity, such as Close Encounters of the Third Kind, ET, *and* Cocoon. *Just remember, as Damon Knight pointed out in his short story, "To Serve Man," a book entitled* To Serve Man *might be a cookbook.*

Early Imaginings

In This Chapter

➤ Early writers speculate on interplanetary travel

➤ Lucian of Samosata was first

➤ Early space-travel stories as thinly disguised social satire

➤ Writers use the scientific knowledge of their day

➤ The moon hoax of 1835

The fascination with "what's out there?" began a long time ago. Many bards and storytellers stretched their imaginations to provide an answer, as did quite a few priests and soothsayers. For many centuries the heavens of the imagination were filled with gods and goddesses, angels, devils, sprites, and other purely supernatural beings. As science began to understand the heavens, however, the storytellers began fitting their stories into the new understandings.

In this chapter we'll look at the earliest space flight fantasies; in the following chapter we'll see what more modern authors have done with the subject.

It Begins with Lucian

The earliest planetary fantasy was probably that of Lucian of Samosata. In his *A True History* (A.D. 165), the hero, aboard a Greek ship, is carried to the moon by a water-spout. The citizens of the moon wear giant phalluses, like the men of some New Guinea tribes, except that these were working models. The rich have their prosthetic private parts made of ivory; the poor have them made of wood. The moon and sun are at war over the colonization of Jupiter. The King of the sun builds a great wall between the moon and the sun, leaving the moon in permanent eclipse. The king of the moon is forced to surrender. The Greeks continue to Venus to build a new colony, and then onward to the Zodiac. They visit Cloud-Cuckoo Land and Lynchopolis, a city between the Pleiades and the Hyades, where the citizens are talkative lamps. They eventually arrive at the Isle of Dreams, where different sorts of dreams are devised, as needed:

> Some we met with that we had seen at home; these came up to and saluted us as their old acquaintance, whilst others putting us first to sleep, treated us most magnificently, and promised that they would make us kings and noblemen; some carried us into our own country, showed us our friends and relations, and brought us back again the same day. Thirty days and nights we remained in this place, being most luxuriously feasted, and fast asleep all the time....

Dream Voyages

Many early accounts of interplanetary voyages were, like the story of Alice falling down the rabbit hole, presented as the dreams of the protagonist. In *Cicero's Somnium Scipionis* ("Scipio's Dream"), Scipio dreams a great vision, which begins at Carthage and continues to an overview of the entire universe and the "Milky Circle," in which he sees "stars which we never see from the earth...all larger than we have ever imagined...indeed, the earth itself seemed to me so small that I was scornful of our empire, which covers only a single point, as it were, upon its surface."

Sighting

Marcus Tullius **Cicero** (106–43 B.C.), one of the greatest Roman statesmen, orators, and philosophers, was in the practice of indulging in the now-common practice of putting words in the mouth of the illustrious dead. Publius Cornelius Scipio Africanus (2376–183 B.C.) was the Roman general who invaded Carthage and decisively defeated the Carthaginian general Hannibal in the battle of Zama in 202 B.C.

Even noted scientists climbed aboard the speculative bandwagon. *Somnium* ("Dream"), by the 17th-century astronomer Johannes Kepler, followed in the sleepytime tradition. His dreamer, Duracotus, reaches the moon. The observations of Duracotus are as scientifically accurate as Kepler could make them. The days on the moon are unbearably hot, the nights unbelievably cold; each lasts for two weeks. But Kepler did allow for life on the moon, although living things "generally begin and end their lives on the same day, with new generations springing up daily."

Flights of Fancy in the 17th and 18th Century

In 1543, when Copernicus put the planets in their proper orbits around the sun, it became clear that the other planets were worlds much like the earth. And speculation immediately began on who or what lived on them. The fabulists, precursors to today's science-fiction writers, immediately began doing their best to answer these speculations. Their depiction of beings on other planets were sometimes merely adventure stories, pure and simple, but often they were satirical commentaries on the society the author lived in. If criticizing the king directly can get you free room and board in the Tower of London for an extended stay, then it is safer (though still risky) to aim your satire at the King of the Lilliputians or the Emperor of the Birds.

Close Encounter.

Political commentary disguised as science fiction was also used by stern, upright, narrow-minded people to reinforce the prejudices of the day. Victorian journalist Percy Greg thought, in his humorless way, that women should stay in their place, and in *Across the Zodiac* he has his Martians say so: "The equalists were driven from one untenable position to another, and forced at last to demand a reduction of the masculine standard of education to the level of feminine capacities. Upon this ground they took their last stand, and were hopelessly beaten. The reaction was so complete that for the last two hundred and forty generations the standard of female education has been lowered to that which by general confession ordinary female brains can stand without violent injury to the physique."

Conversations

In 1686, Bernard Le Bovier de Fontenelle wrote *Conversations upon the Plurality of Worlds*, which became an immediate bestseller in France and England. In it, a philosopher walks through a lovely garden with his pupil, an even more lovely marchioness (the wife of a marquis), and teaches her the newly discovered facts of astronomy. She is delighted to learn that the moon and the other planets are worlds like earth, and that each may well be occupied. The philosopher speculates that in the future humans might visit the moon, or the moon men might visit us.

For the Birds

In 1727, Captain Samuel Brunt [pseud.] published *A Voyage to Cacklogallinia*—pretty much a rip-off of *Gulliver's Travels* except that Brunt ends up in a country of birds whose bird-brained government had an uncanny resemblance to the English government at the time. The birds climb a mountain to accustom themselves to the thin air, and then fly to the moon. Their goal is to mine the gold on the moon to pay for their war debts. Although Brunt knew enough to have an area of weightlessness between the

earth and the moon, it didn't occur to him that there
would be no air in such an area—and why should it
have?

The moon, however, was inhabited by philosophers who
were not interested in gold and refused to permit the
mining. The birds went home empty-taloned.

The Moon Hoax

Many famous murder trials attain notoriety through a
publisher's desire to sell newspapers. And it is said that
the Spanish American War was fought so that William
Randolph Hearst could sell papers. Why not then, the
editor of the *New York Sun* thought, lengthy descriptions
of the fabulous flowers, trees, birds, fish, animals, and intelligent beings that live on
the moon?

In 1835, the famous British astronomer John Herschel, son of Sir William Herschel
who had discovered the planet Uranus, was in Cape Town, South Africa, studying the
southern sky. In the United States, Edgar Allen Poe published a story called "The
Unparalleled Adventures of One Hans Pfall" in the *Southern Literary Messenger*.

In Poe's story, a Dutchman travels to the moon by balloon. These two facts—Poe's
story and Herschel's expedition—came together in the mind of Richard Adams Locke,
a 35-year-old Englishman who had been recently hired to write essays for the *New York
Sun*, a newly established newspaper that needed some excitement in its columns to
attract a readership.

Locke decided the newspaper needed a story that, if true, would get everyone talking, would generate excitement, would be the wonder of the age. Locke decided to perpetrate an outrageous hoax on the readers of the *Sun*, and on the many new readers who would be drawn in by the story. A hoax so outrageous that when the people found out they had been hoaxed they would be too busy laughing to get angry.

The Hoax Begins

He started small, planting a subtle seed in the minds of his readers. On Friday, 21 August 1835, the *Sun* carried the headline: CELESTIAL DISCOVERY. Under it, a short squib:

> *The Edinburgh Courant* says—'We have just learnt from an eminent publisher in this city that Sir John Herschel, at the Cape of Good Hope, has made some astronomical discoveries by means of an immense telescope of an entirely new principle.'

Locke let it sit there for three days. And then, on Tuesday, 25 August, he expanded: GREAT ASTRONOMICAL DISCOVERIES LATELY MADE BY SIR JOHN HERSCHEL, L.I.D., F.R.S.&C. AT THE CAPE OF GOOD HOPE.

The article described how Herschel had made great advances in the art of telescope making, and had produced an instrument so powerful that he could see fine details on the surface of the moon. The telescope, the article explained, had been made in England and shipped to South Africa from St. Catherine's Docks in London.

The Mother of All Telescopes

The telescope, he claimed, was capable of magnifying an image 42,000 times. An image magnified that greatly was very weak, however, so Herschel focused the image on a polished glass plate, and then lit the plate with a powerful lime-light. He then passed the brightened image through a microscope lens and projected it onto a white wall.

This procedure brought the moon's surface, 233,000 miles overhead, to an apparent distance of but five miles. The article was said to be a reprint from the *Edinburgh Journal of Science*. Only the most astute reader would know that there was no *Edinburgh Journal of Science*. To prepare readers for the articles to come, Locke ended this one with the claim that Herschel had "affirmatively settled the question whether this satellite be inhabited, and by what order of beings."

Life on the Moon Observed

With the next article Locke got down to business. The astronomers at the Cape of Good Hope determined that the moon had an atmosphere capable of supporting life. How did they know? They could see the life. The article spoke of "a lunar forest...with trees unlike anything I have seen, except the largest kind of yews in the English

Report from the Field

"Not one person in ten discredited [the moon hoax story], and (strangest point of all!) the doubters were chiefly those who doubted without being able to say why—the ignorant—those uninformed in astronomy—people who *would not* believe, because the thing was so novel, so entirely out of the usual way. A grave professor of mathematics in a Virginia college told me seriously that he had no doubt of the truth of the affair."

—Edgar Allen Poe

churchyards," as well as another forest of firs, dark red flowers, "herds of brown quadrupeds, having all the external characteristics of the bison...but more diminutive." One difference that was seen on the pseudo-bison and on most of the other animals the astronomers observed was "a remarkable fleshy appendage over the eyes, crossing the whole breadth of the forehead and united to the ears. We could most distinctly perceive this hairy veil...lifted and lowered by means of the ears."

The astronomers also reported seeing a goat-like unicorn that seemed to possess some sort of extrasensory perception. When one of the astronomers lifted a hand to the image, as if to touch the animal, it bounded away.

Hut-Building, Fire-Using Beavers

Later installments added wonders to the lunar list. The astronomers saw landscapes full of active and dormant volcanoes, hills "pinnacled with tall quartz crystals, of so rich a yellow and orange hue that we at first supposed them to be pointed flames of fire." And the animals: reindeer, elk, moose, herds of sheep, bears with horns, and a tail-less beaver that walked erect. The beaver "carries its young in its arms like a human being, and moves with an easy gliding motion. Its huts are constructed better and higher than those of many tribes of human savages, and from the appearance of smoke in nearly all of them, there is no doubt of its being acquainted with the use of fire."

Winged Moon Men

Yet more wonders were in store. Under a more powerful resolving lens, flocks of winged creatures unlike any birds turned out to be man-like beings whose wings were retracted when they walked erect.

They averaged four feet in height, were covered, except on the face, with short and glossy copper-colored hair, and had wings composed of a thin membrane, without hair, lying snugly upon their backs, from the top of the shoulders to the calves of the legs. The face, which was of a yellowish flesh color, was a light improvement upon that of the large orang-outang, being more open and intelligent in its expression, and having a much greater expansion of forehead. The mouth, however, was very prominent, though somewhat relieved by a thick beard upon the lower jaw, and by lips far more human than those of any species of the simia genus. In general symmetry of body and limbs they were infinitely superior to the orang-outang.... The hair on the head was a darker color than that of the body, closely curled, but apparently not woolly, and arranged in two curious semi-circles over the temples of the forehead. Their feet could only be seen as they were alternately lifted in walking; but from what we could see of them in so transient a view, they appeared thin, and very protuberant at the heel.

Sex on the Moon

Having pulled every other string he could think of, Locke now eluded to sex, if in a cautious and circumspect way. The report commented on some "habits of these creatures, who were of both sexes, which led to results so very remarkable that they should be laid before the public by Sir John himself in view of the incredulousness with which they would be received." If the reader didn't get it, Locke pushed the point. "They are doubtless innocent and happy creatures, notwithstanding some of their amusements would but ill comport with our terrestrial notions of decorum."

Locke wrote that the astronomers had named this oversexed humanoid *Verpertilio-homo*, or "Batman." They also discovered a race of larger humanoids that went around eating fruit, being nice to the other animals, and creating wondrous works of art.

It Sells Papers

Each day the series ran the sales of the *New York Sun* went up. On 28 August 1835, the paper sold 19,360 copies, making it the largest-selling single issue of any newspaper. The (London) *Times*, the paper with the largest circulation in the world at that time, was selling 17,000 copies a day. Other papers soon started copying the *Sun*'s success by stealing the *Sun*'s stories. They took the precaution of attributing their articles to the *Edinburgh Journal of Science*, of course; how could the *Sun* argue with that? The *New York Times* editorialized that the moon article "display[s] the most extensive and accurate knowledge of astronomy, and the description of Sir John's recently improved instruments, the principle on which the inestimable improvements were founded, the account of the wonderful discoveries in the moon, etc., are all probable and plausible and have an air of intense verisimilitude."

Sighting

Richard Adams Locke stood in the crowd in front of the *New York Sun*'s office one day and overheard a well-dressed gentleman explaining that the *Sun* had made a mistake. The gigantic telescope had not been loaded from St. Catherine's Docks in London for shipment to South Africa. It had been loaded on the East India Docks across the way. The gentleman knew this because he was there at the time and saw the whole thing.

On the Other Hand

Richard Adams Locke's science was not too good, even for the time; a few flaws in the story should have given the game away to the astute observer, of which there were apparently very few among the thousands of readers. The dead giveaway was the many cases of parallel evolution; the deer, bison, one-horned goats, and the rest were pretty much like their earth equivalents except for the flap over their eyes. Highly unlikely, as any exobiologist will tell you.

Indeed, the creatures would have to possess a strange kind of extrasensory perception to be able to detect an astronomer peering at them from the earth. And why were those "works of art" hung in such a fashion as to be visible from a telescope looking down at them? Another error was thoughtlessly built into the story: The telescope is described as having a resolution equal to being five miles away from the lunar landscape. This is a lot better than 233,000 miles, but how much detail could anyone make out from an apparent distance of five miles?

But the weakest part of the tale, as Locke told it, was the brightened image in the telescope. When you shine a bright light on a projected image, you don't brighten the image, you drown it out. (Picture shining a flashlight at a movie screen.)

Report from the Field

"While the setting and characters were romantic, there was a vast amount of "scientific" lore in the *Moon Hoax*, which, couched in technical language, fooled men who should have known better. Locke suffered from the fault of his generation. Struggling for verisimilitude, he piled one scientific detail upon another until the flimsy structure of his tale collapsed under its own weight."

—Marjorie Hope Nicolson, *Voyages to the Moon*

The Word Spreads

After all the articles had appeared, Locke gathered them together into a pamphlet, which sold 60,000 copies in the first month. The story was picked up by newspapers around the world. The French Academy of Sciences debated the truth of these "discoveries." When word finally got back to John Herschel, who had known nothing of the story, he was greatly amused.

The story made its way around the world, its exposure as a hoax always a few weeks behind but never quite catching up to it. Locke later maintained that he always meant the hoax to be transparent and easily discovered, and that the work was really a satire.

The Least You Need to Know

➤ The fascination with the heavens is as old as the human race.

➤ Lucian of Samosata wrote the earliest interplanetary story we know of, taking his hero to the moon on a water spout and then on to the distant stars.

➤ Travel by dream was a popular device; Both Cicero and Kepler adopted this means of locomotion in their stories.

➤ When the heliocentric (sun-centered) view of the solar system emerged, the fiction changed to mirror the facts.

➤ The Moon Hoax of 1835 presented fiction as fact, and the people gladly believed it.

➤ Trees, flowers, animals, and people inhabited the wonderland moon of Locke's hoax.

➤ The series brought the circulation of the *New York Sun* to the highest in the world.

Bug-Eyed Monsters: Aliens in Science Fiction

In This Chapter

➤ The late-19th-century extraterrestrial story

➤ The War of the Worlds

➤ The First Men in the Moon

➤ Edgar Rice Burroughs' Mars novels

➤ Many interesting twists on the theme

When learned professors of science fiction get together, the second great point for discussion, right after *what is science fiction anyway?*, is *when did science fiction begin?* You and I will just bypass the first question. As the Supreme Court decided about pornography, *I don't know how to define it, but I know it when I see it.*

As to when science fiction began, some say back with Lucian of Samosata, some with Cyrano, some with Edgar Allen Poe, some with Mary Shelley's *Frankenstein*, some with Jules Verne's scientific adventures. And, of course, they're all right. But it was toward the second half of the Victorian era, somewhere around the last quarter of the 19th century, that the sort of science fiction that most interests us began to take shape. It was then that writers passed the stage of using the possibility of extraterrestrial beings merely as props for their philosophical or polemical tracts, and seriously began to consider what the existence of extraterrestrial intelligent life might mean to us here on earth.

Use the Vril

In *The Coming Race* (1871), Bulwer-Lytton had his alien race living in great caverns beneath the earth's crust. His hero stumbles across them by falling into a hole in a coal mine. They are the Vril-ya, named after the powerful force that they have learned to control, *Vril*, which enables them to do all sorts of wonderful things. (May the Force be with you!) Their world beneath the world is replete with robots, flying machines, and powerful weapons. Some dangerous animals lurk about this underearth world, and these animals must occasionally be hunted. The Vril-ya let their children do the hunting, however, because, as everyone knows, children are far more ruthless than adults.

Sighting

Edward George Earle Lytton Bulwer, First Baron Lytton (1803–1878), was a prolific novelist, poet, and playwright who wrote fat novels on a bewildering variety of subjects in a variety of styles. He is best known perhaps for his historical novel *The Last Days of Pompeii*, and his crime novel *Eugene Aram*. Occultists will remember *Zanoni*, in which the hero uses occult powers to live for many centuries and to transmute dross metal into gold, but finally gives it all up to marry an opera singer.

One of the aliens, a women named Zee, falls in love with our hero, which he finds to be a quite intimidating experience because these Vril-ya women are bigger and more powerful than surface-of-the-earth women and take the initiative in courtship. He finally escapes from this underground utopia with Zee's assistance and returns to the world upstairs. But he worries about the race he left behind: "The more I think of a people calmly developing, in regions excluded from our sight and deemed uninhabitable by our sages, powers surpassing our most disciplined modes of force, and virtues to which our life, social and political, becomes antagonistic in proportion as our civilization advances—the more deeply I pray that ages may yet elapse before there emerge into sunlight our inevitable destroyers."

The influence of the novel was strong enough so that "Vril" came into the language for a while, and a popular British drink, a beef tea drunk as a health food, was named Bovril, presumably for *bos*, cow and *Vril*, force.

Herbert George Wells

H.G. Wells (1866–1946) was an extremely prolific and popular writer from the later Victorian era until well into the 20th century. He wrote social satire and popularized history and science books, as well as essays on his theories on the best way to run a country—which was not the way it was being run. But he is best known for what in his day were called his pseudo-scientific novels. Wells wrote *The Time Machine* (1895), *The Island of Dr. Moreau* (1896), *The Invisible Man* (1897), *The War of the Worlds* (1898), *The First Men in the Moon* (1900), and *The Shape of Things to Come* (1933). All of them were very successful in their day and were eventually made into movies, some more than once. The two that considered the possibilities of extraterrestrial life were *The War of the Worlds* and *The First Men in the Moon*.

The War of the Worlds

In *The War of the Worlds*, Wells presented a notion that had not really been considered until he wrote about it, but that has become a staple of science fiction today and has, to a certain extent, colored our view of how we might interact with an alien race. Suppose, Wells thought, that aliens desired our planet for their own, and suppose that they were advanced so far beyond us technically that we could do little to stop them.

And suppose that they just hopped over to earth from their home planet (in this case Mars), and proceeded to take it away from us.

The War of the Worlds was serialized in *Pearson's Magazine* in Britain and in *Cosmopolitan* in the United States simultaneously between April and December 1897, and published as a book a year later. Arthur Brisbane, the editor of the New York *Journal* then bought newspaper serialization rights. Without bothering to consult with Wells, Brisbane changed the location of the Martian invasion from southern England to New York and took many other liberties with the text. Wells was not pleased.

In the story, which was an immediate hit on both sides of the Atlantic, the Martians, an ancient, wise, and pitiless race, invade the earth to get our natural resources. They regard humans not so much as people to be conquered and subjugated as vermin to be exterminated. Their spaceships land in England and elsewhere, and from them emerge great walking machines that use powerful heat rays to destroy everything in their path. Nothing the human armies can do seems capable of stopping them, or even slowing them down. The humans were helpless before the superior technology and ruthless intent of the Martian invaders.

Report from the Field

"Across the gulf of space, minds that are to our minds as ours are to those of the beasts that perish, intellects vast and cool and unsympathetic, regarded this earth with envious eyes, and slowly and surely drew their plans against us."

—H.G. Wells, *The War of the Worlds*

Sighting

Many critics have seen what Wells' Martians were doing to England as a metaphor for what Britain and the other European countries were engaged in doing to the "lesser breeds without the law" all over the world.

What finally did the Martian invaders in was earthly microbes. They had no resistance to our diseases, and one by one they succumbed, falling from their great fighting vehicles and dying on the ground.

Close Encounter

The War of the Worlds was so successful here in the United States that Arthur Brisbane, the American publisher, wanted an immediate sequel. Because Wells had no interest in writing a sequel, Brisbane hired hack writer Garrett P. Serviss to do the deed. Serviss produced *Edison's Conquest of Mars*, in which the heads of state on earth along with earth's greatest scientists band together to bring the war to the Martians. They do. They win. Enough said.

The First Men in the Moon

A fair amount of basic scientific facts were known about the moon back in 1900, when Wells wrote *The First Men in the Moon*, and Wells put some thought into what the effect of those facts would be. Wells' two heroes, Cavor and Bedford, experience weightlessness as their glass ball of a ship passes from the effects of the earth's gravity to the moon's. (Actually in outer space you're weightless whenever your ship's engines aren't fighting whatever gravity field you're in, but who's quibbling?)

Gravity on the moon is much less than that on earth, and Wells' characters noted the effect:

> The thrust of my foot that I made in striding would have carried me a yard on earth; on the moon it carried me six....For the moment the thing had something of the effect of one of those nightmares when one falls and falls... I floated through the air and fell down like a feather... I made a step back, and gathered myself together, and leaped with all my might. I seemed to shoot into the air as if I should never come down. It was horrible and delightful, and as wild as a nightmare to go flying off in this fashion.

Wells considered the effects of the moon's rotation: two weeks of light and extreme surface heat, two weeks of dark and total cold. The vegetation, if vegetation there were, would have to grow fast during the long days and then lie dormant for the long nights. Wells describes the moon seeds bursting to life after a lunar night:

> First one and then another had stirred, and down the crack of each of them showed a minute line of yellowish green, thrusting outward to meet the hot encouragement of the newly risen sun. For a moment that was all, and then there stirred and burst a third!

'It is a seed,' said Cavor. And then I heard him whisper, very softly, 'Life!'

The movement was slower than any animal's, swifter than any plant's I have ever seen before. How can I suggest it to you—the way that growth went on? ...Have you ever on a cold day taken a thermometer into your warm hand and watched the little thread of mercury creep up the tube? The moon-plants grew like that.

There is intelligent life on Wells' moon, but you wouldn't want to meet up with it. The Selenites, living in great caverns carved out of the moon's interior, were grotesque insect-like creatures with greatly enlarged brains and the cold, passionless, evil intellect of Wells' Martians. Wells was not too hopeful about what sort of intelligences we might meet when we venture off the earth.

On Two Planets

In 1897, the same year that the magazine version of *The War of the Worlds* came out, a German novelist named Kurd Lasswitz published *Auf zwei Planeten* (On Two Planets), the story of a Martian invasion of earth. Because the stories are different enough, and because the two authors must have been working on their novels at the same time, this seems to be another indication that when an idea is ready it will emerge, sometimes in several places at once.

In Lasswitz's tale, three explorers head for the North Pole in a balloon. They find a Martian station there, and their balloon is destroyed by an "abaric field" created by the Martians. Two of the balloonists are captured and taken back to Mars. When the Martians return to earth, a British battleship sinks their spaceship. They return in force and destroy the British fleet. The power of Britain being thus broken, the Turks massacre all foreigners within their borders. The European countries respond by sending a fleet to shell Istanbul.

Meanwhile back on Mars, two political parties have formed, the Philo-Baten (earth lovers), who believe humans should be treated as equals, and the Anti-Baten, who think humans are no better than animals and should be treated like animals. The anti-Baten forces make their case by demonstrating the human propensity for violence—it's the old "you're too violent, so I'm going to have to beat you up" school of thinking—and the Martians take over the control of Europe, Russia, and the United States.

At one point, one of the lead characters explains that the Martians are winning not because of their superior technology, but because the humans are morally inferior: "...no Martian is able to press the button of the nihilite apparatus if a human stands against him with a firm, moral will, a will that knows nothing but the desire to do what is good."

Then the humans, to prove they're not really violent, rebel and attack the Martian polar stations. Eventually a peace treaty is signed.

This book was a major bestseller in Europe for more than 30 years, and was translated into Czech, Danish, Dutch, Norwegian, and Swedish. For some reason, it was never translated into English.

Burroughs of Mars

Edgar Rice Burroughs' still popular Mars and Venus books (see Chapter 3) are, like the Buck Rogers comic strips, anathema to science-fiction academics. They are what most people who do not read science fiction think of when science fiction is mentioned. The science in them is minimal and flawed, and the stories do not depend on any sort of scientific concept for their existence. They are adventure stories, pure and simple, and like most adventure stories they gain from having an exotic setting. But they've been popular for almost a century now (the first Barsoom book, *A Princess of Mars* was published in 1912) despite their childish science and their sometimes painfully bad writing.

My theory about the popularity of Burroughs' books, the Tarzan books as well as the Mars and Venus books, is that Burroughs' flawed writing skills were still good enough to let his incredible vision come through. It's as though Burroughs were the only one who had been to an incredible land and witnessed some of the most exciting adventures ever seen, and the only way we can find out about this is through his writing. After you arrive at Barsoom in his books, the writing becomes transparent and only the adventure itself remains. Yes, it's the sort of adventure that only a teenage boy can love, but half of the human race will at one time or another be a teenage boy.

Boy Meets Girl, Girl Is Kidnapped by Aliens

The theme of the alien invader, or the alien we humans meet as we propel ourselves into the waiting galaxy, has been a staple of science fiction since the early days of the SF magazines, when the 20th century was less than 20 years old. And not all science-fiction writers are masters of their craft. Trite plotting, recycled ideas, and cardboard characters are as common in science fiction as they are in any other writing genre, including "mainstream." There are many examples of science-fiction stories that transcended the trite plotting, and a number of science-fiction writers who can hold their own in any gathering of masters, but the formula alien story, where the bug-eyed monster wants the girl for reasons of his own, has been all too common. As August Derleth described it in *Writing Fiction* (1946):

Edgar Rice Burroughs' Martian tales are prototypes, and the basic theme seldom varies—motivated by a variety of events such as a terrestrial plague, a vital interest in

Sighting

Years ago at a science-fiction convention a fan asked Ted Sturgeon why 90 percent of science fiction was crap. "Because 90 percent of everything is crap," Sturgeon told the fan. This has become known as Sturgeon's Law, and has stood the test of time.

rocket-ships, the noble impulse to be sacrificed to science, and so forth, the hero and the heroine, who is sometimes a stowaway, set forth bravely into the interstellar spaces. They duly arrive at the moon, Mars, Venus, or some hitherto unknown world or galaxy, and there immediately encounter creatures who are inimical to them…and there begins a titanic struggle for the girl, who, strangely, seems also to be an object of special interest to the insectile or batrachian or reptilian inhabitants of this extraterrestrial place. After a series of harrowing adventures…the hero fetches the heroine back from hideous captivity, and they make the rocket-ship or the interstellar patrol just in time, with a horde of ravening citizens of this alien world at their heels.

More Invasions

The theme of extraterrestrial aliens landing on earth has become a common one in science fiction, and the variants are many. In John W. Campbell, Jr.'s story "Who Goes There?" scientists in Antarctica discover a magnetic anomaly buried under the ice—something that powerfully influences magnetic compasses. They find that, buried 40 feet down, is, "a thing like a submarine without a conning tower or directive vanes, 280 feet long and 45 feet in diameter at its thickest." They determine that it must be a spaceship, and that it must have been buried in the ice for the past 20 million years.

The scientists dig down to the craft and find it made of metals superior to any known on earth. They remove a chunk of ice in which is, presumably, the pilot of the spaceship: a creature with three red eyes and blue hair like crawling worms. When they defrost it, it comes to life—a horrid, evil

Sighting

"Who Goes There" was first published in the August 1938, *Astounding Science Fiction* magazine. It has since been anthologized countless times. In 1951, it was made, with many plot alterations, into the movie called *The Thing From Another World*, usually now just called *The Thing*.

Report from the Field

"Aliens aren't going to invade Earth, and breed human beings for meat animals. It makes a nice background for horror-fantasy, but it's lousy economics. It takes approximately ten years to raise one hundred pounds of human meat, and at that it takes high-cost feed to do it. Beef cattle make better sense—even though that louses up the horror motif.

And that is, of course, assuming the improbable proposition that the alien's metabolism can tolerate terrestrial proteins at all."

—John W. Campbell, Jr.

life. They try to kill it, but it has the ability to take over, to become, any other living thing. They have a hell of a time preventing it from taking them all over; they can't even tell which of them are still human and which have become…monster. This is a real science fiction story, with nothing supernatural or occult in it, and yet it is one of the most effective horror stories I have ever read.

Bugs from Space

Another sort of monster from outer space is dealt with in Michael Crichton's *The Andromeda Strain*, which sort of reverses the idea of *War of the Worlds*. Instead of earth's bacteria destroying an alien invader, the invader is an alien virus. It seems highly unlikely that a virus from anywhere else would be close enough in its DNA structure to be able to replicate in earth animals, or to harm them, but NASA takes the threat seriously enough to have set up quarantine procedures for anything from outer space or any of the planets that our explorations might bring back to earth.

Way back in the 1940s, A. E. Van Vogt wrote the short story "Asylum," in which the aliens who land on earth are vampires, sucking both blood and "life force" from their victims.

In *The Butterfly Kid* (1962), Chester Anderson had the earth invaded by blue lobsters.

In *Anything You Can Do*, Randall Garrett invented the Nipe, an alien who is super-fast, super-smart, and likes to hunt people—and is very good at it.

In Fredric Brown's *Martians Go Home*, the Martians just want to watch us—whatever we do, at any time. And because they can teleport, you can't keep them out.

William Tenn, in the novelette "Firewater," has the earth visited by aliens who flit about from place to place, doing incomprehensible things for their own mysterious reasons and ignoring us humans completely. Anyone who studies them and tries to understand what they are doing goes insane. The aliens are well realized, which seems like a strange thing to say when the whole point is that we can't understand them, but Tenn conveys the essence of their "alienness" thoroughly and well. The story uses the existence of these incomprehensible aliens to explore the behavior of humans.

John Wyndham's *Day of the Triffids* has the earth invaded by giant mobile vegetables with a poisonous sting.

In "Farewell to the Master," which has a last line which is among the most powerful of any short story ever written, a man named Klaatu and a robot named Gnut arrive on earth in a spaceship. The man raises his right arm high in the "universal gesture of peace," and is promptly shot by a lunatic and the robot grieves. This was made into the movie *The Day The Earth Stood Still*—but with a different last line.

A scene from the movie The Day the Earth Stood Still, *based on the story "Farewell to the Master" by Harry Bates.*

Interstellar Adventure

Most writers who have earthmen going out into the galaxy use aliens merely as backdrop, or they are human beings with funny ears. E.E. Smith's *Lensman* series describes many alien species throughout the universe, but they all seem to be humans under whatever odd-colored skin Smith gave them.

Ursula LeGuin's *The Left Hand of Darkness* (1966) manages to do the reverse, and quite neatly. She creates aliens in humanoid skins. The Gethinians look like humans, and behave pretty much like humans most of the time. But they are not human. The major difference is that they are androgynous—both male and female. Not at the same time, but alternately. Most of the time, they are neuter; during "kemmer" (their mating time), however, each Gethinian becomes either male or female, not exactly at random but by some subtle signaling process. Somehow Gethinian couples usually manage to come out with one of each. LeGuin uses this device to explore human gender differences and point out some of its cultural idiocies. This is the sort of science fiction that shows that the genre can say things that are worth hearing, and that would be difficult to put into any other form.

The Least You Need to Know

➤ Early extraterrestrial tales were mostly a vehicle for philosophical speculations about the troubles with humans.

➤ H.G. Wells' *The War of the Worlds,* about an invasion from Mars, established a pattern of earth-invasion stories that is still being used.

➤ Wells' *The First Men in the Moon,* where giant evil insects are found living in caverns under the moon's surface, is a theme still being explored, although the action has been taken far beyond the moon.

➤ In "Who Goes There," John W. Campbell, Jr. created an alien that effectively combined science fiction and pure horror.

➤ Many variants of the alien-lands-on-earth story have been devised.

➤ Some science-fiction writers, such as William Tenn and Ursula LeGuin, manage to transcend the science fiction form in its treatment of extraterrestrials and say something meaningful about the human condition.

Chapter 27

We Control Your TV Set

In This Chapter

➤ The War of the Worlds

➤ Panic in the streets

➤ Television: the anthology shows

➤ Sitcoms: aliens among us

➤ *Star Trek* and *Babylon 5*

➤ *The X-Files*

➤ Reality-based television shows

My theory is that Big Bird, the seven-foot avian puppet on *Sesame Street*, is a model of a real alien. A race of extraterrestrials that look an awful lot like Big Bird have put him on children's television so that all our kids will grow up thinking of seven-foot-tall yellow flightless birds as friendly, helpful, and just a little dumb. When the aliens arrive in force, we'll just hum the *Sesame Street* theme song and go off arm in wing to…to…it's just too horrible to contemplate. I could be wrong. Perhaps the aliens look like plump purple dinosaurs.

Radio and television have been a fruitful ground for the creation of imaginary aliens, both horrific and cuddly, stupid and brilliant, good and evil, and everything in between. Radio had the advantage of using your own mind to create the visual images, which were usually more horrible than anything the special effects people in Hollywood could create. One famous radio broadcast succeeded especially well, creating panic in the streets and a subsequent mistrust of radio. That mistrust, unfortunately, seems to have worn off, judging by the number of radio talk show hosts today who indulge in what Nazi propaganda minister Joseph Goebbels called "the big lie" and garner huge audiences.

Report from the Field

Radio, having only a single dimension, that of sound, may seem to the uninitiated an inadequate vehicle for shows of any kind. Studio photographs showing the cast of "Hamlet" or of "Allen's Alley" standing around the microphone in their street clothes reading from hand-held scripts while a sound-effects man with his crude gadgetry hovers in the background, suggests a pretty static performance, lacking in illusion and imagery. Nothing could be farther from the truth. The listener himself supplied the other necessary dimension—imagination—to fill the stage richly with life, color, and action. As a result, the characters and the situation and the background scenery portrayed on radio were as convincing an illusion as one might gain from a good book.

—Cabell Phillips, *From the Crash to the Blitz: 1929–1939*

The War of the Worlds

On Halloween evening, Sunday, 31 October 1938, Orson Welles and the Mercury Theater on the Air performed a live dramatization of H.G. Wells' 1898 novel, *The War of the Worlds*, which, you will remember from the preceding chapter, is about a Martian invasion of earth. The Mercury Theater had been on the air on CBS for some months, and had already performed dramatizations of such classics as *Treasure Island*, *Julius Caesar*, *The Count of Monte Cristo*, and *A Tale of Two Cities*.

The script for the version of *The War of the Worlds* that night was written by Howard Koch, who did most of the show's scripts. He took it pretty much from the Wells book, except that it was set today (well, the today of 1938) and the action was moved from southern England to the United States. (But that had been done before, in the first American publication of the book; see Chapter 26.)

The Script

Koch and many others in the Mercury Theater company couldn't convince themselves that anyone would care about a bunch of Martians. "It's all too silly. We're going to make fools of ourselves!" the company secretary declared; just the sort of encouraging words a writer needs to hear while working on a script. Koch wrote the first part of the script as though the listener were actually hearing events as they took place to make it seem more authentic.

The story started with Orson Welles narrating but then switched to radio announcers, radio reporters, interviews with astronomers and policemen—all done as though actually happening live on the air. The time scale was collapsed, of course; events that would take weeks in real life were condensed into the first ten minutes of the show. But Koch hoped this new narrative technique would add an air of immediacy to the show that would make the listeners care about what was happening.

He guessed right; the audience cared much more than he or anyone connected with the show could have expected.

The Competition

The show had recently moved to the eight o'clock slot on Sundays, opposite the immensely popular *Edgar Bergen* show. Edgar Bergen, you will remember, was the kindly middle-aged ventriloquist whose ward, Charlie McCarthy, was a spoiled brat, a wise guy, and mostly a dummy. The Mercury Theater wasn't doing well in its new time slot. The week before it had 3.6 percent of the listening audience tuned in while Edgar Bergen had 34.7 percent.

The Show

About a minute past eight, after the introductory music, a few announcements, and the name of the show—there were no commercials because the show didn't yet have a sponsor—came the mellifluous voice of Orson Welles.

> We know now that in the early years of the 20th century this world was being watched closely by intelligences greater than man's and yet as mortal as his own. We know now that as human beings busied themselves about their various concerns they were scrutinized and studied, perhaps almost as narrowly as a man with a microscope might scrutinize the transient creatures that swarm and multiply in a drop of water. With infinite complacence people went to and fro over the earth about their little affairs, serene in the assurance of their dominion over this small spinning fragment of solar driftwood, which, by chance or design, man has inherited out of the dark mystery of time and space. Yet across an immense ethereal gulf, minds that are to our minds as ours are to the beasts in the jungle, intellects vast, cool, and unsympathetic, regarded this earth with envious eyes and slowly and surely drew their plans against us. In the thirty-ninth year of the 20th century came the great disillusionment.

Welles went on with the introduction a bit longer, and then an announcer came on, gave a weather report, and said, "We will now take you to the Meridian Room in the Hotel Park Plaza in downtown New York, where you will be entertained by the music of Ramon Raquello and his orchestra." A short time later, the music (*La Cumparsita*, being played live by the CBS house orchestra) was interrupted for a special bulletin. Astronomers looking at the planet Mars had seen strange puffs of smoke. The announcer interviewed an astronomer, who admitted to not knowing what was happening. Then the orchestra returned.

Nothing very exciting yet, but it was being done with a feel of realism and a sense of immediacy that was new to radio drama.

Then a strange meteor landed at Grovers Mill, New Jersey. Under the watching, horrified eyes of the crowd that had gathered to see the object, a door unscrewed and the grotesque Martians began to emerge.

The Martians

With ever increasing excitement in his voice, the radio announcer described the scene unfolding before his eyes: the door of the spaceship falling aside with a loud clanking sound, something—some *thing*—crawling out of the opening. The announcer described it as it emerged. It had tentacles and was as large as a bear and had a horrible face that the announcer could barely stand to look at; its V-shaped mouth quivered and dripped saliva; its eyes were black and reptilian.

The crowd fell back. Three policemen approached the object, waving a white truce flag. The monster responded by sweeping the area with a heat ray. The announcer shouted that the ray was approaching. Then the radio went dead. A new announcer came on explaining that contact with the mobile unit at Grovers Mill had just been lost.

Twisting the Dial

Now the fates stepped in to add a helping tentacle: The first segment of *The Chase and Sandborn Hour* (Edgar Bergan's show; he *had* a sponsor) had ended at about 12 past the hour, and Edgar and Charlie relinquished the microphone to a singer. This was the perfect time for the listening audience to fiddle with the tuning knobs on their radios—today we call it channel surfing.

It was later estimated by the Hooper rating service that approximately four million people switched from *The Chase and Sandborn Hour* to the Mercury Theater over the next few minutes. Most of them did not realize, however, that they had switched to the Mercury Theater. They heard that Martians in strange killing machines were spreading out over the northern New Jersey landscape. Next they were crossing the Hudson River to New York city, spreading poison gas ahead of them as they went. To many of the listeners it sounded real.

Panic!

As the hour progressed, the pace of the story would have made it clear to anyone who was listening calmly that this was a dramatization. Over the next ten minutes, the body of the Grovers Mill announcer was identified at a Trenton hospital, martial law was declared by the Governor of New Jersey, eight battalions of infantry were assembled and surrounded the Martian at Grovers Mill, and there was a battle fought. The Martian won.

Many people in the audience were no longer listening to the program calmly. Hundreds of people were in the streets of New York and other cities on the CBS network with hastily packed suitcases, headed for the bus stations, the train stations, anywhere to the north, away from the poisonous gas. A woman calling a bus terminal for information told the operator, "Hurry, please, the world is coming to an end and I have a lot to do."

At the half-hour mark, when all of New York city had been destroyed by poisonous gas and there were reports of other Martian machines around the world, the CBS announcer came on.

> You are listening to the CBS presentation of Orson Welles and the Mercury Theater on the Air in an original dramatization of *The War of the Worlds*, by H.G. Wells. The performance will continue after a brief intermission.

By then it was too late. People were barricading themselves in buildings, running up to roof tops to at least die in the open air, and at least one wedding was ruined when all the guests ran wildly into the street to escape the approaching Martian machines.

At this point, no one in the cast or at CBS had any idea of the panic being created by the show. The second half of the show was more like a traditional radio drama; anyone listening to it would know it didn't represent reality. It was too late, however. The damage was done. Many people were already fleeing and didn't hear the rest of the show.

Thousands of Army reservists called their bases to find out where they should report. Police stations and radio and newspaper offices in cities where the show was broadcast were flooded with calls. The mayor of a large Midwestern city telephoned CBS after the broadcast and announced that there were mobs in the streets of his city, and that the churches were filling with people afraid to go home. If this invasion story was some sort of joke, the mayor was going to personally come to New York and punch Orson Welles in the nose. A man found his wife standing in the bathroom with his straight razor; she was getting ready to cut her throat before the Martians could get her.

Report from the Field

"Everybody was excited. I felt as if I was going crazy and kept on saying what can we do, what difference does it make whether we die sooner or later? We were holding each other. Everything seemed unimportant in the face of death. I was afraid to die, just kept on listening."

—A listener, as reported by John Houseman, "The Men From Mars," *Harper's* magazine, December 1948

Sighting

Some UFOlogists theorize that aliens have arrived and that the government knows about it. They won't tell the public, however, because they don't want to start the same panic caused by the Orson Welles broadcast.

Aftermath

After the show the police and the press invaded the CBS building. Reporters questioned the cast unmercifully for an hour, implying that they were directly responsible for countless deaths and much destruction around the country. The police tried to figure out whether they could charge the Mercury players with anything but eventually let them go. A few days later it became clear that, although there were many real incidents of panic around the country, nobody had died as a result and there was little property damage. Some three quarters of a million dollars in damages were claimed in lawsuits filed against the Mercury people for various injuries and property damage. All the lawsuits were eventually dropped, thrown out of court, or won by Mercury and CBS. And only two weeks after the show, the Mercury Theater on the Air picked up a sponsor—Campbell Soups.

Close Encounter

Although some people thought the 1938 panic was the result of a population made nervous by fear, rumors, and reports of war (World War II had already started in Europe), the show seemed capable of provoking the panic reaction elsewhere. In 1944, the show was performed in Spanish in Santiago, Chile, and had people fleeing in the streets. In 1949, the show was broadcast in Quito, Ecuador, and a mob burned down the broadcast building when they discovered it was a hoax, killing six people. In 1988, a crowd in Portugal stormed a radio station after the program was broadcast.

More Radio

No radio series regularly dealt with aliens as a theme, but several science fiction shows had an occasional alien episode. *Buck Rogers in the 25th Century*, which began in 1932, had characters who came from different planets, as did *Flash Gordon*, which appeared later in the 1930s. (Both of these programs began as comic strips in the newspapers but were awfully human in appearance and behavior.) *Dimension X*, which later changed its name to *X Minus 1*, did radio versions of science-fiction short stories, some of which involved beings from elsewhere.

Television

Science fiction came to television early, with the children's show *Captain Video* starting in 1949. The Captain faced evil aliens from outer space for half an hour a day (except for the 12 minutes in the middle of the show when they showed a western serial). Shot live with a small budget and a smaller set, the show still managed to hold its audience of eight year olds enthralled.

Another children's science fiction series with the occasional alien was *Lost in Space*, an Irwin Allen production about the Robinson family (the original name for the series was *Space Family Robinson*), their pilot, the trouble-making Dr. Smith, and the family robot.

Although supposedly stranded on an uninhabited planet, they did manage to run into a number of (mostly nasty) aliens.

Anthology Shows

Two good science fiction anthology shows came into being in the early 1960s: *The Twilight Zone*, which ran from 1959 to 1964, and *Outer Limits*, which ran from 1963 to 1965. *The Twilight Zone* was created by Rod Serling, who wrote many of the scripts. Most of the shows were fantasy, but there were a number of straight science fiction episodes, and aliens figured in a few of them.

Outer Limits tended toward horror shows, but the very first episode, "The Galaxy Being," written and directed by Leslie Stevens, was about an alien composed of energy rather than matter who is accidentally sucked up by an earth radio telescope. An episode written by Harlan Ellison, "Demon With a Glass Hand," is a very evocative, moving tale of an android with all of humanity reduced to a code and carried in his artificial hand, who is being hunted by aliens. The *New Outer Limits* was revived in 1995 and ran for two seasons.

An alien from the Outer Limits *television show.*

Sitcoms

Television situation comedies (sitcoms) such as *My Favorite Martian* and *Mork and Mindy*, or the "Coneheads" segments on *Saturday Night Live*, explored the humor of an alien in a society he didn't understand. Some of the episodes were very clever and funny, but for the most part the alien could have been from Ruritania instead of Aldebaran.

Ray Walston as Bill Bixby's Martian uncle in My Favorite Martian.

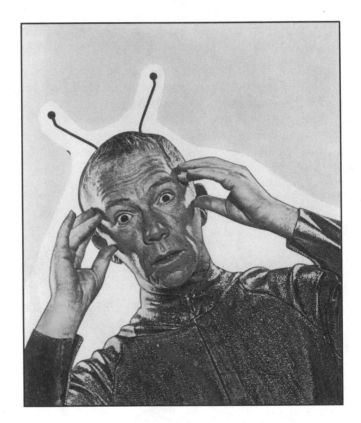

Television Series

Science fiction series on television tend to be regular dramatic or adventure shows disguised as science fiction. This is particularly true of the alien invasion shows such as *V, The Invaders,* and *Earth: Final Conflict,* each of which had aliens that were not particularly alien, and could be recast as France under the Nazis just as well as earth under the aliens.

Star Trek

The granddaddy of all science fiction television series, of course, is the original *Star Trek*, created by Gene Roddenberry, which ran from 1966 to 1968. Set on the great Starship Enterprise, whose seven-year mission of exploration was "to boldly go where no man has gone before," the show featured alien contact as a regular plot element on many of the episodes. Most of the aliens existed only as enemies to be bested. A regular theme was that human compassion or human emotion could beat out alien intelligence any time. It is interesting that the aliens were often pictured as more intelligent than the earthlings. It is also interesting how many planets across the galaxy were occupied by humans.

The well-realized alien in the series was Mr. Spock, the entirely rational Vulcan (although he was half-human). Some effort was made to make Spock, played by Leonard Lemoy, actually think differently from humans.

No one is exactly sure why the series continued to grow in popularity after it had been taken off the air, but grow it did. The first result was an animated cartoon, *Star Trek*, which ran for one season, from 1973 to 1974. The *Star Trek* feature films started to appear, and then the new shows: *Star Trek: The Next Generation*, (quickly called "NextGen" by its fans) about a new Enterprise with a new crew; *Star Trek: Deep Space Nine*, about a space station; and *Star Trek: Voyager*, about a ship lost in space. The new shows have much better special effects, showing the progress of the art in three decades, and high-quality acting. The plots, however, do not transcend the medium.

Babylon 5

An outerspace show with greater than usual intelligence, *Babylon 5*, which began in 1994, tells a continuing story with each episode dependent on what has come before. It creates a picture of an extensive galactic civilization that encompasses many races. The alien civilizations have unique and well-defined cultures, even if the aliens look suspiciously like humans in makeup. And at least one of the races, the Vorlons, have a different atmosphere and have to move about in a complex combination suit and vehicle.

The X-Files

"X-files" are the files maintained by the FBI about unexplained or unexplainable phenomena—or such is the premise of *The X-Files*, the television show that began in 1993 and quickly attracted a faithful following. Special Agent Mulder is put to investigating X-files cases, and, since he is too prone to believe in UFOs or other occult explanations, Special Agent Scully, a doctor and a rationalist, is partnered with him to temper his enthusiasm for the weird explanation, and also to keep tabs on his actions for the Bureau. She soon finds herself as his witting accomplice in investigating the bizarre shadow world revealed by the X-files.

In addition to the occult stories—with their mythological or fantasy explanations: fire starters, vengeful trees, vampires, and the like—is an underlying continuing plot involv-

Report from the Field

"It was the year of fire, the year of destruction, the year we took back what was ours. It was the year of rebirth, the year of great sadness, the year of pain, the year of joy. It was a new age; it was the end of history. It was the year everything changed. The year is 2261. The place: Babylon 5."

—Introduction to the 4th season of *Babylon 5*

ing UFOs, alien abductions, and the secret government conspiracies to conceal, reveal, destroy, and God-knows-what-all. From the basic underlying plot, it seems as though the authors read the stories put forth as truth by Milton William Cooper (see Chapter 13).

But the stories are well told, and the two lead characters, Special Agents Mulder and Scully, are appealing. The convoluted basic plot might just keep you coming back to see if you can figure out what it all means, if anything.

Reality-Based Shows

A crop of what are known as "reality-based" television shows regularly feature segments on UFOs. They have names like *Encounters*, *Sightings*, *The Unexplained*, and *Unsolved Mysteries*. The earliest of these was a show dating back to the 1970s called *In Search Of*, which was hosted by Leonard Nimoy. In addition to shows about UFOs, these shows ran segments on ghosts, the Bermuda Triangle, psychics who solve murders or find lost children, the Loch Ness Monster, Bigfoot, and other fringe science subjects. Some entire shows, such as UPN's *Alien Abduction: Incident in Lake County* (1998), have been written around supposed UFO happenings. The shows are presented as fact but usually run with disclaimers that the network has not attempted to verify any of the information presented. This lack of critical judgment makes it difficult to trust any of the material found on such shows.

"Alien" from the UPN show Alien Abduction: Incident in Lake County.

The Least You Need to Know

➤ My theory is that Big Bird is an alien.

➤ *The War of the Worlds* radio show used a variety of techniques to create a feeling of realism for its audience. It succeeded too well.

➤ Because of a fluke, many people didn't hear the opening announcement that it was a radio drama.

➤ The show, with its realistic reports of Martian war machines spreading poisonous gas, caused a panic throughout its listening area.

➤ In the 1960s, the television anthology shows *The Twilight Zone* and *Outer Limits* occasionally had episodes involving human-alien interaction.

➤ *Star Trek*, the only show to grow more popular the longer it was off the air, had a well-defined alien in the crew of the Enterprise, and many alien villains in different shows. The show's spin-offs are still doing well.

➤ *Babylon 5* has created a world, or rather a universe, with many diverse alien civilizations throughout the galaxy.

➤ The interior plot of the *X-Files* follows one of the more paranoid beliefs about the presence of UFOs here on earth and what their intentions might be. It's a very well-done show.

➤ The reality-based television shows purport to show real incidents, but their standards and level of proof are very low.

Chapter 28

Creatures from the Id: Aliens in the Movies

> ### In This Chapter
>
> ➤ Silent science-fiction movies
>
> ➤ Buck Rogers and Flash Gordon
>
> ➤ The wonderful 1950s
>
> ➤ Special effects make the movie
>
> ➤ *The X-Files: Fight the Future*

The earliest science-fiction movie, *Le Voyage dans la Lune* (A Trip to the Moon) was made by French film pioneer Georges Meliès in 1902. Based loosely on Jules Verne's *De la Terre à la Lune* (From the Earth to the Moon), it was not meant to be taken seriously. A line of laughing chorus girls load a moon missile into the giant cannon; when it hits the moon, it gives the man in the moon a black eye. It was the first attempt to portray extraterrestrials on film.

From the silent classics, *The First Men in the Moon* and *Die Frau im Mond* (Woman on the Moon), to the *X-Files* movie and beyond, extraterrestrial beings have been invading earth or chasing humans about outerspace in movie after movie. Few films have made any attempt to treat the question of extraterrestrial life seriously. In a way, however, this is an unfair complaint. Movies seldom attempt to treat anything seriously; movies are made to provoke emotion, not thought.

Silent Movies on the Moon

J.V. Leigh's *The First Men in the Moon* (1919) was a British adaptation of H.G. Wells' book. There are no known surviving prints of the movie, but it was well reviewed when it came out. One reviewer wrote the following:

> The scenes on the moon, which naturally constitute the outstanding feature of the production, have been staged with genuine skill and imagination.... The landing of the two explorers amidst the wild and desolate lunar mountains, which tower mysteriously in the chill and eerie twilight, is a situation of altogether novel power and suggestiveness. In the picture of the Grand Lunar's glittering palace, Mr. Leigh strikes an almost poetic note. In their grotesque beauty and originality, some of these settings are worthy of the fantastic art of the Russian ballet.

Die Frau im Mond (Woman on the Moon)

Fritz Lang's *Die Frau im Mond* (Woman on the Moon, 1928) was released in English as *By Rocket to the Moon* and *The Girl in the Moon*. It was from a script written by Lang and his wife Thea Von Harbou, based on Von Harbou's original novel. Lang and Von Harbou had done the classic science-fiction movie *Metropolis* together three years earlier, and great things were expected of their next collaboration. The expectations were in part delivered.

The movie had *Verein für Raumschiffahrt* (the German Society for Space Travel) experts Hermann Oberth and Willy Ley as its technical advisors. Willy Ley later came to the United States to avoid the Nazis, and was an important advisor to our space program. Hermann Oberth went on to help design the Nazi V-2 rocket, the first practical long-distance, liquid-fueled rocket. (Today it would be considered a medium-range rocket.) As a result, the technical details of Lang's multi-stage rocket ship are impressively accurate and prescient. The scene in which it moves slowly out of its hanger and approaches the launching pad reminds the viewer of launch preparations at the Kennedy Space Center. The custom of counting down (10, 9, 8...) to a rocket's launch began with this movie. Lang used it to heighten the suspense, which it certainly does even in real life.

The scenes on the moon are not as impressive as the efforts to get there. The moon's surface looks an awful lot like the Swiss Alps, and the difference between the earth's and the moon's gravity and atmosphere, and even the great temperature swings known to exist on the moon, are ignored. Complaining about small points three-quarters of a century later is unfair, however; for its time *Die Frau im Mond* was an impressive piece of work.

The Queen of Mars

The Russian film *Aelita* (1924), directed by Yakov A. Protazanov, is based on a play by Alexei Tolstoi. It features Soviet cosmonauts rocketing to Mars, where one of them falls in love with Aelita, the Queen of Mars. He and his companions quickly discover the Martian workers are being exploited by the Martian aristocrats and bourgeoisie, and they provoke a revolution among the workers. The film is good science fiction submerged in Soviet propaganda.

Flash and Buck

The term "space opera" was coined in the 1930s to describe the stories that appeared in the science-fiction pulp magazines and that were the science-fiction equivalents of the "horse opera" westerns then being published in the western pulps. These were straight adventure stories, aimed at 14-year-old boys, with the trappings of science fiction—spaceships, ray guns, aliens, scantily clad beautiful girls—to give them a suitably exotic setting.

Sighting

The *Buck Rogers* comic strip and movie were based on Philip Francis Nowlan's stories "Armageddon 2419 AD," and "The Airlords of Han," which were serialized in *Amazing Stories* in 1928 and 1929, respectively.

The newspaper comic strips *Flash Gordon*, created, drawn, and written by Alex Raymond, and *Buck Rogers in the 25th Century*, created by John Flint Dille and written by Philip Francis Nowlan, were the comic equivalent of the pulp magazine stories. They were both turned into serial films in the 1930s.

Flash Gordon

The first space opera film was the 1936 serial *Flash Gordon*, starring Buster Crabbe as the heroic Flash, Jean Rogers as his girlfriend Dale Arden, and Charles Middleton as the evil Ming the Merciless. The plot involves Flash, Dale, and Flash's scientist sidekick, Dr. Zarkov, taking a homemade spaceship to Mongo, the planet from which the evil Ming plots to take over the earth. After facing shark-men, clay-men, and various monsters for 13 episodes, they finally defeat Ming and make it back to earth. The film had two sequels, *Flash Gordon's Trip to Mars* (1938) and *Flash Gordon Conquers the Universe* (1940), which follow basically the same story. The special effects were primitive and unbelievable, but suspending disbelief is easy for a 14-year-old, and the sight of Flash's spaceship taking off from the rocky terrain of Mongo, billowing smoke and popping sparks out the back, was as exciting then as a full, wide-screen view of the Millennium Falcon is today.

Sighting

Charles Middleton was one of the greatest villains of all time. The sight of him seated on his throne, waving a casual hand at his minions, who are holding a struggling Flash Gordon and saying in a bored voice, "Take him to the brain destroyer," is one of the greatest moments in the history of space opera.

Buck Rogers in the 25th Century

The second great space opera serial, *Buck Rogers in the 25th Century*, also starred Buster Crabbe. In this take off on the comic strip, Buck wakes up after a 500-year sleep and discovers that Killer Kane and the evil Zuggs from Saturn have invaded the earth. The 12 episodes of the series have the usual spaceship chases, clanking robots, ray guns, and near-death experiences, as Buck goes to Saturn to confront and defeat the evil Zuggs.

The Wonderful 1950s

The 1950s ushered in the great era of alien invasion movies. From *The Day the Earth Stood Still* to *Invaders from Mars* to George Pal's wonderful adaptation of *The War of the Worlds*, moviegoers could be scared out of their minds week after week by evil, grotesque aliens pillaging, burning, and generally acting up. Occasionally, as in *The Day the Earth Stood Still*, the movies focused on narrow-minded earthmen attacking the friendly aliens.

The Day the Earth Stood Still

The 1951 movie version of the Harry Bates short story, "Farewell to the Master," *The Day the Earth Stood Still*, written by Edmund H. North and directed by Robert Wise, told the story of Klaatu arriving on earth with his eight-foot tall robot Gort to warn earthlings to behave and to practice nonviolence. Before he can deliver the message, however, he is wounded by one of the soldiers surrounding his spaceship, and flees the area. Befriended by an earth woman, he finally makes it back to his spaceship and sets up a demonstration of his race's powers—stopping all the machinery in the world. As he tries to deliver the message, however, he is shot and killed. His female friend activates Gort the robot, who retrieves and reanimates the body, whereupon his message is delivered to our planet.

Sighting

Although the directorial credit for *The Thing* was given to Christian Nyby, the film was actually directed by Howard Hawks. Nyby was Hawks' film editor, and Hawks arranged for Nyby to get the directorial credit.

A much better movie than this bald description of the plot makes it sound, the film is directed and acted with a fine restraint that makes it very effective.

The Thing

Howard Hawks' 1951 horror film, with screenplay by Charles Lederer, and based on John W. Campbell, Jr.'s "Who Goes There?", was released as *The Thing* and as *The Thing from Another World*. Under either name it is easily one of the scariest movies ever made. At a United States military base in Greenland, a group of scientists discover a flying saucer that has been buried in the ice for many centuries. Unwisely, they defrost it, and an all-too-human vegetable emerges and terrorizes the base and audience. In the end the creature is defeated, but the questions of where it came from and whether there are any more like it at home remain. The last, haunting, line of the movie is: "Watch the skies!"

Invaders from Mars

A strange movie in which a young boy wakes up in the middle of the night and sees a flying saucer land behind his house, and aliens take over the bodies of his parents and then move on to take over the whole town, William Cameron Menzies' *Invaders from Mars* (1953) seems to be an overly paranoid fantasy brought on by the communist scares of the 1950s. The basic idea is that everyone looks normal, but no one knows whom to trust. In an interesting twist, after the aliens are defeated by the army, the boy awakes and realizes that it was all a dream. Before he has a chance to breathe a sigh of relief, however, the boy once again sees the aliens land behind his house.

The poster for the 1953 movie Invaders From Mars.

The War of the Worlds

You've read about the H.G. Wells book (Chapter 26) and the Orson Welles radio show (Chapter 27), now what about the movie? Cecil B. De Mille bought the movie rights to *The War of the Worlds* in 1925 but decided there were too many technical problems to make the movie. In 1930, Paramount offered the Russian director Sergei Eisenstein a chance, and he actually wrote a script before abandoning the project. The film, however, didn't get made until 1953.

Sighting

The recent movie *Independence Day* was effectively an uncredited remake of *The War of the Worlds.*

A George Pal production, the movie was written by Barré Lyndon and directed by Byron Haskin. Probably the finest alien invasion movie made up to that time, it was worth waiting for. The script followed the Wells book fairly well, except for the necessary updating and a mandatory love interest. The Martian's war machines were manta-ray–looking flying machines instead of walkers, and did a creditable job of destroying everything in sight with their heat rays. As in the book, the Martians are invincible to anything the puny earthlings can do, but they are brought down by earth's bacteria, to which they are not immune.

A Martian war machine from the 1953 movie, The War of the Worlds.

This Island Earth

Raymond F. Jones wrote the novel, *This Island Earth*, which appeared as a serial in "Thrilling Wonder Stories" in 1949–1950. The movie version, directed by Joseph Newman in 1955, has one of the more complicated plots for what is essentially a true space opera. Using parts bought from a strange electronics parts catalog, scientist Cal Meacham builds an "interociter,"—a sort of two-way television—with which he communicates with Exeter, an alien who is on earth to devise a way to save his doomed planet Metaluna. He joins a band of earth and alien scientists who are working on this project in a secret laboratory, and meets Dr. Ruth Adams, the love interest.

The scientists take a trip to Metaluna in a giant flying saucer, just in time to see the planet in the final stages of being destroyed by their enemy aliens, the Zhagon, who are guiding giant meteors to crash into Metaluna. The flying saucer descends to a great city under the surface, and they meet the Monitor, head of the planet. He takes an instant dislike to them and orders them to be destroyed, but they escape. The movie would have been better had it more closely followed the Raymond F. Jones novel, but the special effects are okay.

Close Encounter

Outer space has been a great location for aliens in many a movie. The titles using this location, or a variant, over the years include: *Phantom from Space* (1953), *Fire Maidens from Outer Space* (1954), *I Married a Monster from Outer Space* (1957), *It! The Terror From Beyond Space* (1958), *Invaders from Space* (1962), *They Came from Beyond Space* (1967), *Battle in Outer Space* (1975), *Bloodsuckers from Outer Space* (1984), *Hermano del espacio* (Brother from Space, 1986), and *Killer Klowns from Outer Space* (1988).

Forbidden Planet

Proving it's easy (or at least easier) to produce a classic when you start with a classic, director Fred McLeod Wilcox based *Forbidden Planet* (1956) on Shakespeare's *The Tempest* (1611). Morbius (the Prospero figure if you know your Shakespeare) and his daughter Altaira are the sole survivors of a colony on the planet Altair Four. With the aid of their robot, Robbie, they manage to survive until a rescue ship, the United Planets Cruiser C57D, and its crew, headed by Commander Adams, arrives. There is a mysterious buried city left by a race called the Krel, with many wonders to explore, and a love interest between the commander and Altaira. There is also a menacing and intangible monster that turns out to be a "creature from the Id," unwittingly created by Morbius with the aid of the Krel machinery. The movie, which critics often mention as a precursor to *Star Trek*, is visually interesting and holds up well.

Earth vs. the Flying Saucers

Based on a short story by Curt Siodmak, *Earth vs. the Flying Saucers* (1956) was written by George Worthing Yates and Raymond T. Marcus, and directed by Fred F. Sears.

Flying saucers menace Paris in the 1956 film, Earth vs. the Flying Saucers.

Aliens from a "disintegrated solar system" need earth and its resources, and want humans to surrender quickly so that they can land their waiting fleet and take over. Their giant saucers attack and destroy everything around, until an earth scientist discovers how to build an ultrasonic beam that will disrupt the saucers' anti-gravity fields. The movie features wonderful shots of the saucers crashing into the Washington Monument and the Capitol, all done on a minuscule budget by the master special effects creator, Ray Harryhausen.

Five Million Years to Earth

A remake of the 1958 British television series *Quartermass and the Pit*, the 1968 British movie *Five Million Years to Earth*, directed by Roy Ward Baker, is one of the strangest and most compelling alien invasion stories ever made. A spaceship buried under London is discovered by workmen digging a great hole for a new underground (subway) station. The ship contains the skulls of long-extinct ape men. Professor Quartermass correctly concludes that the ship must be at least five million years old. His nemesis, however, a rigid and narrow-minded army officer named Colonel Breen, thinks the ship is some kind of Nazi missile that crashed during the World War II blitz of London.

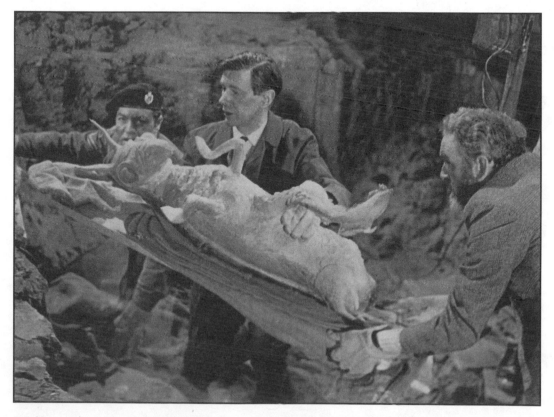

Professor Quartermass inspects an ancient alien in Five Million Years to Earth.

Then, in the forward part of the ship, they find the bodies of insect-like creatures that clearly were in control of the ship and, therefore, intelligent. In the meantime, the people living in the area over the dig, Hob's Lane, have an increase in the scary psychic manifestations from which they have suffered for some time.

Quartermass figures out that the insectoids are Martians who came to earth five million years previously because their planet was dying. They kidnapped a bunch of ape men and genetically altered them, implanting their (the Martians) racial memories so that those men would become, at least mentally, Martians. The race of Martians would continue, once removed, in the bodies of men.

Meanwhile, the buried spaceship comes alive, feeding off the power of a television cable laid across it, and causes humans in an ever-increasing radius around the underground hole in the ground to go crazy. Those with the Martian gene did their best to kill those without it.

The special effects by Les Bowie, especially those of widespread poltergeist phenomena, are subtle, effective, and disturbing.

Special Effects Win the Day

Modern science-fiction movies have become more and more dependent on special effects to keep the viewer's interest. The special effects have improved to the point where anything that can be conceived of can be shown on-screen. Personally, I still prefer a good plot and believable motivation, but those space ships sure are impressive.

2001: A Space Odyssey

Stanley Kubrick's *2001: A Space Odyssey* (1968) had the greatest special effects to be seen on the big screen until *Star Wars* came out a decade later. Based on Arthur C. Clarke's short story "The Sentinel," the film is equal parts science fiction, mysticism, and incredible views of outer space. The plot involves astronauts who discover a huge black monolith on the moon that has apparently been left there by some alien race four million years ago. Its function is either to aid in some undefined fashion in human evolution or to signal the aliens when humans reach some particular point in evolution—or possibly both, possibly neither. The astronaut who makes it to Jupiter (his companions are killed by a rogue computer on the way) sees the monolith as he dies—or does he die?—and then a kaleidoscopic montage of space and color with a baby—a space child?—floating in its midst ends the movie. Some years ago, I asked Mr. Clarke what the ending was meant to signify. He had asked Kubrick the same thing and thought he had understood the answer at the time. Later, however, he wasn't sure.

The Star Wars Trilogy

The *Star Wars* trilogy movies are the finest space adventure movies I've ever seen. Despite some flaws in plot and dialog, George Lucas' *Star Wars* (1977) and its two (so far) sequels, *The Empire Strikes Back* (1980) and *Return of the Jedi* (1983), succeed at the willing suspension of disbelief better than any of their predecessors. This is accomplished with believable, if a bit simplistic, characters, action that never stops, great attention to detail, and the finest special effects that have ever graced the movie screen. When those two suns were in the sky, there were two suns in the sky. And Jabba the Hud was grossly effective. When shooting the famous bar scene, Lucas must have hired alien actors; there's no other explanation.

Close Encounters of the Third Kind

Steven Spielberg's 1978 movie *Close Encounters of the Third Kind* is a trite, thoughtless evocation of the UFO myth. The aliens are inconsistent, the humans are incapable of thought, and the denouement makes no sense whatsoever. If the aliens understood people, which it seems they must have, why did they need that elaborate music and light show at the end? If they didn't understand people, how did anyone know to prepare that elaborate music and light show, or know just what music and/or light to use?

E.T. The Extra-Terrestrial is a movie about a cute little animal, who happens to be an extraterrestrial instead of a puppy. The theme of the movie seems to be that you can't trust adults. Which, as far as I'm concerned, goes for the adults who made the movie.

Star Trek: The Motion Picture and All the Little Star Treks

I feel obliged to mention the *Star Trek* movies, and here is the mention. There are no credible aliens in the *Star Trek* universe. There are many credible humans, some of whom wear funny clothes and masks, and pretend to be alien. We all know they're really human; they can't kid us. Even Spock and Data, with their emotionless facade, are human underneath. This is wonderful and good if you like that, but this is a book about alien contact.

All the Little Aliens

In the 1958 film *It! The Terror From Beyond Space*, written by Jerome Bixby and directed by Edward Cahn, a spaceship crew discovers that a blood-sucking monster has boarded the ship, is attacking crew members, and is stowing their bodies in the ship's ventilation system. One by one, the crew members are murdered. In the 1979 film *Alien*, written by Dan O'Bannon and directed by Ridley Scott, a spaceship crew discovers...well, you see where I'm going, don't you?

The plots are the same, but the movies are quite different, thanks to Ridley Scott, the incredible special effects and sets—particularly the derelict alien space ship—and the star, Sigourney Weaver. And, of course, the alien, who is one of the most horrendous creatures ever devised by man. The sequels, *Aliens*, *Alien 3*, and *Alien: Resurrection*, are more of the same. Although *Alien* was clearly a horror movie, *Aliens* is more of an adventure movie, with Weaver fighting the alien creature mother-to-mother in some of the most exciting fight sequences ever filmed. Ripley (Weaver) dies in *Alien 3*, but that can't keep her down when there's a sequel to be made. *Alien: Resurrection* takes place 200 years later, and a newly cloned Ripley once again fights an alien queen—also freshly cloned for the encounter. As usual, Weaver and the alien queen steal the movie.

The X-Files: Fight the Future

The X-Files: Fight the Future, written by Chris Carter and directed by Rob Bowman, was perhaps the most hyped movie since *Gone With the Wind*. The movie might live up to the hype if you're a true-blue fan of the *X-Files* television show. For the rest of us, however, it's too busy, too diffuse, and full of too many characters who are there only so that the regular *X-Files* television show viewer will have the thrill of recognition.

The movie starts some 5,000 years ago with aliens attacking a cave man. It switches to modern-day Texas, where a young boy finds a Neanderthal skull and becomes infected with a weird virus called "black oil." Mulder and Sculley, two FBI agents and the movie's hero and heroine, are in Dallas investigating a bomb scare. They are now working in the anti-terrorism unit, the X-Files operation having been officially disbanded. The bomb explodes, and we are led to believe that it was intended to cover up something about the existence of aliens.

After reprising many elements from the television show, and several of the characters with no names, just habits—the Cigarette-Smoking Man, the Well-Manicured Man—the movie finally arrives at an alien spaceship under the ice in Antarctica. The aliens are reminiscent of those in *Alien*: very scary. Mulder, sort of by accident, fouls the aliens' plans while rescuing Sculley from the ship, and the giant flying saucer takes off from the Antarctic ice.

And So It Goes

If I haven't mentioned one of your favorite shows in this run-down, I'm sorry. But in trying to show the good and bad in the history of the movie industry's representation of extraterrestrial life in this brief space, I had to be selective. I selected the films I liked the best or disliked the most. For a fuller list of titles, see Appendix E.

The Least You Need to Know

➤ The early science-fiction, space-travel movies were mostly about trips to the moon, although Mars also figured in one or two.

➤ The children's serials *Flash Gordon* and *Buck Rogers*, based on newspaper comic strips, were the original "space opera" movies.

➤ The 1950s produced dozens of alien invasion movies, and a few, such as *The Day the Earth Stood Still* and *The War of the Worlds*, were actually pretty good.

➤ The British movie *Five Million Years to Earth* manages to be scary and effective on a small budget.

➤ Made in 1968, Stanley Kubrick's *2001: A Space Odyssey* is still a masterful film as far as overall impact and special effects go. The plot was never its strong point.

➤ The *Star Wars* series is the best space opera to date. The aliens in it, from Jabba the Hud to the gathering in the bar scene, had the distinction of being more than men in funny suits; they were truly alien.

➤ The *X-Files: Fight the Future* movie was good if you like the *X-Files* television show.

Glossary

Abductee   One who has been, or believes he or she has been, abducted by aliens. (*See:* Contactee)

Alien   In this usage, an intelligent being from another planet.

Ancient astronauts   Visitors from another planet who some believe have come to earth in prehistoric times. These visitors have been credited with everything from "seeding" the life on this planet to building the pyramids.

Archetype   A person or object that represents and stands for an entire class of things. Superman is the archetypical strong man, for example.

Bandwidth   The bandwidth of a radio signal is the span from the number of hertz (cycles per second) at the low end of the signal to the number of hertz at the high end. An FM radio station listed as broadcasting at 88.5 MHz (megahertz: million cycles per second) can probably be heard from 88.3 to 88.7 MHz or more. Its bandwidth, therefore, is at least 0.4 MHz.

Casuistry   The study of problems of conscience and morality, and how to resolve them.

Cepheid variables   Stars that periodically vary in brightness. They were so called because the first one discovered was in the constellation Cepheus (named after the mythical father of Andromeda). In 1912, the American astronomer Henrietta Swan Leavitt discovered that Cepheids with the same period—that take the same length of time from bright to dim and back—have the same brightness. This enabled astronomers to calculate the distance from the earth to the Cepheids; if you know how bright something is, you can measure how far away it is.

Cherubim   Winged creatures associated with Jehovah. The Hebrew root word, *krubim*, means "full of knowledge."

Close encounter   An interaction with a UFO or alien. The four kinds of close encounters are as follows:

Close Encounter of the First Kind   When UFOs are seen at close range, and possibly heard, but you don't touch them and they don't touch you. They depart without leaving behind any sign of their presence. This sort of experience may leave you with disturbing memories, despite the lack of physical contact.

Close Encounter of the Second Kind   Like the Close Encounter of the First Kind with the addition of physical indications of their presence. Some common possibilities are scorched ground where the UFO landed, flattened vegetation, or broken tree limbs. Car engines or radios may suddenly stop, and electronic devices may not work while the UFO is present. These effects typically end after the UFO leaves.

Close Encounter of the Third Kind   Involves the observer seeing intelligent alien beings in or around a (usually landed) UFO. The possibilities of a third-kind encounter range from merely watching the beings to speaking with them (usually telepathically) or having some other interaction.

Close Encounter of the Fourth Kind   Also called "alien abductions," these are cases where aliens take humans aboard a craft against their will to examine them physically and/or mentally, and possibly talk with them (usually telepathically) before returning them whence they came. These experiences are often accompanied by loss of memory for a specific period of time, as well as powerful psychological reactions.

Contactee   A person who has, or claims to have, hobnobbed with the extraterrestrial crew of a UFO. Typically, the extraterrestrial crew tells the contactee how the universe works, and gives him or her advice to share with the rest of mankind.

Cyclotron   A device that accelerates atomic particles (usually protons) around a circular course, guiding them with powerful magnets, until they achieve high speed and energy and smash into a target. Sometimes called an "atom smasher," the cyclotron was developed by physicist Ernest Lawrence in 1930.

Diffraction grating   Bends light passed through it as though it was a prism. Made of closely spaced thin wires or fine lines scratched on a glass plate, it was invented by Joseph von Fraunhofer in 1820.

Dirigible   A lighter-than-air craft that has a rigid frame, is capable of powered flight, and can be steered.

Ecosphere   The range of orbits around a star that are suitable for a life-bearing planet.

Exobiology   The study of the biology of organisms originating outside the earth. Since we have not yet located any such organisms, the problems of exobiologists now concentrate on deciding just what sorts of life are possible in alien environments. (Some scientists have recently claimed that a rock found in Antarctica and believed to have originated on Mars has traces of microscopic life.)

Exogeology   The study of the mineral and rock composition of a planet, and how it got that way. A surprising amount of information can be gathered by unmanned spacecraft circling a planet and using sophisticated sensors to study the ground below. Knowledge of how other planets formed can greatly aid our understanding of our own planet.

Exometeorology   The study of the weather on other planets.

Extraterrestrial (E.T.)   A being or life-form from another planet.

Flying saucer   A disc-shaped flying object possibly piloted by extraterrestrials; or, by extension, any UFO.

Foo Fighters   Mysterious small discs or globes of light that played tag with both Allied and Axis powers' airplanes during World War II.

Geoglyphs   From the Greek for earth-writing, geoglyphs are figures drawn on the ground. They are not necessarily cut very deep into the earth; they might just have the top layer of dirt removed to reveal a different colored clay or rock underneath; or they may be created from pebbles or stones. Many geoglyphs are very large—some of them are hundreds of feet long—and seem to have been created to be seen from above.

Half-life   The amount of time it takes for half of a radioactive element, such as plutonium, to decay (change) into another element. If half of it decays in, say, 100 years, another half will decay in the next 100 years. In 200 years, three-quarters of the original mass will have changed into something else. And so on.

Lenticular clouds   Clouds that form in the shape ovals or circles. They can have distinct edges and look convincingly like solid objects.

Men In Black (MIB)   Conservatively dressed men who occasionally show up at the site of a UFO incident to interview, or some say intimidate, the observers. Some UFOlogists believe Men In Black are government agents; some believe they are aliens; some believe they are imaginary.

Metabolism   The processes necessary to maintain life. This includes the processes of growing, such as tissue and muscle building, as well as the processes of breaking down, such as the burning of body sugars to make energy.

Myth   A story, often about a god or a hero, that somehow speaks to the human condition. Perhaps it teaches something of what it is to be a member of the society that created the myth.

Nebula   From the word "nebulous," which means cloudy or indistinct, nebula was the name given to small, indistinct, cloudy patches in the night sky. As telescopes improved, many of them turned out to be distant galaxies, while others were expanding clouds of interstellar gas, possibly from exploding stars.

Organic   In the sense used in this book, organic means formed from the same complex carbon compounds produced by the processes of life. Some of the compounds, such as various amino acids (the basis for the proteins that are the building blocks of life), have been shown to be produced by natural processes.

Paleontologists   Scientists who study fossils, which are the remains, in whatever form, of long-dead things that were once alive.

Pantheism   The belief that God and the universe are one, that God is everything and everything is God.

Parallax   The apparent change in position of an object in relation to its background as the viewer's position changes. Watch a tree as you pass it in a car, and see how it seems to move across the mountains behind it as the car moves.

Perihelion   The orbits of planets around the sun are not perfectly round, but are slightly elliptical (shaped like a racetrack). The point in their orbit where they are closest to the sun is their perihelion.

Polytheism   The belief in many gods.

Prandtl, Ludwig (1875–1953)   Considered the father of aerodynamic theory, Prandtl developed mathematical models for how air flows over the surface of a wing at various speeds.

Pulsars   Stars that regularly emit bursts of radio waves toward the earth—so regular that radio astronomers originally thought they might have found intelligent communication. As regular as they are, however, the bursts contain no information. Pulsars are now considered as rapidly spinning neutron stars—very dense stars perhaps left over from a supernova explosion—that are emitting a beam of energy. Each time the beam sweeps by our radio telescopes record a pulse.

Quasars   Quasars (quasi-stellar radio source) are distant objects that emit tremendous amounts of energy—in some cases more than an entire galaxy—but that seem to be not much larger than stars. Quasars remain one of the great mysteries of the universe.

Summer solstice   The moment when the earth reaches the place in its orbit around the sun that the sun appears at its farthest northern point in the sky for that year. This is caused by the tilting of the earth's axis so that at one point in its orbit the North Pole leans toward the sun and at the opposite point it leans away from the sun.

Sun dogs   Apparitions of the sun, like mirages, that occur when atmospheric inversions cause the image of the sun to be refracted to a different position. Two or more sun dogs are occasionally visible on both sides of the real sun.

Sun spots   Dark patches on the surface of the sun believed to have been caused by the upwelling of hot gasses from the sun's interior. The number of spots increases and decreases in an 11-year cycle. At their highest number, sunspots have been known to cause disruption of radio transmission on earth.

UFO   UFO, or Unidentified Flying Object, as become synonymous with "flying saucer." UFOs, however, come in all shapes and sizes.

UFOlogist   One who studies UFOs seriously.

Ziggurats   Step pyramids, named for the temple-towers of ancient Babylonia and Assyria.

Reporting UFOs

Air Force Regulation 200-2 specifies a report form for UFO sightings. It went through several revisions; the following is a portion of the 12 August 1954 version.

INTELLIGENCE
Unidentified Flying Objects Reporting

(1) Purpose and Scope: This Regulation establishes procedures for reporting information and evidence pertaining to unidentified flying objects and sets forth the responsibility of Air Force activities in this regard. It applies to all Air Force activities.

(2) Definitions:

    a. *Unidentified Flying Objects (UFOB)*. Relates to any airborne object which by performance, aerodynamic characteristics, or unusual features does not conform to any presently known aircraft or missile type, or which cannot be positively identified as a familiar object.

    b. *Familiar Objects*. Includes balloons, astronomical bodies, birds, and so forth.

(3) Objectives: Air Force interest in unidentified flying objects is two-fold: First as a possible threat to the security of the United States and its forces, and secondly, to determine technical aspects involved.

    ...   .

(4) Responsibility:

    a. *Reporting*. Commanders of Air Force activities will report all information and evidence that may come to their attention, including that received from adjacent commands of the other services and from civilians.

    b. *Investigation*. Air Defense Command will conduct all field investigations within the ZI to determine the identity of any UFOB.

c. *Analysis.* The Air Technical Intelligence Center (ATIC), Wright-Patterson Air Force Base, Ohio, will analyze and evaluate: All information and evidence reported within the ZI after the Air Defense Command has exhausted all efforts to identify the UFOB; and all information and evidence collected in oversea areas.

d. *Cooperation.* All activities will cooperate with Air Defense Command representatives to ensure the economical and prompt success of an investigation, including the furnishing of air and ground transportation, when feasible.

...   .

(7) Reporting: All information relating to UFOB's will be reported promptly.

...   .

d. *Report* Format. Reports will include the following numbered items:

1. Description of the object(s):
   a. Shape.
   b. Size compared to a known object (use one of the following terms: Head of a pin, pea, dime, nickel, quarter, half dollar, silver dollar, baseball, grapefruit, or basketball) held in the hand at about arms length.
   c. Color.
   d. Number.
   e. Formation, if more than one.
   f. Any discernible features or details.
   g. Tail, trail, or exhaust, including size of same compared to size of object(s).
   h. Sound. If heard, describe sound.
   i. Other pertinent or unusual features.

2. Description of course of object(s):
   a. What first called the attention of observer(s) to the object(s)?
   b. Angle of elevation and azimuth of the object(s) when first observed.
   c. Angle of elevation and azimuth of the object(s) upon disappearance.
   d. Description of flight path and maneuvers of object(s).
   e. Manner of disappearance of object(s).
   f. Length of time in sight.

3. Manner of observation:
   a. Use of one or any combination of the following items: Ground-visual, ground-electronic, air-electronic. (If electronic, specify type of radar.)
   b. Statement as to optical aids (telescopes, binoculars, and so forth) used and description thereof.

   c. If the sighting is made while airborne, give type of aircraft, identification number, altitude, heading, speed, and home station.

4. Time and date of sighting:
   a. Zulu time-date group of sighting.
   b. Light conditions (use one of the following terms): night, day, dawn, dusk.

5. Locations of observer(s). Exact latitude and longitude of each observer, or Georef position, or position with reverence to a known landmark.

6. Identifying information of all observer(s):
   a. Civilian—Name, age, mailing address, occupation.
   b. Military—Name, grade, organization, duty, and estimate of reliability.

7. Weather and winds-aloft conditions at time and place of sightings:
   a. Observer(s) account of weather conditions.
   b. Reports from nearest AWS or U.S. Weather Bureau Office of wind direction and velocity in degrees and knots at surface, 6,000', 10,000', 16,000', 20,000', 30,000', 50,000', and 80,000', if available.
   c. Ceiling.
   d. Visibility.
   e. Amount of cloud cover.
   f. Thunderstorms in area and quadrant in which located.

8. Any other unusual activity or condition, meteorological, astronomical, or otherwise, which might account for the sighting.

9. Interception or identification action taken (such action may be taken whenever feasible, complying with existing air defense directives).

10. Location of any air traffic in the area at time of sighting.

11. Position title and comments of the preparing officer, including his preliminary analysis of the possible cause of the sighting(s).

12. Existence of physical evidence, such as materials and photographs.

(8) Evidence: The existence of physical evidence (photographs or materiel) will be promptly reported.

   a. Photographic:

1. Visual. The negative and two prints will be forwarded; all original film, including wherever possible both prints and negatives, will be titled or otherwise properly identified as to place, time, and date of the incident (see "Intelligence Collection Instructions" (ICI) June 1954).

2. Radar. Two copies of each print will be forwarded. Prints of radarscope photography will be titled in accordance with AFR 95-7 and forwarded in compliance with AFR 95-6.

b. *Materiel*. Suspected or actual items of materiel which come into possession of any Air Force echelon will be safeguarded in such a manner as to prevent any defacing or alteration which might reduce its value for intelligence examination and analysis.

(9) Release of Facts: Headquarters USAF will release summaries of evaluated data which will inform the public on this subject. In response to local inquiries, it is permissible to inform news media representatives on UFOB's when the object is positively identified as a familiar object (see paragraph 2b), except that the following type of data warrants protection and should not be revealed: Names of principles, intercept and investigation procedures, and classified radar data. For those objects which are not explainable, only the fact that ATIC will analyze the data is worthy of release, due to the many unknowns involved.

—By Order of the Secretary of the Air Force

UFO-Related Organizations and Web Sites

UFOs

The UFO Coalition (CUFOS, FUFOR, and MUFON)

The UFO Coalition is made up of CUFOS, FUFOR, and MUFON.

CUFOS, the J. Allen Hynek Center for UFO Studies, was founded in 1973 in Chicago, where its co-founder, the late Dr. J. Allen Hynek, was a professor of astronomy at Northwestern University. CUFOS publishes the quarterly *International UFO Reporter*, the annual refereed, *Journal of UFO Studies*, and the occasional monograph and book. Annual membership dues are $25 and include a subscription to *International UFO Reporter*.

Address: CUFOS, 2457 West Peterson Avenue, Chicago, IL, 60659

FUFOR, the Fund for UFO Research, was established in 1979. FUFOR is not a membership organization per se. Instead, it raises and disperses research funds for proposals approved by a national board. Each year the fund also awards a cash prize, the Donald E. Keyhoe Journalism Award, to both the print and electronic media journalist whose work about UFOs is judged the best among those submitted. For further information, or an application for the Fund's journalism award, write:

Address: The Fund for UFO Research, PO Box 227, Mount Ranier, MD, 20712

MUFON, The Mutual UFO Network, was established in 1969. One of the oldest UFO groups around, it is headquartered in Seguin, Texas and has over 5,000 members, field investigators, and research consultants worldwide. It publishes the monthly *MUFON/UFO Journal* and an annual collection of *Symposium Proceedings*. Membership, which includes a subscription to the Journal, is $30 annually.

Address: MUFON, 103 Oldtowne Road, Seguin, TX, 78155-4099

Web site: http://hotx.com/ansen/mufon/

Other Organizations

BUFORA, the British UFO Research Association publishes *UFO Times*.

Address: BM BUFORA, London, WC1N3XX, UK

CAUS, the Citizens Against UFO Secrecy conducts Freedom of Information Act inquiries to obtain government-held information on UFOs. CAUS also publishes a quarterly journal, *Just Cause*.

Address: CAUS, PO Box 176, Stoneham, MA, 02180

MOTHERSHIP maintains a Web site with frequently updated information on UFOs as well as other paranormal interests. It has a good list of links to other sites.

Web site: www.ufomind.com

The National UFO Reporting Center takes reports on UFO sightings on a 24-hour telephone hotline as well as on a well thought-out reporting form at its Web site.

Address: National UFO Reporting Center, PO Box 45623, University Station, Seattle, WA, 98145

Hotline: 206-722-3000

Web site: www.nwlink.com/~ufocntr/

E-mail: ufocntr@nwlink.com

SSE, the Society for Scientific Exploration, publishes the quarterly, refereed *Journal of Scientific Exploration*, which contains UFO-related articles, among others.

Address: ERL 306, Stanford University, Stanford, CA, 94305

You can order Betty Hill's book, *A Common Sense Approach to UFOs* (ISBN 0-9648243-0-2) directly from:

Betty Hill
PO Box 55
Greenland, New Hampshire 03840

The price is $15.95 (plus postage).

Crop Circles and Animal Mutilations

If you are interested in the "hard" scientific research available regarding physical alterations to plants and soils at crop formations, unusual animal deaths (the so-called "cattle mutilation phenomenon"), and apparent UFO-trace cases, contact:

Nancy TalbottBLT Research Team

Address: Box 127, Cambridge, MA 02140

Telephone: 617-492-0415

Fax: 617-492-0414

Abductions

Stephanie Kelley, of the University of Kansas, is doing a study on alien abductions. Or, as she puts it, "a rhetorical analysis using abduction narratives as my texts." Any information she gathers will be kept completely confidential, and could be helpful in understanding the phenomenon. If you are, or believe you have been, an abductee and are willing to participate in a study, contact Ms. Kelley.

Address: Stephanie Kelley, Principal Investigator, Department of Communication Studies, 3090 Wescoe Hall, University of Kansas, Lawrence, KS, 66045

Telephone: 785-864-9897

E-mail: skelley@falcon.cc.ukans.edu

Radio Shows

Several national talk radio shows are dedicated to the discussion of UFOs and other paranormal phenomena. Check their Web sites to find what station they are on in your area. Among the better known are the following:

Sightings with Jeff Rense	www.sightings.com/
X-Zone with Rob McConnell	www.x-chronicles.com/
Coast to Coast with Art Bell	www.artbell.com/

SETI-Related Organizations and Web Sites

The SETI Institute

A non-profit corporation founded in 1984, the SETI Institute, according to its literature, "serves as an institutional home for scientific and educational projects relevant to the nature, distribution, and prevalence of life in the universe. The Institute conducts and/or encourages research and related activities in a large number of fields, including but not limited to, all science and technology aspects of astronomy and the planetary sciences, chemical evolution, the origin of life, biological evolution, and cultural evolution. The Institute also has a primary goal to conduct and encourage public information and education related to these topics."

Address	SETI Institute
	2035 Landings Road
	Mountain View, CA 94043
E-mail	info@seti-inst.edu
Web site	www.seti-inst.edu

The SETI League

An organization "of, by, and for the amateur radio astronomer," the SETI League consists of members who search for extraterrestrial life with radio telescopes in their own backyards. The SETI League will tell you where to get the necessary radio equipment, help you get started, and keep you informed as the search continues.

Address	The SETI League
	433 Liberty Street
	Little Ferry, NJ 07643
Mailing address	The SETI League
	P.O. Box 555
	Little Ferry, NJ 07643
Telephone	201-641-1770
Fax	201-641-1771
Membership hotline	800-TAU-SETI
General e-mail	info@setileague.org
Memberships	join@setileague.org

The Friends of SERENDIP

Headed by science and fiction writer Arthur C. Clarke, and headquartered at the University of California at Berkeley, the organization supports the continued efforts of Project Serendip (*S*earch for *E*xtraterrestrial *R*adio *E*missions from *N*earby *D*eveloped *I*ntelligent *P*opulations). The project operates as a "piggyback" SETI system on the 1,000-foot dish at Arecibo Observatory in Puerto Rico. Without interrupting any radio astronomy observations, SERENDIP takes a feed of the telescope's output and passes it through the SERENDIP spectrum analyzer and looks at millions of narrow-band chunks to see if any of the signals overheard show signs of intelligence (see Chapter 23).

For information, send e-mail to sereninfo@ssl.berkeley.edu.

Alien-Inspired Movies

The following is an alphabetical listing of important or interesting movies that have a strong extraterrestrial influence. The movies marked with an asterisk (*) are discussed in Chapter 28.

20 Million Miles to Earth (1957)

2001: A Space Odyssey (1968)*

Aelita (1924)*

Alien (1979)*

Aliens (1986)*

Alien 3 (1992)*

The Andromeda Strain (1971)

Battle in Outer Space (1975)*

Bloodsuckers from Outer Space (1984)*

Buck Rogers (1939)

Close Encounters of the Third Kind (1978)*

Cocoon (1985)

Cocoon: The Return (1988)

Communion (1989)

Coneheads (1993)

Contact (1997)

Dark Star (1973)

The Day the Earth Stood Still (1951)

Die Frau im Mond (Woman on the Moon) (1928)*

E.T. The Extra-Terrestrial (1982)

Earth Girls Are Easy (1989)

Earth vs. the Flying Saucers (1956)*

The Empire Strikes Back (1980) *

Fire Maidens from Outer Space (1954)*

The First Men on the Moon (1919)*

Five Million Years to Earth (1968)*

Flash Gordon (1936)*

Flash Gordon Conquers the Universe (1940)*

Flash Gordon's Trip to Mars (1938)*

Forbidden Planet (1956)*

The Grays (1991)

Hermano del espacio (Brother from Space, 1968)

I Married a Monster from Outer Space (1957)*

Independence Day (1997)*

Invaders from Mars (1953)*

Invaders from Space (1962)*

Invasion of the Body Snatchers (1956)

It Came from Outer Space (1953)

It! The Terror from Beyond Space (1958)*

Killer Klowns from Outer Space (1988)*

Le Voyage dans la Lune (A Trip to the Moon) (1902)*

Mars Attacks! (1996)

Men in Black (1997)

Phantom from Space (1953)*

Predator (1987)

Predator II (1990)

Return of the Jedi (1983)*

Santa Claus Conquers the Martians (1989)

Slaughterhouse Five (1972)

Star Trek: The Final Frontier (1989)

Star Trek: The Motion Picture (1979)*

Star Trek: The Next Generation (1994)

Star Trek II: The Wrath of Khan (1982)

Star Trek III: The Search for Spock (1984)

Star Trek IV: The Voyage Home (1986)

Star Wars (1977)*

Starman (1984)

Starship Troopers (1997)*

They Came from Beyond Space (1967)

The Thing (1951)*

This Island Earth (1955)*

The War of the Worlds (1953)*

The X-files: Fight the Future (1998)*

Index

Symbols

1950s science fiction movies, 290

19th-century UFO sightings, 73-82

2001: A Space Odyssey, 296

5-5-5 reliability scale, 142-143

A

A Princess of Mars (Edgar Rice Burroughs), 270

A True History (Lucian of Samosata), 27

abductees, 11, 151

abduction, 151
    Betty and Barney Hill, 146-150
    hypnotic regression, 159
    indicators, 152
    problems with hypnosis, 160
    reliability of hypnosis, 153
    types of people abducted, 153
    typical scenario, 154-155, 158
    validity of encounters, 190

acceleration, barrier to interstellar travel, 245

accidents, UFOs, Roswell Incident, 120, 123-124

Adamski, George, contactee, 175, 176

Aetherius Society, 178

Air Force
    Regulation 200-2, reporting UFO sightings, 305, 307
    UFO investigations, 114-116

airships, 73-82

ALFs (Alien Life Forms), 140

Alien (film), 297

alien abduction, 134, 143, 151
    Betty and Barney Hill, 146-150
    hypnotic regression, 159
    indicators, 152
    problems with hypnosis, 160
    reliability of hypnosis, 153
    types of people abducted, 153
    typical scenario, 154-155, 158
    validity of encounters, 190

alien autopsies, 128

alien stories
    Biblical, 57-60
    Book of Mormon, 57
    Rig-Veda, 61

aliens, 11
    Bible stories, 56
    invaders in science fiction, 270
    reincarnation, 56
    related movies, 315
    salvation, 55
    theories on existence, 17-19
    varieties reported, 156
    visitations in past, searching for proof, 47

Alpha Centauri, 225

alternate explanations for UFOs, 163
    archetypes, 170
    demons, 164
    fallen angels, 164
    hollow earth theory, 165
    occult aspects, 166-167
    parallel universes, 168
    paraphysical aspects, 168-169

alternate universe theory of UFOs, 19

ambivalent nature of UFO question, 186

amino acids, 209

Anaxagoras, solar theory, 25

ancient astronaut theory, 10
    Erich Von Däniken, 48
    Great Pyramid, 49, 51
    Great Sphinx, 51, 52
    Pyramid of Inscriptions, 53
    searching for proof, 47
    Yonaguni-Jima pyramid, 53

ancient myths and legends, 15, 33

ancient scientific analysis of universe, 25

ancient theories of the universe, 23-24